Protest
and Politics

Protest and Politics

*Christianity and
Contemporary Affairs*

Edited by
ROBERT G. CLOUSE
ROBERT D. LINDER
RICHARD V. PIERARD

THE ATTIC PRESS, INC.
Greenwood, S. C.
1968

Acknowledgments

The editors wish to thank the following people who helped to prepare the manuscript of this book: Dennis Harrell, Jacqueline Moore, Charlene Pierard, Nancy Proctor, Helenann Coffel, and Jean Ann Linder. We wish also to thank Donald Scheick and Donald Hawthorne who have greatly encouraged us in our work.

Permission to quote from the following copyright material is gratefully acknowledged:

The Military Establishment, by John R. Swomley, Jr. Copyright 1964, Beacon Press.

From State Church to Pluralism, by Franklin H. Littell. Copyright 1962, by Doubleday & Co., Inc.

Church and State in the United States, by Anson P. Stokes and Leo Pfeffer. Copyright 1964, Harper & Row.

The Great Ascent, by Robert Heilbroner. Copyright 1963, by Harper & Row.

Vietnam: Lotus in a Sea of Fire, by Thich Nhat Hanh. Copyright 1967, by Hill & Wang.

Shall We Overcome? A Message to Negro and White Christians, by Howard O. Jones. Copyright 1966, by Howard O. Jones.

Liberty in the Balance: Current Issues in Civil Liberties, by H. Frank Way, Jr. Copyright 1964, by McGraw-Hill Book Co.

The Interplay of East and West, by Barbara Ward. Copyright 1957, by Barbara Ward. Reprinted by permission of Barbara Ward and W. W. Norton & Co., Inc.

The New Cold War, by Edward Crankshaw. Copyright 1963, by Penguin Books.

The State of War, by Stanley Hoffman. Copyright 1965, by Frederick A. Praeger.

The Smaller Dragon: A Political History of Vietnam, by Joseph Buttinger. Copyright 1958, by Frederick A. Praeger.

A Southern Moderate Speaks, by Brooks Hays. Copyright 1959, by University of North Carolina Press.

The Church as a Social Institution, by David O. Moberg. Copyright 1962, by Prentice-Hall, Inc.

A History of Militarism, by Alfred Vagts. Copyright 1967, by World Publishing Co.

The Scripture quotations in this publication are from the Revised Standard Version of the Bible, copyrighted 1946 and 1952 by the Division of Christian Education of the National Council of the Churches of Christ in the U.S.A. and used by permission.

R.G.C.
R.D.L.
R.V.P.

Contents

Introduction

A rising tempo of protest against political, economic, and social injustice is one of the most striking characteristics of the present day. The new sense of activism and involvement which contrasts so sharply with the cautious indifference of the post-war decade in the United States is evidenced by the mounting number of demonstrations, boycotts, petitions, sit-ins, and picket lines. Christians have become increasingly involved in this movement of social protest, and many church groups are standing in the forefront of struggles which aim at such things as ending racial segregation, alleviating poverty, and securing peace in the world. Although a large number of religious activists have been identified with ecclesiastical bodies that are basically theologically liberal in nature, the interest in political and social problems by people associated with the "evangelical" wing of Protestant Christianity has not been so conspicuous.

Since there is some confusion as to what an evangelical is, it seems most appropriate to utilize a definition advanced in what is currently the leading spokesman for the evangelical position, the bi-weekly religious journal *Christianity Today*. According to a recent editorial in this publication, the common ground on which evangelicals stand is a "belief in biblical authority and in individual spiritual regeneration as being of the very essence of Christianity."[1] In another place the editor elaborates on this point by asserting that evangelicals believe the Bible has correctly described man's spiritual condition as lost without Christ and separated from God. They affirm that Christ died to atone for the sins of mankind and rose triumphantly from the dead. This Gospel message, which should be proclaimed to all men, brings peace with God, fellowship with other Christians, entrance into a new life and spiritual joy and moral growth, and assurance of life with Christ beyond the grave.[2] However, even using this rather broad definition, it is still sometimes difficult to classify various Christians as "evangelicals." It is not unusual to see individuals who have been designated as fundamentalists, conservatives, or neo-orthodox placed in this category, and most of them probably would accept the label.

1

There are certainly large numbers of evangelical Christians in nearly every Protestant denomination.

Evangelicals have generally not been noted for their involvement in social issues because certain articulate publications, church groups, and individual spokesmen have closely linked evangelical Christianity with their own doctrinaire conservative political ideology. These include such widely circulated periodicals as *Christianity Today*, *Christian Economics*, and *United Evangelical Action*; such organizations as the Christian Anti-Communism Crusade, American Council of Christian Churches, Christian Crusade, and Church League of America; and such schools as Bob Jones University, Harding College, and Grove City College. A few examples should suffice to illustrate this contention. Rex Turner, president of Alabama Christian College, recently declared that the Christian must never cause "excitement" or "support change in a society."[3] J. Howard Pew, a prominent Christian layman often associated with evangelical causes and chairman of the board of Sun Oil Company, flatly proclaimed to millions of Americans in *Readers Digest* that Christ "refused to enmesh himself or his followers in the economic, social and political problems of his day—problems certainly as serious as those we face today. . . . He made it crystal clear that we are to seek 'first the kingdom of God and His righteousness'—carefully pointing out that 'the kingdom is within you.' "[4] The editor of *Christianity Today* affirmed on March 17, 1967 that the church "forsakes the spirit of Christ" when it uses "picketing, demonstration, and boycott" to pressure business leaders to hire more Negroes in their firms.[5] The social philosophy expressed by the above-mentioned individuals, organizations, and publications has prompted a reputable scholar of the history of American revivalism, Professor William G. McLoughlin of Brown University, to make the accusation that the evangelicals "are the spiritual hard-core of the radical right."[6]

In spite of this situation, there is a significant group of younger men of moderate persuasion in the evangelical movement who refuse to be categorized as doctrinaire political conservatives. Eleven of us who are displeased with the calloused indifference on the part of so many of our fellow evangelicals to the vital political, social, and economic problems of the day have decided to speak out in protest. Seven of us are historians and four are political scientists, and we have been closely associated with the academic community during our professional careers. Some of us occupy positions in colleges and universities while others are active in public life. All of us identify with either the Democratic or Republican Party and in some way have participated in political campaigns. We are speaking, therefore, not only as evangelical Christians, but also as concerned citizens and practicing scholars.

We are profoundly disturbed about the state of affairs which exists today in evangelical circles. On all sides we hear evangelical spokesmen mouthing the pious phrases and slogans of a bygone era and yet they say little of relevance to the needs and concerns of our day. Whenever the Christian church in the past was a vital and dynamic organism, it was always valiantly dealing with the problems of its time. Today we live in a world of revolutionary change and unparalleled challenge, and the task is now before organized Christianity to minister to the needs of modern man. Unfortunately, altogether too many evangelicals are more concerned with their own status in society, and they find themselves in the position of either opposing social change or at least ignoring it. These people live in a segmented, compartmentalized world in which the Christian faith has only to do with one's internal well-being and post-historical destiny. Their lives in the "secular" sphere of activity are regulated by unquestioned political, social, and economic traditions together with considerations of personal self-interest. These traditions are all too frequently linked with Christianity to produce what President David A. Hubbard of Fuller Theological Seminary aptly has labelled "a package-deal faith."[7] For these people adherence to such traditions as the laissez-faire free enterprise system, the principle of racial segregation, armed intervention in the internal affairs of other states, and the deep-seated fear of any expansion of the activities of the federal government comes to occupy a prominent position in the body of Christian dogma.

Each of the contributors to this collection of essays is keenly aware of the dangers inherent in such a compartmentalized and package-deal Christianity. For example, from time to time every one of us has sadly witnessed the departure of friends and associates from the ranks of evangelical Christianity. Many of them came to feel that evangelicalism was no longer meaningful because it was tied to seemingly outmoded traditions, and they are now seeking satisfaction either in another form of Christianity or in no religion at all. Worse still, the recent history of Germany has revealed how a modern hell can come on earth when the evangelical church simply lives contentedly to itself and leaves men to grope alone and unaided in the everyday world of work and politics. Christ exhorted his followers to be the "salt of the earth" and the "light of the world." If we fail to provide an effective ministry to the needs of men in the contemporary world, we are guilty of incomplete obedience to the directives of Christ. In short, out of conscience's sake we feel compelled to speak out about this reprehensible state of affairs which characterizes much of evangelical Christianity at the present time.

Designed to promote dialogue among evangelicals, the essays contained in this collection are scholarly analyses of selected problems in current affairs. They offer from a Christian point of view a general approach to questions of political involvement and stimulating discussions of several pressing domestic and foreign problems. Senator *Mark O. Hatfield* of Oregon, an outspoken Christian layman and former political science professor, leads off with a hard-hitting essay on the timely topic of Christian political ethics which deals with the basic moral issues confronting a Christian who is active in public life. Another political scientist, *Walfred H. Peterson*, formerly a staff member of the Baptist Joint Committee on Public Affairs and now a university professor, analyzes the responsibilities of a Christian voter and points out that he has a definite influence which can and should be exercised intelligently. A historian well acquainted with the agony which overtook Germany in this century, *Richard V. Pierard*, examines the threat of the Radical Right to American democracy and presents a number of cogent reasons why evangelicals should take a more moderate position.

The next four essays deal with specific domestic issues. *William W. Cuthbertson*, an American historian, concentrates on the increasing presence of militarism in this country and the serious danger which the growth of the military establishment holds for American democracy. In a penetrating essay on the welfare state, social historian *James E. Johnson* pleads eloquently for evangelicals to acknowledge that the federal government can and should be used to meet the economic needs of people today. *Robert D. Linder*, an authority on the history of the Reformation and Christianity, surveys the civil rights movement in the United States and forcefully argues that it is both morally and spiritually right for evangelicals to support this current drive for racial equality. An American intellectual historian, *Donald E. Pitzer*, treats the question of the place of religion in the public schools and in a lucid manner shows that the recent Supreme Court decisions concerning the separation of church and state are definitely beneficial, not harmful, to evangelical Christianity in the United States.

The last four contributions deal with problems that are confined not merely to the borders of this country. *Earl J. Reeves*, acting director of the Center of Community and Metropolitan Studies, University of Missouri at St. Louis, reveals the devastating impact of the population explosion on people throughout the world as well as in the United States and contends that evangelicals must be prepared to support government financed and administered population control programs. A specialist on communism and the Soviet Union, *William W. Adams, Jr.*, examines some widespread misconceptions about communism and suggests that a "human view" of communism eliminates the apparent contradiction between the demands of political realism and Christian conscience in dealing with the radical left. Historian *George Giacumakis, Jr.*, a Middle-Eastern specialist, provides an assessment of the complex Arab-Israeli conflict and suggests attitudes which the American Christian might adopt regarding this question. In the concluding essay *Robert G. Clouse*, a Reformation and Church historian, closely examines the Vietnam War and proposes an alternative position to that of uncritical support of the American involvement in the conflict which the evangelical might in clear conscience accept.

The points of view expressed in the essays are those of the individuals contributing them, and they do not necessarily reflect the views of the editors or of other contributors. The editors were of the conviction that each author should be allowed a maximum amount of freedom of expression on these crucial issues, and thus editorial changes have been restricted to a bare minimum.

It is hoped that this collection of essays will not only enjoy a wide reading public among individual evangelical Christians but also that churches, discussion groups, colleges, and seminaries will use it as a resource book for the study of contemporary affairs. This volume has been specifically designed to offer the thoughtful Christian options for his consideration and to stimulate him to constructive social action. Those who have participated in this project are firmly convinced that the historic theology of the Christian church is as valid and relevant as ever to the problems of the rapidly changing world of the twentieth century. We have endeavored to be temperate in our statements and admonitions because we are speaking out of a deep sense of Christian concern. We have not meant to offend or antagonize our fellow evangelicals but rather to encourage them to rethink some of their assumptions about the contemporary world. Undoubtedly, the answers given will not satisfy some of the readers of this book, but it has been the intention of the authors that these answers provide a basis for intelligent discussion of the problems.

NOTES

1. "Somehow, Let's Get Together," *Christianity Today*, XI (June 9, 1967), p. 24.
2. "Who Are the Evangelicals?" *Christianity Today*, XI (June 23, 1967), p. 22.
3. Quoted in Robert Meyers, ed., *Voices of Concern: Critical Studies in Church of Christism* (St. Louis: Mission Messenger, 1966), p. 72.
4. J. Howard Pew, "Should the Church 'Meddle' in Civil Affairs?" *Readers Digest*, LXXXVIII (May 1966), p. 53.
5. "Equality by Boycott," *Christianity Today*, XI (Mar. 17, 1967), p. 27.
6. William G. McLoughlin, "Is There a Third Force in Christendom?" *Daedalus*, (Winter 1967), p. 61.
7. David A. Hubbard, "The Package Is Shattered," *Eternity*, XVIII (June 1967), p. 10.

Mark O. Hatfield is the junior United States Senator from the state of Oregon. He was born in Dallas, Oregon, on June 12, 1922 and attended Willamette University where he received a B.A. degree in 1943. He then entered the United States Navy and participated in the South Pacific campaign and the invasions of Iwo Jima and Okinawa. After returning to civilian life, he obtained an M.A. at Stanford University and joined the faculty of Willamette University as an instructor in political science. He was subsequently promoted to assistant and associate professor and in addition served as dean from 1950 to 1956.

Mr. Hatfield is best-known for his long and distinguished career in public life. He entered politics on the state level and served as a State Representative, 1951–55; State Senator, 1955–57; Secretary of State, 1957–59; and finally as Governor of Oregon, 1959–67. He entered the United States Senate in 1967 and is now a member of the Committee on Agriculture and Forestry, Committee on Interior and Insular Affairs, and Select Committee on Small Business. Senator Hatfield has been quite active in Republican Party politics. He was a precinct committeeman, an alternate county chairman, and has been a member of the Oregon delegation at every Republican National Convention since 1952. He nominated Richard M. Nixon for President in 1960, and at the 1964 convention he served as the temporary chairman and delivered the keynote address. In 1968 he was widely mentioned as a possible Republican Vice-Presidential candidate.

He has been the recipient of numerous citations and awards, including fifteen honorary doctorates. He was selected by *Life* magazine in 1962 as one of the most important young men in America, nominated for Vice President by fourteen collegiate mock conventions in 1964, and named an honorary member of the Japanese Diet in 1964. Senator Hatfield has travelled extensively in Europe, Asia, and South America. He also belongs to several service and fraternal organizations and is a member and former moderator of the First Baptist Church of Salem, Oregon. He is the author of a political autobiography, *Not Quite So Simple*, which was published by Harper & Row in mid-1968.

MARK O. HATFIELD

How Can A Christian Be in Politics?

Two out of every three Americans believe that Congressional misuse of government funds is fairly common. So says a recent Gallup Poll.

Members of a PTA group in a large suburban high school were once asked to list in order of preference the occupations they would want their children to enter. Doctor and lawyer were at the top. Elected public official was toward the bottom.

In the minds of most people there is a latent suspicion that politicians are somehow dishonest or at least very flexible ethically. Reports of the misconduct of public officials, which always receive front page attention in the newspapers, serve to support the popular notion that all office-holders are less than completely honest if not just plain crooked. Disclosures of influence-peddling, misuse of funds, and falsifying government pay records by trusted public servants cause great damage to the people's trust of government officials.

I have often been asked: "How can you be a Christian and be in politics?" There is inherent in this question the popular idea that politics is dirty and that no honest person would get himself involved. Have you ever heard a doctor or a lawyer asked that question? Yet certainly there are as many cases of professional or ethical misconduct in their occupations as among politicians.

The great concern about the malfeasance of an officeholder stems, it seems, from three things. The first thing is the power he can use or misuse in office; that is, his authority to compel obedience to the law and his access to large sums of public money. The second is the concept that an official of the government holds a special trust from the people. He is their representative. He acts with authority delegated from them. He is to serve their—the public's—interests. And third, there is the fact that an

7

officeholder lives, so to speak, in a fishbowl. We have come to refer to a government official as being in "public life." There are probing eyes and listening ears to pick up every aspect of a politician's life. Some regard officeholders as public property—to be used without regard to personal considerations.

The difficulties in all of these areas comes in the ill-defined conflicts of interest. In the use of power, for example, how can a violation simply of good judgment be distinguished from one of ethics and morals? In the conflict between public and private interests, where is the line to be drawn between clear violations of the law and other "gray" areas where the distinction is not so easy? In the matter of the public life, where does privacy become a cover for clandestine activities rather than simply the wish to be left alone?

View Of History

Our ideals of civic duty and the responsibility of carrying the public trust probably find their origins in the two roots of western culture. These are the traditions of Israel and of Greece and Rome. The theological and ideological heritages of these two traditions become immediately apparent. The judges and kings of ancient Israel ruled by appointment from God. Their authority was broad and virtually absolute. We see the origin of human government as an instrument of the will of God in the Scriptures.

It is significant, I believe, that we even have recorded in the accounts of the lives of Israel's rulers the details of their flaws and misconduct, both public and private. These misdeeds were viewed as violations of God's commandments. They even were described as breaches of the personal trust and relationship between God and man. When a ruler in Israel was accused of some misconduct he would be condemned for violating God's holy law rather than for simply acting against the public interest. In the economy of the Old Testament, God's will was the public interest.

The history of Israel teaches us another interesting principle. This is that the people could turn to God for relief from an oppressive and evil ruler. We should note two things in this. The first is that herein lies the seed of the political philosophy of the right of revolution. The idea that a people can appeal to God for protection and justification in altering or overthrowing their unjust government and rulers finds eloquent expression in the documents of the American Revolution. The roots are in ancient Scriptures. The second point is that frequently in its history Israel suffered under oppressive rulers as a direct result of its own evil conduct and disobedience to God's commandments. In other words, the corrupt and evil government resulted from the moral degeneration of the people themselves. This is a point to remember when we begin to judge the ethical conduct of public officials in our own country.

From the Greeks and from the Romans we inherited our commitment to the ideals of reason, order, and moderation. The public good, the common interest—especially in the Greek city-states—was the principal motivation for morality in public office. In Athens it was the custom to conduct a public examination (*dokimasia*) of a candidate's character before he could be selected for public office. His entire life was open to challenge by any citizen. He had to prove freedom from physical defect and from scandal, the pious honoring of his ancestors, and the full payment of his taxes. His record of military duty was also closely examined. If he passed these tests and was selected for office, usually by lot, he would swear an oath to perform the obligations of his office and to avoid accepting bribes and presents.

Instruction in the responsibilities of citizenship and the nobility of public service was an essential part of the education of the young men in Athens. The swearing of the Ephebian oath committed them to high ethical conduct in public service and admitted them to full citizenship in the city. It was expected that every citizen of Athens would serve at least one year in public office. Civic duty was an accepted part of Greek life. Even though the oath of public office was taken on the altars of the Greek gods, a violation of the oath was considered a breach of the public trust, rather than a sin against God—as was the case of Israel.

Thucydides, the Greek historian, reported that the Greeks were more anxious to be called clever than honest, however. There was hardly a man in Athenian public life who was not charged with crookedness. The legend of Diogenes searching with his lantern, when the sun was high, for an honest man may be closer to fact than one realizes.

The great Greek philosopher Plato proposed a society, in his *Republic*, in which only the most qualified and wise ruled. These philosopher-kings alone knew what was good for men and states. There was no need for law because these wise rulers were the law. In Plato's view, of course, these rulers acted for the total good because they alone knew what was absolutely good and right. Pure reason, embodied in the philosopher-king, prevailed. Plato felt that the purpose of the State was to produce the highest type of human being. This idea ran quite contrary to the deep convictions of the Greeks about the moral value of freedom under the law and of the participation by the citizens in the task of self-government.

Aristotle, Plato's equally famous pupil, emphasized the Greek idea of a government of laws rather than of men—no matter how wise and good the men might be. He felt that there should be a moral equality between the ruler and the ruled in that they both must obey the law.

The Greek ideals of public service and civic pride and duty have influenced us to a large extent. Yet the Greeks became loosened from their own ethical traditions. Public morality declined, carried out on the tide of private degeneration.

The Romans built the world's greatest empire on the grand excellence of military might and administrative proficiency. The legions of the emperors were not known for their mercy, but for their brutal efficiency. Justice in the courts was accorded only to those fortunate enough to be citizens of the Empire. The Christian missionary Paul of Tarsus was one of these. Officials of the Roman Empire were not responsible to the public interest in their conduct of business. Their major allegiance was to the emperor and his provincial governors. With great administrative genius the Romans ruled a diverse and far-flung empire. An elaborate system of inspection and record-keeping was developed to check on the efficiency and honesty of their officials.

In the early years of the Empire the Roman philosopher and statesman, Cicero, articulated the idea of an eternal, unchangeable law which was universally binding upon all peoples. This law, based in right reason, was authored by God. It was natural law. Only irrational men would attempt to violate it. Cicero insisted that, in the light of this eternal law, all men were equal. The true political state was a community for ethical purposes, and unless it were held together by moral ties, it would be nothing but anarchy on a large scale. The commonwealth—"the affair of the people" —was composed of men united by common agreement about law and rights and participation in mutual advantages. For Cicero, a life of political service was the crown of human happiness and achievement. Reasonable men who were altruistically motivated should be called to public service. He insisted that such individuals would rule with integrity and high ethics.

Seneca, the Roman philosopher and dramatist who lived in the first century of the Christian era, was more pessimistic. He reasoned that because the mass of men were so vicious and corrupt, a despotism was preferable to any form of popular government. He felt, therefore, that a political career had little to offer the good man except the annihilation of his goodness. The good man could do little for his fellows by holding political office. Seneca's idea is quite popular among Americans, both in and out of the churches.

By no means, however, did Seneca feel that the wise and good man ought to withdraw from the community. He insisted, as did Cicero, upon the moral obligation of the good man to offer his services in some capacity or other. He rejected the popular Epicurean idea of pursuing private satisfaction at the cost of neglecting the public interests. Public service in his view did not necessarily have to take the form of political office. A good man could render service to humanity even though he had no political power. Here are the seeds of the unique American idea of voluntary private action for the benefit of the community.

Here in these experiences and thoughts of the Hebrews and of the Greeks and Romans are the roots of our own ideals of political morality and the ethics of public office. These roots reached into Medieval Christian Europe. They blossomed, grew, and were pruned by the Renaissance, the Reformation, and the Age of Reason. The seeds of the old world found new life in the new world, and a unique society with unique political concepts flourished.

The American Experiment

The American concept of politics and of public ethics draws heavily from those ancient ideas of Israel, Greece, and Rome. Ours is a refined combination. It was with great optimism in the perfectibility of man that our founding fathers created the American nation. They recognized that the task of building a new society, based on the principles of self-government, would require the exercise of the highest and most noble qualities of man. Both the citizen and the public official had to act in a selfless, loyal, and dedicated manner in order to make the new democracy work. This fact was most clearly stated in the closing words of the Declaration of Independence: "And for the support of this Declaration, with a firm Reliance on the Protection of divine Providence, we mutually pledge to each other our Lives, our Fortunes, and our sacred Honor." There is in this simple and eloquent statement the combination of the two concepts of public duty of which we have spoken earlier. Reliance on God's protection (Judeo-Christian) and a mutual pledge of life, fortune, and honor for the common or public interest (Greco-Roman).

There was the basic assumption by our nation's authors that a democratic society would free the best spirit within man. This spirit, motivated by God, and educated in Biblical truths, could create the greatest good for the greatest number of people. There was also the recognition that man can be selfish, dishonest, and tyrannical. And so the government was structured to safeguard against tyranny and to protect the people from the selfishness of their governors.

Daniel Webster summed up the attitude of the nation's early leaders by saying that "whatever makes men good Christians, makes them good citizens."[1] There was a feeling, a hope that the nobleness and integrity in the spirit of men would rise to the surface in the American society. There was even the hope that the spiritual motivation of men could be transferred into a sort of civic religion and zeal for freedom. Whatever it was that made men good Christians and good citizens was to be encouraged and nurtured in the American family, the churches, and the schools in the hope that these qualities of individual life would create the new citizens for the new society.

Our Founding Fathers, however, were practical men. They had been through experiences which taught them to distrust the nature of man— at least men in political power. They had witnessed tyranny over the mind, the body, and the spirit. Consequently they wanted to construct a system of constitutional government to insure that tyranny could not take root in the new world. Therefore, today we have a political system which allows for the peaceful debate between conflicting interests. James Madison in Number Ten of the *Federalist Papers* explained the function of what we now know as the political parties as the balancing of various group interests against one another in order to arrive at the common good.

We have today a political system that recognizes, in a general way at least, that God rules in the affairs of men. We recognize that a public official is a servant of the people and a trustee of their delegated sovereign power. We acknowledge the need for loyalty to common goals and ideals of government by both officials and citizens of the nation. And we have grown accustomed to expecting our public officials to be men of honor, integrity, and decency.

The Citizen's Responsibility For Morality In Government

These are our ideals, our traditions, our roots. But what of our practices, our works? As we weigh our ideals against our present performance, we find that the scales are tipped out of balance. Our newspaper headlines gives us new reasons to suspect that few public officeholders are honest. We are stunned to hear a sub-cabinet official state that the government has the right to lie to the people. We hear constantly of the "credibility gap" in the government—the distance between the truth and what is told to the nation. Scandalous revelations of the misconduct and dishonesty of United States Congressmen and Senators remind us often of the moral frailty of men. Influence-peddling and fraud by government employees and their friends cause us to wonder what has become of integrity in public service.

The standard reaction to all of this by the American public has been to draw a general rule from the specific cases and to condemn everyone in public office as a crook. For many who take seriously their moral convictions and Christian faith there is a grave question as to whether a "good man" or a Christian could enter politics and still keep his faith. Because of this, many good, honest people avoid politics and seek "safer" vocations. This approach creates a serious vacuum of morality in places of public leadership.

While condemning their public officials for misconduct, most Americans fail to realize that they are pointing their fingers at the "representatives" of the people. These men hold office because we, the people, put them there. We helped to elect them—the good ones and the bad ones— either by voting or failing to vote; by making our views known or by withholding our comments and complaining only where we could not be heard.

Keep this in mind, my fellow Americans: The Congress, the executive branch—indeed, government at all levels—is no better than the demands of the citizens. If the people pursue excellence, they can require it from their public officials. If the nation seeks after righteousness, then its leaders should surely point the way. If each of us, as citizens, expects moral and ethical leadership in government, we ought to be prepared to render that kind of service ourselves whenever called on to do so. By the quality of our own personal ethical and spiritual character we ought to be setting the standards for conduct, both private and public.

There is an old saying: "All that is necessary for evil to triumph is for good men to do nothing." This is precisely where we find ourselves today in the matter of Christian ethics and political morality. For too many political generations too many good men have done nothing. They have stood by as neutral observers while the contest was fought in the political arena. This is true in the local community, it is widespread on the state level, and it is certainly the case in national politics.

Many Christians have forgotten that we are engaged in a cosmic battle between the forces of good and the forces of evil. The Scriptures speak often of the conflict between good and evil within the human heart and soul and conscience. What we often forget is that this personal battle is translated into social battles in the community, into conflicts between classes, races, economic interest groups, and ultimately, into conflicts between nations.

If the message of the transforming power of God in Christ is applicable to the individual human being, then it must have an effect upon the social man and his community. A man's view of the world and his relationships to those around him must change when he is confronted with the message of the Gospel. Changed men must build a changed world. Christians must become involved in the processes of transformation in our world, as God leads them. One of the major processes for orderly change in our world is politics—the art and science of human government.

For the Christian man to reason that God does not want him in politics because there are too many evil men in government is as insensitive as for a Christian doctor to turn his back on an epidemic because there are too many germs there. For the Christian to say that he will not enter politics because he might lose his faith is the same as for the physician to say that he will not heal men because he might catch their diseases.

John Stuart Mill in chapter two of his treatise on *Representative Government* wrote:

> If we ask ourselves on what causes and conditions good government in all its senses, from the humblest to the most exalted, depends, we find that the principal of them, the one which transcends all others, *is the qualities of the human beings composing the society over which the government is exercised.*[2]

The American people have made the kind of government which they have today. If there is evil, immorality, and unethical behavior in government, it is because the American people have allowed it to develop. Where there is nobleness, honesty, integrity, and goodness, the American people are responsible for that too.

The solution to the problem of immorality in public office begins with the character of the people of this nation. It must begin with us as we search our own hearts and consciences. Ask yourself this question: "If everyone else in America were just like I am, what kind of country would this be? If everyone took the same interest in government that I do, what kind of government would we have? If everyone obeyed the law, including traffic laws, with the same faithfulness that I do, what kind of crime rate would we have? If everyone accepted public service or community work with the same attitude that I do, how much would get done for the public good? If everyone obeyed his conscience and the spiritual commandments of God with the same faithfulness and courage that I do, what kind of world would this be?" John Stuart Mill goes on in his work to say that "whenever the general disposition of the people is such that each individual regards those only of his interests which are selfish, and does not dwell on, or concern himself for, his share of the general interest, in such a state of things good government is impossible."[3]

All will agree that the selfishness of men accounts for most of our social, political, and economic problems. The founders of our nation knew this fact too, and they attempted to construct a political system in which the selfish interests of one group would be balanced off against those of another. They saw to it that the selfishness, if we may call it that, of the executive branch of government would be balanced with that of the legislative and judicial branches and vice versa. We call this the separation of powers in our government.

Our government "of laws, rather than men" is really an institution in which we have sought to embody in statutes the best of the ideal conduct of men. John Stuart Mill, again in his treatise on *Representative Government*, puts it this way:

> All government which aims at being good is an organisation of some part of the good qualities existing in the individual members of the community for the conduct of its collective affairs. A representative constitution is a means of bringing the general standing of intelligence and honesty existing in the community, and the individual intellect and virtue of its wisest members, more directly to bear upon the government. . . . . Such influence as they do have is the source of all good that there is in the government, and the hinderance of every evil that there is not. The greater the amount of these good qualities which the institutions of a country succeed in organising, and the better the mode of organisation, the better will be the government.[4]

Though we Americans have sought to organize the best that is in the nation, we find that we have not always succeeded. We see indications that the worst qualities of man appear to gain in power and influence. It is easy to become cynical and mourn the defeat of our idealism. It is this cynicism which causes many Christians to avoid entering public service.

There is a reluctance among those who call themselves Christians to believe that the ultimate victory belongs to Christ. We fail to understand that God is at work in history and that all human affairs will one day be consummated in Jesus Christ. We have in the revealed truth of God the assurance of his power and the promise of its application in our daily lives. This fact gives us the kind of security and stability which allows us to risk ourselves in the service of mankind. Christ said that it is only when we lose our lives that we truly find them (Mt. 10:39). It is when we turn our eyes from the anxious anticipation of circumstances surrounding us and lift them to see the power and dominion of God in Christ that we gain the perspective and leverage to change the world in which we live.

This then is the two-fold challenge to the citizen-Christian. First, it is to redeem the citizens of our society and thereby to build a better foundation for government. This can be done by obedience to the Great Commission, the teaching of the Gospel of Christ. The second challenge is to be willing to serve God in politics and government if that is where he wants you. The great experiment that is America calls to each generation for the kind of men and women who will dare to make this nation what it was meant to be. The call is to service, to loyalty, to sacrifice, and to opportunity. The crisis is in the dearth of leadership. The greatest need of our times is for men who will give of themselves and who will serve unselfishly in a position of public trust. The call is for leaders who will be led by God.

The Christian As A Public Servant

Let us turn now from this discussion of the citizen's responsibility for morality in government to some thoughts about the relationship of a leader's personal spiritual life to his public service. Of course, the need for personal faith is not limited merely to those involved in public service. The trials, the temptations, the sense of void and loneliness can be present in any person's life, regardless of his profession.

There are certain problems, however, which are perhaps intensified by a political career. Among these is the temptation of the ego. There are tremendous pressures in public service to fixate upon one's own importance. The man who falls in love with his own image loses all touch with real human needs. He loses all perspective of his own capacities. The political leader with an inflated ego makes no room for God in his life and suffers from the blasphemous delusion that he has no such need. In my own life, I know of no solution except a personal, daily relationship with Jesus Christ. If we cease to believe in a personal deity because of the inflation of our own ego, God does not die, but we die when our lives cease to be daily renewed by the steady radiance of his love. Dag Hammarskjöld once wrote: "Your position never gives you the right to command. It only imposes on you the duty of so living your life that others can receive your orders without being humiliated."[5] Men need God in their lives to live in that manner. For, the ego is always humbled before God.

Another intensified problem for the public servant is that it is easy to forget what it means to serve. True service involves neither condescension nor exploitation. The imagery of the "public servant" is a fundamental part of the Christian-Judaic tradition. From the servant image of Isaiah to the commands of Christ, we are called to serve others—"the public." Our call to service is not because service has been earned, but rather because each man is of divine worth. Christ provides the example for the Christian in public service. "If I then, your Lord and Teacher, have washed your feet, you also ought to wash one another's feet" (Jn. 13:14). One's spiritual life should help to renew daily a personal sense of "servant-hood."

The personal spiritual life of a public servant should be a constant source of strength. The need for strength is great. Abraham Lincoln admitted: "I have been driven many times upon my knees by the overwhelming conviction that I had nowhere else to go."[6] A daily relationship with God in prayer helps us not to confuse our will with his will. Any person in public life who thinks that he can "go it alone" is tragically mistaken. No man has enough love, enough concern, enough humility, enough strength, enough courage. In an individual's friendship with God there comes each day the humility of having fallen short, the joy of being forgiven, and the strength of being renewed.

Because Christianity is a relationship, not a dogma, it provides a dynamic absolute for one's life. The temptation to lose sight of any absolute is particularly intensified in the political arena. Our democratic system holds that the best political policy is not derived from some political absolute, but formulated through the legal clash of many relative views. In such a system, many political leaders can see no absolute which does not change with the situational context.

I can accept neither simplistic dogmatism nor total relativity. My relationship with Christ gives me a base—an absolute—both for my personal and my public life. This is the one constant factor running through all of life. The dynamics of this relationship can give the Christian both an absolute foundation and the freedom to deal with the relativity of the political sphere. There is a perspective, an equilibrium, and a total world view which the Christian can achieve, and this gives him the capacity to deal with relative and changing circumstances.

Let us turn for a moment to how Christian belief affects the mechanics of government. According to our pledge of allegiance, we are "one nation under God." I think that too often we misunderstand what it means to be "under God." It does not mean that somehow "God is on our side." As Voltaire sarcastically put it: "It is said that God is always for the big battalions."[7] Being "under God" does not mean that our Constitution should affirm a particular faith. Nor does it mean that this country is uniquely under his protection. We have not always been right, and we cannot claim the approval of God upon everything we have done. Thomas Jefferson once said: "I tremble for my country when I reflect that God is just."[8] It is neither necessarily unpatriotic to believe that God could bring his judgment upon the United States of America, nor is it in our best interests to remain silent when we consider government policies and actions wrong. The ancient prophets of Israel certainly did not spare the rod in pointing to the sins of the rulers as well as to those of the people. Like each of us as individuals, our country is of man as well as of God.

A clearer understanding of "under God" is found in the phrase which appears on all our coins: "In *God* we trust." A nation cannot "trust in God" unless its people and its leaders are committed to that trust. Christian belief only affects the mechanics of government as individuals approach the system with this trust. In this connection, two things are important for us to remember. First, there can be no peace where God is not in the hearts of men. This is individual trust. Second, "there will be no peace so long as God remains unseated at the conference table," in the words of William Peck. This is national trust manifested through individuals as they relate to the governmental system. This relationship between individual morality and trust and national ethics and trust is clearly stated in II Chronicles 7:14: "If my people who are called by my name humble themselves, and pray and seek my face, and turn from their wicked ways," (individual trust and repentance) "then I will hear from heaven, and will forgive their sin and heal their land" (national trust and repentance).

Only when it is "In *God* we trust" will we be able truly to say that we are "one nation *under* God." What does this mean in practical terms? As a public official, I have as much responsibility to the Christian as to the non-Christian. I firmly support the full separation of church and state. Yet, Christ asks each of us to involve ourselves with mankind. This includes a very real responsibility to the institutions of our secular life. The responsibility of the public servant is not to Christianize the institutions of government, but to bring the influence of Christ to bear upon them. Whenever we are successful in institutionalizing a particular article of our faith by enacting it into law, we seem to lose the vitality, spirit, and freshness of it. There often is an abdication of our individual responsibility. Christ recognized this human tendency toward institutionalism when he forbade Peter from building the three monuments on the Mount of Transfiguration. We cannot capture great spiritual truths in concrete, or in law. Both statues and statutes can become forms of idolatry. No amount of government legislation can replace the function of the church which is to change men's hearts by the power of Christ. The church has no other mission. It betrays its Lord when it seeks merely to act as a power bloc in the political arena. It falls short of its high calling when it serves only as another of the many community welfare organizations.

If the Christian faith is to have any effect on the mechanics of government, it must be through the lives of public officials coming together in God. There are numerous opportunities for this throughout our government. The prayer breakfast groups in the Senate and House of Representatives create a kind of fellowship in which we can humble ourselves together before God. There are similar groups of public officials and civic leaders in every state of the Union and in most of the countries of the world. They meet out of a recognition that they need God's guidance and grace in carrying out their public duties. I have had reports of situations where public policy controversies have been settled when the leaders of the opposing sides were able to reconcile their differences in prayer. A unique spiritual bond is formed between public officials who can come together in prayer before God. I have seen this take place between leaders of different nations. The personal lives of public men are changed by these encounters with God. This is fundamental; the Christian faith cannot affect the mechanics of government except as it affects the lives of individual men who bear influence on these institutions.

Our view of man and his relationship to the state and the government has been greatly influenced by our Christian-Judaic tradition. We begin with God—as Creator, and as law giver. We view man as a divine creation. Not only is each man created by God, but also he is created in the image of God, with a creative potential of his own. Christianity affirms that each man is of divine worth. An individual is of infinite worth not because he earned it, but because he is created, sustained, and loved by God. We love each other only because he first loved us. We recognize the value of men as creatures of God, having the same direct access to God that we have. Since we believe in our own value as creatures of God, we respect the worth of others.

The state—the institution of human government—has been ordained by God to serve the individual. We must remember that the individual was not ordained to serve the state. It is the duty of government to provide and to permit the opportunities and freedoms by which man can fulfill his creative potential. In this delicate relationship between God, man, and the government, it is easy to lose sight of God. When this happens the relationship between man and government becomes distorted. Governments that lose the view of man as a creature of divine worth often force him to bow to service to the state without regard for his obligation to God. When governments fail to recognize man's allegiance to God, they court revolution. When men fail to recognize their allegiance to God, they court tyranny.

The Christian And Political Ideology

We cannot discuss the subject of Christian ethics and politics without touching briefly upon the matter of how men can be faithful Christians and still differ politically. As to the possibility of this, I have no doubt. There are many fine Christians who disagree with each other on political questions.

This often becomes a problem of great concern to some Christians.

They cannot understand how a public official could disagree with them on a political issue and still claim to be a Christian. This view is caused, I think, when we allow ourselves to fall into the idolatry of marrying our particular brand of theology to a certain political philosophy. The typical examples of this are the liberal theology-liberal politics blend, and the orthodox theology-conservative politics mixture.

It is dangerous for us to read into the Scriptures any particular political point of view. Christ's teachings, and the letters of St. Paul, are very clear. We must be willing to be disturbed enough by what we read in the Bible to allow the Spirit of God to change us as individuals so that we may change our world.

We must also recognize the ultimate hand of God in the affairs of men. If two Christians disagree on a matter of political policy, they both could be wrong. They both need to recognize that God is at work in history and that his will is to be accomplished regardless of their political opinions. Our duty must remain that of being faithful to God above all else and following him as he guides us through prayer, the Scriptures, and his Holy Spirit. Ultimately, we shall see as we are seen and then God will show us the breadth of his will and the extent of his kingdom. And the great question asked of us will not be whether we stood on the right or on the left, politically, but whether we stood in the shadow of the Cross of Christ.

No matter how we regard the politics of our government, the commandment of Christ and the teaching of St. Paul indicate clearly that we are to obey the appointed authorities in all points over which they have rightful authority. Christ admonished his disciples to "render to Caesar the things that are Caesar's, and to God the things that are God's" (Lk. 20:25). St. Paul exhorted Timothy:

> First of all, then, I urge that supplications, prayers, intercessions, and thanksgivings be made for all men, for kings and all who are in high positions, that we may lead a quiet and peaceable life, godly and respectful in every way. This is good, and it is acceptable in the sight of God our Savior.   (I Tim. 2:1–3).

It is much easier for us to criticize and condemn our public officials than it is for us to pray for them. We find it difficult to pray for those with whom we disagree. Yet this is God's will in order that "we may lead a quiet and peaceable life, godly and respectful in every way."

This is a practical point of departure from which we can begin to have an influence upon our government and upon its public officials. Prayer changes men. Your prayers can change men who make history. Your faithfulness to God as a citizen and as a Christian can mean the difference in the destiny of the United States of America—"one nation under God."

NOTES

1. Daniel Webster, *The Writings and Speeches of Daniel Webster* (Boston: Little, Brown, 1903), I, p. 220.

2. John Stuart Mill, *Considerations on Representative Government* (Oxford: Basil Blackwell, 1940), p. 125. Italics mine.

3. *Ibid.*, p. 126.

4. *Ibid.*, pp. 128–29.

5. Dag Hammarskjöld, *Markings* (New York: Alfred A. Knopf, 1964), p. 105.

6. Quoted in Noah Brooks, "Personal Recollections of Abraham Lincoln," *Harper's Magazine*, XXXI (July 1865), p. 226.

7. *Oeuvres Complètes de Voltaire* (Paris: Garnier Frères, 1882), XLVI, p. 551.

8. Thomas Jefferson, *Notes on the State of Virginia* (Philadelphia: Pritchard and Hall, 1788), p. 173.

Walfred H. Peterson is Professor of Political Science at Washington State University, Pullman, Washington. He was born in Moline, Illinois, on December 28, 1924 and received his undergraduate education at the University of Minnesota where he was elected to Phi Beta Kappa and awarded the B.A. degree in 1947. He obtained an M.A. from this institution in 1949 and did further graduate work at the University of Washington in 1950–51. The Ph.D. degree in political science was conferred upon him by the University of Minnesota in 1957.

Mr. Peterson joined the faculty of Bethel College, St. Paul, Minnesota, in 1951 and rose to the rank of Professor of Political Science. In 1965 he became Director of Research Services for the Baptist Joint Committee on Public Affairs in Washington, D.C. He assumed his present post at Washington State University in 1968. He served as a visiting professor there in 1960–61 and has also held visiting appointments at the University of Minnesota and Lewis and Clark College. He is a specialist in the areas of political parties, political theory, and public law. Memberships in professional organizations include the American Political Science Association and the American Academy of Political and Social Science.

His articles have appeared in a number of scholarly journals, among which are *Religious Education, Western Political Quarterly, Foundations*, and the *Journal of the Minnesota Academy of Science*. He has edited a series of conference study books for the Religious Liberty Conference of the Baptist Joint Committee on Public Affairs and has written extensively for Baptist magazines and agencies publishing Baptist study materials. His special interest in church-state relations has led him to write pamphlets on aspects of that theme for the Baptist Joint Committee on Public Affairs and several other church agencies, and he has lectured extensively on these topics at college convocations and at church and student conferences. Although officially a Democratic Party member, Mr. Peterson has actively worked in political campaigns for both Republican and Democratic candidates. He is a Baptist and has been active in his local church and on Baptist and interdenominational committees on public affairs.

WALFRED H. PETERSON

The Responsibility of
the Christian Voter

Opportunities for Influence

Representative democracy in the United States gives people, individually or collectively, many opportunities to exert political influence. The means of influence are varied: the right to vote, to run for office, to organize parties and pressure groups, to lobby, to petition, to publish, to speak and demonstrate on political issues, and to compete by examination for appointed office. If the list were broken down into subcategories, it would be much longer.

In spite of all this, some people feel alienated from the political system. These people speak of it as a distant machine "run" by "those politicians" or "them," and their tone rings with hostility. But this alienation and hostility are not created by the system's unwillingness to include people in its workings. To the contrary, people are begged to vote, to work in a party, to join political action and political education groups, to support candidates, and to participate in displays of political unity.

This alienation from our political life springs largely from some deficiency in the alienated person. He cannot fit into political groups as a leader or follower, or he cannot accept the general policies that dominant groups are trying to promote and implement. The reasons for this inability to fit in or to accept are many and their quality varies. Some people are too busy with other things, some are too uninformed, some are too garrulous, some are not gregarious, some are too perfectionist to compromise, and some are too saintly. At first glance, the reasons may be good or bad. But the persons who feel alienated ought to recognize that in the total American political establishment is found a very wide range of persons with different abilities, personalities, political and ethical codes. Politics has its busy people, it "loners," its perfectionists, its saints, and its lefts and rights. It has almost all kinds of people.[1] A person who cannot find a niche in our political system at some level will not readily find his place in any mass organization.

The task of this essay is to discuss the system's broadest means of participation, the franchise, and to ask how the Christian should relate to it. A reminder of the scope of the franchise in American politics will be the starting point, for it is broader than in most other large democratic societies and therefore presents special opportunities and problems for people and groups. In this country, adult citizens can vote in all elections related to the political units of their residence. "Adult" is arbitrarily defined by age with different states using 18, 19, 20, and 21. Possession of American citizenship is now a uniform requirement, but in the past aliens who had obtained their papers were enfranchised in some states. The states set these and other requirements subject to the federal constitutional limits (Fourteenth, Fifteenth, and Nineteenth Amendments) which deny them the power to restrict voting on grounds of race, color, and sex. These few facts remind us that the battle for universal suffrage has been long and hard in American history. The poor, Negroes, and women had to struggle for it. People who discount its purpose might do well to review the arguments and the fervor of those who worked for its extension.

The words "all elections" used above have many meanings, for the American voter has many tasks. At regular elections he must pass judgment on candidates for three levels of government. The local level includes a wide variety of county, city, township, and school board posts. Furthermore, at the state and local level he may vote on constitutions and charters, amendments to both of these, referenda, and a multiplicity of bond issues. In some states he also may have to make decisions on initiative and recall petitions. At primary elections he must choose party officers and nominees for the final election, and in a few states there will be a run-off primary if the nominees do not receive a specified percentage of the vote.

If anything, the American voter has too many responsibilities. In some primary elections even the rather well-informed voter will feel uninformed about the scores of candidates and issues. In some state and local elections, several long and technical constitutional and charter amendments may be presented to the voter in language only a lawyer could comprehend. As a result, most political scientists have come to agree that many state and local ballots should be much shorter. In what follows, these criticisms of the election system should be kept in mind, for they make it almost impossible for even the conscientious voter to be as responsible as he might wish to be.

The Stewardship of Influence

What the wide franchise and the scope of the election system mean for the Christian is this: he has the opportunity to be influential in politics. In short, he has power. His acts help decide the who and, more importantly, the what of our political life.

Of course, it would be absurd to pretend that the power or influence of one voter is large. It is, in fact, very small. However, disparagement about the influence of a voter can show a basic misunderstanding of the working of representative democracy in a nation with a population of two hundred million, or it can even reveal an opposition to democracy. Democracy is supposed to reflect the thoughts of the many with small power. How can it be otherwise? If it does not do so, then the political system is dictatorial or oligarchic.

Of course, democracies actually operate in ways which make it possible for a few people to acquire a large amount of power. But this condition is not necessarily a criticism of democracy if the competition between citizens to become powerful is reasonably free and if the powerful person can be tumbled from his position by the concerted action of weaker persons. In fact, all government, whether of the state, the church, industry, or of education, is oligarchic in nature; that is, government enables some men to become more powerful than others. But there is a significant difference between governments that have a democratic check on the very powerful citizens and governments that do not.

The check works in two ways: first, elections choose the top policy-making personnel of government. This is important, in spite of what some people might say to the contrary. Certainly, the landslide victory for President Lyndon B. Johnson and the Democratic Party in 1964 produced a different domestic program than would have been the case if Senator Barry Goldwater had won the presidency and carried a Republican Congress with him into power. Second, elections give the politician an indication of the general mood of the public. In spite of the fact that the Republican resurgence of 1966 was not much stronger than normal for an off-year election, especially when the huge Democratic victory of 1964 is considered, the Democrats assumed a more conservative posture in the ninetieth than in the eighty-ninth Congress. They took note of the shift in voter mood.

It is true that the policy differences occasioned by the victory of the Democratic or Republican Party could easily be exaggerated. Political forces make their impact along with other forces that may be more long-term and basic such as the technological, economic, sociological, and military. Also, in a two party system the quest for victory drives politicians toward the moderate or center position. But the parties have had significant differences at many points in American political history, and the voters' choices have made a difference in the nation's life.[2]

That the ordinary citizen has power and can use this to check governmental authorities is central to our concerns. Christian ethics has always maintained that power of any sort must be used responsibly. To put it in the words of C. Emanuel Carlson of the Baptist Joint Committee on Public Affairs, there must be a *stewardship of influence*. It is to the problems of exercising this stewardship that we now turn.

The Centrality of Issues

Democracy makes sense only if the voter acts on issues. The basic reason for voting is that voters help to determine the general policy of their nation, state, or locality. The *what* of democratic politics is primary, not the *who*. If voters are deciding merely between the attractiveness of personalities, they are only dispensing patronage, not exercising self-government.

In the actual working of the complex American election system, of course, there are circumstances in which the voter cannot act on issues. Some offices, such as clerk of the county court or registrar of wills, are elective in many places. For this kind of office, no genuine issues can be advanced, barring manifest incompetency in one of the candidates. And, in a specific election for a given office there may be no differences between the candidates as far as the voter can determine. Because of this, some elections seem pointless, and especially at the local level where issues are less exciting than at the national level, voter participation often falls off sharply. Sometimes, there is too much lamenting of low voter participation. Low participation that reflects an absence of issues is not an evil, and high participation that is not issue-oriented is not a good. After all, Nazis and Communists can turn out over 95 percent of the enfranchised populace every election.

Voting on the basis of judgments about political issues has implications that make the voter's task difficult. Three will be described here because an understanding of them is necessary to responsible citizenship. First, such voting implies that nonpolitical affiliations of candidates should normally not determine how the voter casts his ballot. This is hard for many people to accept—including many well-meaning church folk. If a candidate is a good Methodist, for example, he should not automatically receive the votes of Methodists nor should he receive the endorsement of his church. The reason relates to policy. He may be, let us say, a political conservative. A politically liberal Methodist would make a mistake in voting for such a candidate if there were another one in the competition more akin to his position. And, a Methodist church would be in error if it endorsed the man in a way that aligned it with the candidate's political position. Of course, the same would hold true if the candidate were a political liberal. Any candidate, however capable and however good a churchman, ought not to be divorced from his political policies in a democratic election.

To be sure, some nonpolitical affiliations may indicate something about the man's policy position. But church membership is not a reliable indicator of policy. There are good Quakers who support war as well as good Roman Catholics who support a wide separation of church and state. A responsible voter must look beyond the nonpolitical labels a candidate wears. The American Constitution took an unequivocal position respecting religious affiliation in 1789. In Article VI it decreed that ". . . no religious Test shall ever be required as a qualification to any Office or public Trust under the United States." Yet as late as 1960 many citizens who claimed to be protecting the Constitution tried to make Senator John F. Kennedy's religion the sole touchstone of the election. In spite of the victory of Mr. Kennedy, some careful studies have shown that in many states his religion hurt him seriously. Apparently, if he had not been a Catholic he would have won by a clear margin.[3] By 1964, however, there was much less overt opposition on religious grounds to the candidacy of Representative William Miller for vice president. Does this imply that the American electorate is coming abreast of 1789, or is it that people do not get excited about vice presidents?

Does the rejection of religious affiliation as a grounds for voting mean that religion is unimportant in a candidate's life? Not at all. What it means is that affiliation with this or that denomination does not indicate specific things about the candidate's political beliefs. Within any large denomination there is a wide range of political positions and there is almost always opposition to the denomination's official stands. What a candidate believes is something that the campaign and his public record should reveal; for example, a Quaker should be asked about his view of war, a Catholic about church-state relations, a Methodist about his attitude toward prohibition, and a Mormon about racial equality. Candidates must accept the fact that their religious connections make certain questions likely. They should be prepared to answer them in good grace, and voters should accept the answers given in like manner.

Second, voting on the basis of political issues implies that even political affiliation should not necessarily determine how an individual ought to cast his vote. Does not party membership indicate where a candidate stands? The answer is both yes and no. In some localities and states the party label which a candidate carries may say something in general about his political views. But in the United States there is the tradition of the political maverick and of local party autonomy. This means the party label is not a fully reliable indicator of a given candidate. Senator Wayne Morse has been a Republican and is now a Democrat, but as a Democrat he is attacking his own party's policy in Vietnam with great regularity. Perhaps he is an exceptional example, but each party has its liberals and conservatives. The range of the two parties overlaps considerably.

The voter must also remember that the primary election system, however democratic it is, makes it possible for anyone to capture a party's nomination. Middle-of-the-roaders, rock-bound conservatives, and wild-eyed liberals can all seek the party's nomination for an office if they can raise the modest filing fee. In this manner, even John Birchers or Trotsky-ites can take over a political party and obtain the use of its name. There is no sure way within our system to make candidates pledge support for the party platform. They may and sometimes do proudly run against the platform of "their" party.

This point is especially important for a people as mobile as Americans. An informed voter should be aware that when he moves from one locality to another he may be changing his political climate. The G.O.P. in Minnesota and Wisconsin is not the same party as the G.O.P. in Georgia, Iowa, or California, and the Democratic party shows a similar inconsistency. A responsible voter must continually look to see if his general opinions about a party are correct. This is written with some pain. I recently changed my state of residence, voted largely on the basis of party label, and now find that those I voted for do not hold my general political position. My only comfort is that from my point of view the other candidates were even less attractive.

The reader should not take this discussion to mean that there are no grounds for defending party loyalty. The existence of political parties is essential in a large democracy. The parties help recruit candidates, organize and finance campaigns, and define issues. They are a cohesive force within the government that expedites government work. In general, they indicate something about the policies of a candidate. In contrast with the party candidate, most independent candidates are without identifiable political position. Thus, party should count for much. What is argued here is that it should not count for all.

The third implication of voting on the basis of policy is much more controversial among Christians. A candidate for public office should be judged primarily on public policy considerations, not on the basis of the quality of his private life. Of course, this statement needs qualification, as the word "primarily" implies. If the candidate is a grossly immoral person, he does not merit support *if* there is any reasonable alternative. But, certainly, Christians should not decide for or against a candidate on the basis of some detailed Christian code of personal ethics. For example, the fact that one man uses alcoholic beverages and another one does not should not be the basis of a voter's decision. Society in general accepts drinking, and unless the candidate is an alcoholic, this should not be a determinant of how one casts his vote. The same can be said about going to the race track or divorce.

A few years ago the news of Governor Nelson Rockefeller's impending divorce was revealed on a Saturday. The next day in a church in a large metropolitan area a Sunday School teacher told his adult class that no Christian could ever again support the governor. Similar remarks had been current during Governor Stevenson's 1952 and 1956 campaigns for the presidency. This is too rigid an approach, for to society as a whole divorce, while frowned upon, is acceptable. The fact that Governor Rockefeller seems to have weathered the storm caused by the breakup of his first marriage and the lack of attention given to Ronald Reagan's divorce shows that this acceptance may be widening.

The Christian can scarcely apply the purest standards of the household of faith to people in society at large. Puritan efforts to restrict power to the "elect" did not fit American democracy which found these standards too demanding a century and a half ago. Today, the Christian must admit in all modesty that even in the more pious and homogeneous denominations, standards concerning drinking, gambling, and divorce are not rigidly enforced or accepted. Moreover, the Believer should not become the proponent of a rigid legalism that has a priority system of sins by which all men are judged.

Multiplicity of Issues

Responsible Christian citizenship recognizes not only the centrality of issues but also the multiplicity of issues. In any election many issues are potentially at stake, because elected officials must pass judgment on a wide variety of matters. For example, a state legislator must vote on matters regarding public health, education, welfare, conservation, governmental structure, civil rights, taxation, public works, alcohol control, Sunday laws, gambling regulation, criminal codes, and divorce law. Unhappily, the list of possible issues that confronts a state legislator is so long that it makes his work, as well as the task of a conscientious voter, almost forbidding.

This multiplicity signifies several things for the voter. First, it means that except in the rarest cases it is folly to pass judgment on a candidate on the basis of just a single issue. If a legislator is to decide on a dozen matters that affect society, can the society only examine how he stands on one of them? The answer seems obvious, but over and over again campaigns become "single-issue" campaigns. For example, a little-known Democratic candidate, George Mahoney who ran in Maryland in 1966, scored an upset by winning the primary election for governor against two strong and well-financed opponents. He used a time-worn slogan against "open occupancy" or "fair housing" laws, repeating over and over again on the radio: "A man's home is his castle." Newspapers and other news media discussed only this issue in connection with his candidacy, and even in the general election campaign reporters could not obtain statements from him on many other pivotal questions. He was defeated by only a small margin, thus indicating that a single-issue candidate can go a long way. The illustrations used earlier concerning the religious issue in John F. Kennedy's presidential campaign and the divorce issue concerning Governor Rockefeller could be mentioned again. Even if a man's religion and his private life are treated as issues, it cannot be argued that these matters are the only problems. Yet these concerns became the whole matter for some influential churchmen.

In American political history, the Prohibition Party is often treated as the classic single-issue party. When in the 1900 campaign William Jennings Bryan, a Democrat, was arguing that the American acquisition and subjugation of the Philippines was the "paramount" issue and President McKinley and other Republicans were saying they were responsible for the "full dinner pail," leading Prohibitionists maintained that these and other questions were so inconsequential compared to the issue of the "liquor traffic" that they could be ignored. Christians who become so tunnel-visioned as this are cause for weeping.[4]

On the current American political scene, two groups that center on church-state issues tend to promote the single-issue approach. One is Citizens for Educational Freedom (CEF), a group which urges state aid to private and parochial schools, and the other is Protestants and Other Americans United for Separation of Church and State (POAU), a group that calls itself, ". . . the only organization in the nation exclusively dedicated to church-state separation. . . ."[5] In contrast to CEF, this group opposes all state financial aid to such schools. Candidates for elected office are often classified as acceptable or unacceptable by spokesmen for these groups solely on the issue of the meaning of the separation of church and state as it relates to support of private education. While most people will agree that church-state relations in education are important, a position that makes them all-important is problematic for a democratic system. It can produce elected officials whose serious interest in politics is much more narrow than their total responsibility. Thus, the voter who uses materials produced by these groups (and some of these materials are excellent) should recognize their narrow interests.

The multiplicity of issues means, secondly, that the voter must be content with less than the ideal candidate. If the voter is interested in, let us say, a half dozen issues and if he can find statements by candidates on these issues that are not glittering generalities, he will very likely find that no candidate is really in agreement with him on all points. His problem then becomes one of finding the candidate who most often agrees with him on the most important questions. This may sound obvious and elementary, but some voters despair when they find that all their tastes are not suited.

At this point an issue should be mentioned that bothers some Christians when they study the political scene. Can they compromise their ideals? Can they vote for or electioneer on behalf of a candidate with whom they generally agree but with the exception of some points? Can they join or support a party knowing that it is right on only seven issues out of ten? Sometimes the problem is raised in caricature by a contrast between a "man of principle" and a "man of party."

The Christian should not have trouble with this issue at the level of ideas. He starts with the Biblical understanding that the present world is not ideal, indeed, it is a mixture of good and bad, and all man's efforts are finally inadequate. He knows that even the church on this earth falls terribly short of perfection. Thus the Christian ought to be aware that the demand for an earthly ideal, while necessary as a prod, is utopian and cannot be achieved. For the here and now, the Christian must accept and work within a framework of the relatively good. Those who cannot do so should retreat into a monastery or an agrarian sect, when and if they can find one that is perfect.

In short, the way all human society operates means that the voter must accept the relatively good candidate or, if worst comes to worst, the least bad candidate. Refusal of voters of high ideals to accept this fact leaves open the route to power by the most corrupt. If the good men retreat from the field of battle because they cannot tolerate its noises, who will win the day?

French politics give us some of the best examples of difficult choices between bad and worse. There a politically moderate Protestant who opposes state aid to church schools may find himself in a district where the only candidates with a chance of election are a politically reactionary

Roman Catholic who supports such aid and a hard-line Communist who opposes it. An extreme example? Perhaps it is. Yet a sensitive voter must often vote with tears in his eyes, but these tears should not deter him from voting.

Sources of Political Information

The multiplicity of issues together with the wide scope of the American election system puts the voter in a trying position. He can scarcely hope to make responsible judgments about all the candidates and issues. He cannot get firsthand knowledge even if he tries. This means the voter must rely on others for the information on which he bases his political judgments. This reliance requires some care if it is to be prudent. What sources of information are reliable? The best answer is that no single source of political information is dependable. The person who intends to use his political influence responsibly must accept the fact that all opinion-shaping agencies in the society have their political biases. People select and interpret news on the basis of those biases. The family, social club, gang at work, church, press, television, radio, and motion pictures—all sift the political news and color it according to preconceptions.

Optimistically, the biases of different sources of information will balance each other out and supplement each other by chance. In some cases this is true. But for many people in the society, this balancing and supplementing does not occur. The local newspapers may have a given bias that is reinforced by the editorial policies of the national magazines to which his family has long subscribed. If the organizations to which he belongs have a leadership of similar political disposition, the individual's slanted view of things will be further buttressed. But chance circumstances are only a part of the means by which people develop and reinforce a political predisposition. Many or most people will consciously or unconsciously choose certain reading material, radio and TV programs, and social contacts because these are congenial to an original bent in their thought. That is, they screen out that which challenges their bias and let in that which reinforces it.[6]

If a person seriously tries to control the information he receives in order that he may obtain information reflecting several points of view, he must deliberately choose to see or hear a broad range of sources. The range must be consciously selected, and its sweep cannot be left to chance. To be sure, some sources of information are relatively unbiased and complete—the *New York Times*, for example. But one study of its fine work has revealed that its most faithful readers can be woefully led astray even on a subject it covers rather thoroughly.[7]

These observations are, of course, pertinent to any person who takes his democratic responsibility seriously. Should something special be said to the Christian on this? At least this ought to be pointed out. Churches, denominations, interdenominational agencies, religious journals, and church leaders have no immunity from the diseases of unknown or deliberate bias in politics. Indeed, because they believe themselves to be striving disinterestedly for the common good and for God's will in the world, they run the special risk of the arrogance of assuming and implying that their opinion and their "facts" are preferred in the divine order of things.

With all due recognition of the fact that words like "liberal" and "conservative" are among the most amorphous in the English language, let us specifically illustrate the point about political bias in religious agencies. Experienced political observers agree that in its general tendency, the National Association of Evangelicals is politically conservative and the National Council of Churches is politically liberal. Materials both groups produce, resolutions both adopt, and the speakers which their agencies directly or indirectly sponsor reveal their general positions rather consistently and clearly. Or, to categorize magazines on the basis of the articles they carry and their editorials: *Christian Century* is generally on the liberal side of political issues, while *Christianity Today* is usually conservative. *Eternity* stands somewhere between the two. One reason for the establishment of *Christianity and Crisis* was the feeling of its original editors that the then consistently pacificist bent of the *Christian Century* should be countered by a Christian journal that accepted the propriety of war in certain circumstances. Or to take denominations on the basis of long term positions: the writer recently attended a meeting of church groups on a military draft law which had just been reported out of the House Military Affairs Committee. Representatives of the Friends, Mennonites, and Brethren were present, and true to their customary patterns of behavior, they objected to a provision that would induct all persons eligible for the draft into the army before, rather than after, the conscientious objectors among them are allowed to begin their alternative service programs. In the same manner objections would be voiced by Seventh-Day Adventists on Sunday closing laws, Christian Scientists on laws requiring medical care, and many Methodist and Baptist groups on liquor control legislation.

The point should be clear that church and religious agencies do not come to political issues with an immunity from bias. The Christian who relies on a single church, denomination, or religious journal for his political knowledge will have a knowledge that reflects the predispositions of those who shape that agency's political thought. Therefore, the same rules apply to public affairs material produced by church or religious groups

that are applicable to secular material: (1) Any single source is not reliable for a balanced view of political life; and (2) a range of sources
must be deliberately selected if a person wishes to vote responsibly.

These observations must be related to earlier comments about the danger of judging a candidate for office on the basis of religious connections,
because what has been said may seem contradictory. If religious materials
have political biases, will not candidates of a given religion share these
views? The answer is yes and no. The candidate learns his political ideas
from many sources. He may be a Presbyterian and read his church's publications that deal with social problems. But before entering public office
he was, perhaps, a labor union official who read labor magazines which
covered social matters much more thoroughly and consistently than his
church's publications ever did, or a banker who relied on banking journals for most of his political information. The devout churchman can all
too easily assume that another person's religious connection is formative
in his life. For many (should it be said most?) people, religious affiliation
is not formative at all. Is this not what the devout mean when they say
we live in a secular age?

What about the clergyman as a source of political information? He too
is not immune from political bias. And this is true even when he bases his
political judgments on a supposedly careful interpretation of Scripture.
Well-meaning clergymen who sincerely believed that they were solidly
grounded on Biblical insights have argued for feudalism, capitalism, socialism, monarchy, aristocracy, and democracy. Some supported the South
and some the North in the Civil War. Currently, some support a racially
segregated society while others support an integrated society. The Vietnam War has produced both hawks and doves among the clergy. In most
instances the social, economic, political, ethnic, and geographic milieu in
which a clergyman was raised and now lives will orient his general political thought more decisively than will his study of the Holy Scriptures.

Perhaps a further caution concerning the political views of the clergy
is in order. Many of them are not well-educated in those disciplines which
would help them to speak more perceptively on political matters. This is
not meant as blanket criticism of them or of theological education. The
ministerial student must be exposed to so many areas of knowledge that
he can only touch some superficially. Because of this and because seminaries do not require that their entrants have a well-rounded social science
background, many graduate from seminary with only the most rudimen-
tary knowledge of such tempting pulpit topics as the national debt, laws
on obscenity, the statistics of crime, or the data on divorce. Thus they
may be expected to spread some folklore when they talk on such subjects.
To be sure, courses in economics, constitutional law, and social statistics

do not guarantee immunity from error, while at the same time, some men become self-educated with remarkable facility. However, formalized education does help, and too often those who lack it in the social sciences are not aware of the seriousness of their deficiency.

Conclusion

What has been said here may seem discouraging. People are always being told that they must assume their responsibilities, that these are not easily executed, and that their execution requires purposeful effort. The formula is the same for the many roles we play: student, spouse, parent, employer, employee, and citizen. It becomes at times rather wearying.

Wearying or not, the theme is valid. Since we possess the opportunity to make a difference in the affairs of men, we have the responsibility to do so and to do the best we can. What if the best difference in social and political affairs in this generation is not easily identified or achieved? What if a given person's opportunity to make a difference is small? The responsibility is nevertheless there. Even the servant with one talent is called to answer for his stewardship. The question is what, not how much, was done.

The Christian comes to the responsibilities discussed above with certain advantages. First, he possesses the needed motivation, for he knows that to love God, his lodestone, also involves loving his fellowmen. He, therefore, should be deeply concerned with the public affairs that so decisively mold the lives and determine the welfare of his fellows. This concern ought to give a dynamic dimension to his activities as an enfranchised citizen. Second, he has the capacity to rise above the level of self-interest that debases much in public life because he has experienced the paradox involved in losing and finding one's life. Third, he has a perspective that allows him to assume his civic duty, since he knows that his best and his worst freely devised efforts are executed within a divine order of things that gives hope and meaning. Since he possesses these unique spiritual endowments, the Christian should be expected to exercise his stewardship of influence. The obligation cannot be shirked or ignored because it is the will of his Heavenly Father.

NOTES

1. For discussions of political participation see Seymour M. Lipset, *Political Man* (New York: Doubleday, 1959); and Robert E. Lane, *Political Life* (Glencoe, Ill.: Free Press, 1959).

2. For further information on the degree of party divergence see Part II of

V. O. Key, Jr., *Politics, Parties, and Pressure Groups* (New York: Thomas Y. Crowell, 1958); and Hugh A. Bone, *American Politics and the Party System* (New York: McGraw-Hill, 1965), chap. 5. The *Congressional Quarterly* regularly carries tallies of roll call votes by party on issues which the editors classify as crucial. Use of several years' studies from this source will show consistencies in party differences.

3. See Philip E. Converse, Angus Campbell, Warren E. Miller, and Donald E. Stokes, "Stability and Change in 1960: A Reinstating Election," *American Political Science Review*, LV (June 1961), pp. 269–80.

4. A review of the Prohibition Party's platforms shows that the party did raise a few other issues on most occasions, but these were relatively insignificant compared to the overriding concern of prohibition. See Kirk H. Porter and Donald B. Johnson, *National Party Platforms, 1840–1960* (Urbana: University of Illinois Press, 1961).

5. Undated advertisement folder and undated letter of advertisement signed by Glenn L. Archer, Executive Director, received in April 1967.

6. A leading source book for issues related to political opinion formation is V. O. Key, Jr., *Public Opinion and American Democracy* (New York: Knopf, 1961).

7. See the discussion of the *New York Times'* work in Irving Kristol, "The Underdeveloped Profession," *The Public Interest*, no. 6 (Winter 1967), pp. 36–52.

Richard V. Pierard is Associate Professor of History at Indiana State University, Terre Haute, Indiana. He was born in Chicago, Illinois on May 29, 1934 and spent the major portion of his youth in the state of Washington. After serving two years in Japan as an enlisted man in the United States Army, he obtained his undergraduate education at Westmont College and California State College at Los Angeles, and in 1958 the latter institution awarded him the B.A. degree with high honor. He obtained an M.A. from California State College at Los Angeles in 1959 and a Ph.D. in history from the University of Iowa in 1964. In 1962–63 he was also the recipient of a Fulbright grant for advanced study at the University of Hamburg in Germany.

Mr. Pierard was a teaching assistant in the Department of History at the University of Iowa for four years and was an instructor in this department in the summer of 1964. He joined the faculty of Indiana State University in 1964 as an assistant professor and was promoted to associate professor in 1967. He was a participant in the Earlham College African Institute in 1965, and presently he is a member of the instructional staff of the NDEA Institute for Advanced Study in Non-Western History sponsored by Indiana State University. During the summer of 1967 Professor Pierard spent several weeks in research and travel in Germany and Central Europe.

His primary areas of interest are the history of Modern Germany and European overseas expansion in the nineteenth and twentieth centuries. Mr. Pierard is the author of *Sylvanus F. Bowser* (Fort Wayne, Ind., 1964), and he has contributed articles to the *Standard, Eternity, Teachers College Journal, Tanzania Notes and Records,* and *Scandinavian Economic History Review.* His book on the German Colonial Society will be published shortly. He is a member of the American Historical Association, Conference Group for Central European History, African Studies Association, and American Association of University Professors. His denominational preference is Baptist, and he is also a registered Republican voter.

RICHARD V. PIERARD

Christianity, Democracy, and the Radical Right

A serious malady presently afflicts a substantial segment of evangelical Christianity, namely, a close identification with the so-called "Radical Right." Not only does this tragic situation hinder the effectiveness of the evangelical witness, but also it threatens to negate many of the basic principles of Christianity itself. Because the relationship with the Radical Right is sapping the very lifeblood of the Christian faith, it is imperative that evangelicals become aware of the perils of Right-wing extremism and that they take immediate and forthright steps to combat this plague which has infected the body of Christ. Evangelical spokesmen and publications, with the striking exception of the courageous magazine *Eternity*, have unfortunately not done enough to inform their constituencies about the menace of the Radical Right. Therefore, this essay will examine the nature of the Far Right in America and demonstrate that the movement is both incompatible with and absolutely inimical to the interests of evangelical Christianity.

What is the Radical Right?

Although it is extremely difficult to formulate an acceptable definition of the term Radical Right, it would be helpful to distinguish between what is generally regarded as responsible conservatism and Right-wing extremism. The difference lies basically in two broad areas, namely, their conceptions of the nature of the communist conspiracy and their approaches to achieving their aims. Radical Rightists are convinced of the absoluteness of the communist menace. Everything in the world is seen in terms of a life and death struggle between "slavery" and "freedom," and the communists are winning because they recognize the true nature of the contest. Implicit in this is the idea of conspiracy. Communism is primar-

39

ily an internal threat because its adherents are seeking to gain control of the institutions of government, education, and religion. Rightists believe in the existence of a gigantic "control apparatus" in the government which is endeavoring to transform the country into a "collectivist" state by gradual encroachment in the economic sphere and to destroy the old-fashioned American belief in Christianity and rugged individualism. When the time is ripe, the Soviet Union will move in, take over the United States, and complete the task of enslaving the American population. Responsible conservatives also decry the decline of traditional values and feel that every president since 1933 has manifested socialist leanings and softness toward communism, but they attribute this primarily to the blindness and bungling stupidity of the liberals who allegedly had charge of the government rather than to some insidious, internal communist conspiracy.

Radical Rightists, moreover, are committed to the use of "direct action" to combat the communist threat to the American way of life. According to their view, the enemy is already in the gates and one must mount the counterattack immediately. Secret communists must be ferreted out and exposed by every means available. All forms of government intervention in the social and economic realm must be blocked. Almost any tactic that will shock complacent Americans into action to save their rapidly disappearing freedoms is acceptable to the Rightists. Responsible conservatives, on the other hand, prefer to operate within the framework of American democratic procedures, and they shy away from the alarmist methods of the Radicals. They are willing and able to use the techniques of free speech and debate without resorting to hysterical name calling and smear tactics.[1]

It is somewhat difficult to categorize individuals and organizations as Radical Rightist, but undoubtedly there are a great number of them. The 1962 edition of the *First National Directory of "Rightist" Groups, Publications and Some Individuals in the United States* (San Francisco: Noontide Press) lists 824 supposedly Rightist organizations. The Forster-Epstein study (sponsored by the Anti-Defamation League of B'nai B'rith) contends that around 500 local and national groups fall into the Rightist category but only about two dozen can be regarded as major organizations.[2] The best known of these are the: John Birch Society, Christian Anti-Communism Crusade, Christian Crusade, National Educational Program, Twentieth Century Reformation Hour, Manion Forum, Life Line Foundation, Church League of America, Conservative Society of America, Liberty Amendment Committee of the U.S.A., Ku Klux Klan, Minutemen, Circuit Riders, Inc., and Liberty Lobby. A number of other extremely conservative groups are designated by Forster and Epstein as "fellow travelers" of the Radical Right.[3]

Estimates vary as to the number of people who are Right-wing extremists. Forster and Epstein suggest a figure of twenty per cent of the American electorate while sociologist Seymour Lipset declares that public opinion poll data indicate the existence of five to seven million political, racial, and religious extremists (both right and left wing) in the United States.[4] Particularly numerous in the ranks of the Radical Right are wealthy businessmen who provide the seemingly inexhaustible financial resources which support the myriad of organizations, radio and television programs, publications, lecture series, and seminars. Because of the vast influence which the Radical Right is capable of exercising in American society, it would be well to probe deeper into the movement to determine what kind of people are attracted to it, what specific objectives it has, and what methods it utilizes.

Personality Traits Found in Right-Wing Extremists

Devoted adherents to Radical Right movements tend to manifest a number of disturbing personality traits. The first of these is *simplism*, that is, a tendency to reduce all problems to a false simplicity by ignoring complicating factors. The Rightist usually sees people, ideas, and events in stark black-and-white terms. In his mind things stand in absolute "either-or" relationships; either communism or capitalism, surrender or war, black power or segregation. He seems to have a compelling need for firm, stereotyped views of people and events and thus rejects any ambivalence, compromises, or half-measures. With his all-or-nothing attitude, the extremist cannot tolerate any divergent view. He never subjects his simplistic, closed system to doubt or testing in the open marketplace of ideas, and he feels constrained to reinforce it continually with new, ever more fantastic details and explanations in order to forestall possible threats to it. To use Eric Hoffer's terminology, he erects a "fact-proof screen" to filter out ideas and facts which contradict his doctrine and thus is able to insulate himself from the uncertainties and unpleasant realities of the world around him.[5]

A second and particularly noteworthy trait is that of *paranoia*. One psychologist has even gone so far as to suggest that the United States is threatened by the danger of a "possible mass insanity" because of the paranoid nature of the Radical Right.[6] The paranoid is basically an insecure and suspicious person who feels himself the victim of injustice and persecution. As he seeks to find his imaginary enemies, he falls victim to mounting anxieties. When he manifests his strong feelings of suspicion, other people become either more cautious around him or actually hostile to him, and this only confirms his fears. The paranoid then embarks upon more and more desperate moves to identify the enemy and protect himself. Rapidly he comes to believe in the existence of a huge conspiracy directed at him personally, and he devotes his entire energy to the struggle against it.

The Radical Right position is particularly congenial to such a personality type, and it is no mere coincidence that so many people with paranoid tendencies are found in the ranks of Rightist movements. Richard Hofstadter has aptly pointed out that the "paranoid style" has the central image of "a vast and sinister conspiracy, a gigantic and yet subtle machinery of influence set in motion to undermine and destroy a way of life."[7] History is seen as a conspiracy which is directed by a demonic power, but the paranoid is aware of this and can perhaps defeat the forces of evil if he moves quickly and decisively in an all-out campaign. Since the struggle is between absolute good and absolute evil, one must work for complete victory. The enemy, however, is a free agent who has control of the mechanism of history and deflects its course in an evil way. He has charge of the effective means of power such as the press, educational system, and government, thus making the struggle even more difficult. The paranoid individual, already beset by personal anxiety and insecurity, easily falls prey to Right-wing demagogues and wholeheartedly joins the crusade to save America from the communist conspiracy. Before, he was suspicious of his friends and neighbors, but now he distrusts his government, the normal processes of law, and anyone who urges moderation or compromise.

A third trait common to most Radical Right-wingers is a *sense of alienation* from modern society. This is partially due to the frustrations and anxieties growing out of life in an age of revolution and potential world destruction. Moreover, the upward mobility of the lower class groups of recent immigrant stock in the cities is threatening the social status of the so-called native Anglo-Saxon Americans, and the latter are accordingly quite insecure about their own positions in contemporary society. Added to this is the development of a mass society with its drive toward a state of sameness and conformity in which the individual loses his sense of personal identity. The result is that many feel helpless and threatened in the modern world, and they long for the idealized simple, rural, and individualistic society of a by-gone era.[8]

The appeal of the Right-wing ideology to such people is strong. It offers them an organizational relationship in which the alienated individual can find meaning. It pinpoints and personifies his enemy as a great evil and provides him with a means to combat it. The individual gains status and importance because he is engaged in a cause that is noble and good, namely, bringing about the destruction of communism. At the same time, he is working to recover the traditional American way of life which he so fervently desires.

A fourth character trait of Rightists is *hostility*. They tend to express a substantial amount of hate and aggression toward their alleged enemies, particularly the political, social, and intellectual leaders of the community. They react vehemently to any criticism of their views or actions, and as anyone who follows the activities of the Radical Right is painfully aware, they frequently resort to the most unethical hit-and-run tactics and even outright violence. Closely related to this is *ego defense*. Rightists usually blame others for their own personal and social failures and indulge in the most deplorable forms of scapegoating to conceal their shortcomings.

It is evident from the foregoing discussion that the Radical Right tends to attract people who suffer from serious personality maladjustment and manifest a cluster of traits commonly labelled as authoritarian.[9] The famous study of personality traits of extreme conservatives made at the University of Minnesota by political scientist Herbert McClosky draws a similar conclusion. After presenting an impressive body of data which demonstrates the presence of the above mentioned traits, he goes on to declare that the Rightist ideology is:

> Far more characteristic of social isolates, of people who think poorly of themselves, who suffer personal disgruntlement and frustration, who are submissive, timid, and wanting in confidence, who lack a clear sense of direction and purpose, who are uncertain about their values, and who are generally bewildered by the alarming task of having to thread their way through a society which seems to them too complex to fathom.[10]

Objectives of Radical Right Movements

Although the specific aims of the Radical Right are practically as numerous as the stars in the sky, it is possible to detect some basic common denominators among them. First, the Right-wing extremists are trying to politicize every aspect of life. The Overstreets have indicated that everything the Rightists do or say, even in their daily lives, takes on political significance.[11] Whether they are going to church, talking with a neighbor, joining a PTA organization, or simply reading a book, they make political action a constant focus of life. Even though the Rightists are committed to unceasing political endeavor, they nevertheless reject the present political system in the United States. They denounce politicians, the major parties, and the give and take of political compromise, all of which they believe are diverting the attention of the American people from the really fundamental issue of communist subversion.

A second objective of Radical Right extremists is the repudiation of the American democratic process. In spite of his oft-repeated cliché: "The only -ism for me is Americanism," the Rightist seeks to destroy the American concept of civil liberties and attempts to silence all those who disagree with him or oppose his position. The Overstreets refer to this attitude as "a Communist-type intolerance marked by a will to demolish and liquidate" and show that the Rightists would rather "demolish than reform" all disliked programs and institutions, regardless of whether they be labor unions, public schools, foreign aid, mental health programs, the income tax, or the United Nations.[12] Instead of serving as a loyal opposition which works to bring about peaceful, gradual change within the framework of American democracy, the Far Right seeks to impose its will through such devices as intimidation, subversion, and the offering of radical panaceas. A perceptive conservative commentator, William S. White, has correctly stated that the Far Right is a complex and sophisticated form of "political nihilism."[13]

In the third place, Rightists wish to restore the simple virtues and traditional morality of rural America, above all, Protestant fundamentalism, nativist nationalism, close family relationships, rigid sexual standards, individual initiative, and self-reliance. For them, this would involve such actions as dismantling social security and welfare state programs, elimination of the income tax, drastically reducing the role of the federal government in the economic life of the country, and returning to state and local governments the primary responsibility for labor, welfare, and similar legislation. Daniel Bell points out that the Right-wing is really fighting "modernity," namely, "the belief in rational assessment, rather than established custom, for the evaluation of social change" and that it seeks to defend "its fading dominance, exercised once through the institutions of small-town America, over the control of social change."[14] Since there is a sequential association of such events as a declining interest in religion, a weakening of traditional family and sexual norms, an increase in the crime rate, the substitution of one-worldism for patriotism, and the passing of laissez-faire individualism, Rightists find it extremely easy to assume that this association is also causally related. Communism serves as a convenient scapegoat for the Radical Right, and thus the blame for the decline of the traditional values (and with it rural control of American political and social life) can be pinned on an alleged communist conspiracy to subvert the United States from within. Although the Rightist purports to be resisting the threat, he is in reality trying to recover the way of life of a former period of American history.

Finally, in spite of the fact that the Right is essentially isolationist in its outlook, it urges the assertion of American diplomatic and military power to defeat international communism. For example, Rightist spokesmen demand that the United States withdraw from the United Nations and other international organizations, discontinue foreign aid programs at once, and refrain from participating in disarmament conferences. But when it comes to relations with communist countries, the Rightists assume a surprisingly bellicose stance. They call for an end to diplomatic recognition of these regimes, the encouragement of revolts in the Soviet bloc countries, an immediate invasion of Cuba, a decisive military victory in Vietnam, and even the destruction of Red China. They contend that the American arms budget should be increased and her preparedness for war stepped up. The "no-win" policy must be abandoned and a preventive war to save "freedom" should be launched. Critic Brooks Walker cynically refers to this as the one "positive" plank in the Right-wing platform, and he appropriately designates its supporters as the "wipe-em-out contingent" of the Far Right and the "death makers."[15]

Methods Utilized by Right Extremists

To obtain these objectives, the Radical Right resorts to a number of methods which are, to say the least, questionable and in the more extreme cases utterly foreign to the basic procedures of American democracy. A prominent device of the Right is the formation of tightly organized groups which are characterized by extreme secrecy and strict vows of obedience. The most famous example is, of course, the John Birch Society. The Birch Society members are organized into small cells known as "chapters" and supervised by professional cadres called "coordinators." The party line is handed down from the society's headquarters in Belmont, Massachusetts, and no deviation from this is permitted. It fosters a cult of the leader, and the rank and file members act as a sort of task force which carries out orders without question. Since the group can expel members at any time, its ranks are kept free of dissidents and independent thinkers. Even data concerning membership and finances are kept strictly confidential.[16] Most of the other groups on the Far Right, however, have not been able to achieve the high degree of organizational efficiency of the Birch Society, and thus their nefarious activities are more open to public scrutiny.

Rightists, particularly Birchers, customarily endeavor to infiltrate the political party structure and the organizational fabric of American society such as PTA's, school boards, civic and service clubs, and churches. For this reason a high value is placed upon secrecy and most individual Birch Society members attempt to conceal the fact of their membership. Epstein and Forster demonstrate that the influence of the Radical Right is "most effective, most easily seen, and most keenly felt at the grass-roots level of American life." The reason for this is that infiltration and the capture of influential positions are more easily and effectively accomplished at the local level. Moreover, public apathy and indifference make it simpler for extremists to capture elective offices. Emotional issues which can be exploited are more readily available such as neighborhood racial tensions, a proposal to fluoridate the municipal water supply, or the presence of a provocative social studies teacher in the high school. Also, greater political weight can be brought to bear on local officials and businessmen through saturation campaigns.[17] When the Radical Right finally obtains control of a local group, they proceed to infect it with intolerance and militancy and to subject liberals and moderates in the community to constant vilification and innuendo.

The Radical Rightists have especially concentrated their energies on infiltrating the Republican Party. There is no question that the entrenchment of Rightists at the grass-roots levels was the pivotal factor in the nomination of Barry Goldwater in 1964. Rightist figures and organizations assumed prominent roles in the campaign, and vast quantities of Rightist literature were distributed under Republican auspices. For example, the Vigo County (Indiana) Goldwater headquarters openly disseminated along with its regular campaign literature a shoddy tract by John Stormer titled *None Dare Call It Treason*, an alleged exposé of communist subversion in the United States. Moreover, large numbers of Rightists continue to occupy positions of power at the precinct and county levels even today and incessantly inject their ideological poison into the veins of the party of Abraham Lincoln and Theodore Roosevelt. Even though the party's national leaders, Thruston Morton, Everett Dirksen, and Gerald Ford, attacked the John Birch Society in the fall of 1965, local groups such as the Los Angeles County Young Republicans rallied to the defense of the society. Numerous other examples could be cited of specific Birchite activities in the local Republican organizations, especially in California, Washington, North Dakota, and the South.[18]

Furthermore, the election of 1966 resulted in a strengthening, not weakening, of the Radical Right position in American political life. A study made by Group Research, a liberal-oriented agency, revealed that not a single spokesman for the extreme Right was defeated in the election. The ultra-conservative organization, Americans for Constitutional Action, boasted that 180 out of the 225 candidates whom it endorsed were victorious. Only one of the 121 congressmen up for re-election who possessed an ACA voting rating of 60% or higher was defeated, and this individual was a Republican running in an Alabama district.[19] It is therefore reasonable to assume that the Radical Right's infiltration of the Republican Party has been quite extensive and that it will continue to affect the posture of the party for some time to come.

A typical method of the Right-wing extremist is the one-sided approach to the discussion of issues. Such people see the struggle against communism as one in which viewpoints which are absolutely false must be defeated by their opposites which are absolutely true. Any fair, balanced presentation of ideas might neutralize people or even instill doubts in them. Facts never speak for themselves; they must be arranged in such a way that they will support conclusions which have already been drawn. Thus, the Rightist has a compelling need for "experts" and "leading authorities" to make facts do what they should. The world of Radical Rightism is a steady parade of quasi-experts, study groups, monographs, statistics, documents, footnotes, and bibliographies. The most highly esteemed figures are those who have had access to some unusual source of information, such as a former Communist Party member or ex-FBI agent. Such qualifications usually entitle these individuals to be permanent authorities on all matters.[20]

It is remarkable to observe the ease with which the Rightist twists and misuses his facts in spite of the presence of so much scholarly apparatus. Facts and non-facts often stand side by side in the writings of these people. Again and again the documentary evidence cited to establish the pro-communist and treasonous activities of individuals occupying high positions are the literary productions of other Rightists or reports of the Rightist-controlled House Committee on Un-American Activities and Senate Internal Security Subcommittee.[21] Also, only those materials are utilized which give support to the author's preconceptions about domestic and foreign policy matters.

A technique commonly used is that of raising suspicions about a particular group of people. The Rightist may say that "only a few teachers are communists" and thereby plants the idea that some are. Since subversive teachers are somewhere, they must be looked for everywhere. This creates an atmosphere of doubt which soon leads to witch hunts, smears, and mass hysteria. The same tactic can be applied to any other group such as ministers or elected officials. A classic instance of the latter occurred in 1962. For some time Rightists had been circulating a statement attributed to Nikita Khrushchev which read: "We cannot expect the Americans to jump from capitalism to communism, but we can assist their elected leaders in giving Americans small doses of socialism, until they suddenly awake to find they have communism." Alarmed by the implications of this assertion, Senator Lee Metcalf of Montana initiated an investigation to determine its authenticity and found it to be spurious. Then he lashed out against the Rightists in a Senate speech on March 8, 1962 and accused them of using the false statement to show people that their public officials were communist stooges. He forthrightly declared they had used a lie to perpetrate a greater lie and contended they were cut from the same cloth as communists and fascists.[22]

Another noteworthy instance of this type of behavior was the celebrated Air Force Manual controversy of 1960. It was discovered that a newly issued training manual for non-commissioned officers in the Air Reserves openly asserted that a number of communists had infiltrated the National Council of Churches and that 30 of the 95 persons who had participated in the translation of the Revised Standard Version of the Bible had been affiliated with communist front organizations or activities. This revelation caused a public furor, but the utter falsehood of these allegations was soon demonstrated and the manual was withdrawn. Nevertheless, seeds of doubt about the clergy as a profession had been sown, and the Rightists had left a nagging fear in the minds of many that the National Council was somehow under the influence of communists.[23]

A good illustration of the manner in which the Radical Right-winger tends to twist facts to make them fit his preconceived ideas is Fred Schwarz's description of communism as a series of concentric circles. According to this "eminent authority," in the center of the concentric circles stands the Communist Party, a small group of organized, disciplined, and dedicated people. Surrounding this is the "zone of fellow travellers," those who approve of the communist philosophy, objectives, organization, and tactics but do not submit to total party discipline. Beyond this is the "zone of sympathizers," various pacifists, collaborators, and socialists who disapprove of the brutality and denial of individual liberty of communism but who feel that communism has many good features and that it is possible to associate with them in some worthy project. Next comes the "zone of pseudo-liberals," professors and pseudo-intellectuals in the colleges and universities who uphold the right of communists to teach and defend the use of the Fifth Amendment by them. Finally, there is the "zone of dupes," genuinely patriotic Americans who simply have been deceived and have fallen into traps set by communists.[24] Of course, any person who possesses even an elementary understanding of communism will be struck by the absurdity of this facile explanation.

If Rightists merely utilized the persuasive power of tongue and pen in the open marketplace of ideas, they would be nothing more than a minor nuisance. Unfortunately, they often resort to high-pressure tactics and outright intimidation to obtain their objectives. A frequent device used is that of a well-planned heckling campaign at a public meeting. Another tactic is the indiscriminate use of the big lie and the wanton smear to discredit opponents. Character assassination in the form of a whispering campaign is often an effective device. Others who go afoul of the Rightists become the target of abusive telephone calls at all hours of the day and night. To put pressure on law-makers, Right-wing extremists unleash avalanches of "look-alike" letters to influence the passage or defeat of legislation, and they utilize economic weapons such as the boycott against uncooperative merchants and businessmen. Even violence is not out of the question as is graphically illustrated by a pair of incidents which occurred in 1962. Crudely made bombs were exploded at the homes of two Los Angeles ministers who were highly critical of the Radical Right, and a fire bomb was hurled into the office of the *Midlothian* (Texas) *Mirror* after the newspaper's editor, W. Penn Jones, had protested a "John Birch Society-type speech" delivered at a high school assembly in his community.[25] Of all the methods adopted by the Far Right to obtain its objectives, these devices of intimidation offer the most serious threat to an orderly, democratic society.

Identification With Protestant Fundamentalism

One of the most disturbing aspects of the Radical Right is its close relationship with American Protestant Christianity. Nearly every commentator on Right-wing extremism has called attention to the large number of fundamentalists who are associated with the movement. Such prominent figures of the Far Right as Billy James Hargis, Carl McIntire, Fred Schwarz, George Benson, and Edgar Bundy are all practicing fundamentalists while Robert Welch came out of this background and expresses sympathy for the position. The rank and file members of the various Rightist organizations are overwhelmingly fundamentalists in their religious convictions. Certain major Protestant denominations generally associated with fundamentalism, such as the Southern Baptist Convention and the Churches of Christ, seem to furnish an inordinately large number of supporters for Rightist movements.

In turn, the prophets of the Right direct many of their appeals to these people and identify their work with Christianity. They speak of "Christian Americanism" and of the struggle against "godless communism." The new Christian patriots declare that "our side is God's side" and equate American capitalism with Christianity itself. The strongly laissez-faire oriented publication, *Christian Economics*, editorialized: "Would not we do well if we henceforth speak of the American Way as the Chris-

tian Way?" while Robert E. Kofahl, president of Highland College, a
staunchly fundamentalist school in California, said that the free enterprise
system is "established by the Ten Commandments and the teaching of
Jesus Christ and His apostles."[26]

The Radical Right attracts fundamentalists for a number of reasons.
Communism is presented as a twentieth century abomination which
serves as the catch-all for everything that is evil and undesirable in the
affluent, sophisticated, and easy-going life of modern urban society. By
equating the struggle against communism with a war against sin and
atheism, the Rightist appeals to the crusading tendencies of fundamentalists. The moralistic quality of the Rightist economic ideas seems to
harmonize with the basic asceticism of the fundamentalist world view.
Most of them have traditionally believed that a person's life ought to be
characterized by such qualities as prudence, economy, and diligence and
that he is rewarded for virtue and hard work and punished for vice and
laziness. The fundamentalist is profoundly disturbed because these values
are seriously questioned today, and he rallies to the support of those who
are trying to uphold them.[27]

Moreover, the Right has taken over the revivalistic techniques which
are so familiar to the fundamentalist. A Rightist rally or "crusade" features the singing of stirring religious and patriotic hymns, passionate appeals for funds to support anti-communist organizations, and speakers
who utilize all the oratorical tricks of an old-fashioned evangelist. For
instance, the portly prophet of anti-communism, Billy James Hargis, repeatedly uses in his public addresses and radio sermons such phrases as
"counterattack with prayer" and "the Word of God is one of the weapons
most feared by anti-Christ communism." Another master of the technique
of "political revivalism" is the Australian-born psychiatrist, Dr. Fred
Schwarz, a modern day Jeremiah who by means of his Christian Anti-
Communism Crusade is attempting to rescue Americans from imminent
destruction. Here are some examples of his platform oratory:

> Christian, to arms! The enemy is at the gate. Buckle on the armor
> of the Christian and go forth to battle.

> With education, evangelism and dedication let us smite the Com-
> munist foe and if necessary give up our lives in this noble Cause!

> ... We cry, "We shall not yield! Lift high the blood-stained banner
> of the Cross and on to Victory!"

> ... Co-existence is impossible. ... Communism is total evil ...
> its methods are evil and its ends are evil. ... We must hurl this thing
> back into the pit from whence it came![28]

Further, the Radical Rightists have sought with considerable success to divert the enthusiasm and missionary zeal commonly present among fundamentalists into essentially non-religious channels. Individually and in teams, nightly and over weekends, the apostles of the Far Right fan out over the countryside with tape recorders, movie projectors, and suitcases of books and pamphlets to carry out their mission of spreading the gospel of "Americanism." An illustration of this was provided by a Congregational minister in the Los Angeles subcommunity of Diamond Bar who had experienced the efforts of Right-wingers to infiltrate his congregation and substitute their doctrines for those of his church. Amazed at the fervor of the young people in this movement, he declared: "Would that this passion might be devoted to the service of Christ!"[29]

As the Overstreets have so wisely pointed out, it is wrong to conclude "that religious fundamentalism and Radical Rightism just naturally go in tandem."[30] The Rightists are actually misrepresenting fundamentalism and appropriating its doctrines, techniques, and emotional fervor for their own ends. Therefore, it is necessary that the principles and practices of the Far Right be examined in the light of Biblical Christianity. Only then will one become fully aware of the heretical nature of this new religion which is operating under the guise of fundamentalism and sapping the strength of evangelical Christianity.

Biblical Principles and the Radical Right

The Radical Right departs from the basic tenets of Christianity at a number of significant points. First, the Rightist denies the mutual responsibility of men for one another. He blindly ignores the Scriptural injunction *to do good to all men* (Gal. 6:10) and forgets that if the Christian shows partiality, he has committed a sin. (Jas. 2:9) Christ not only echoed the Old Testament command to love one's neighbor as oneself (Lev. 19:18; Mk. 12:31), but also offered the touching story of the Good Samaritan as an example of how one should express this love. Moreover, when Christ condemned those who supposedly did not give him food, drink, or clothing when he needed it, welcome him when he was a stranger, or take care of him when he was in prison, he firmly declared: "As you did it not to one of the least of these [my brethren], you did it not to me." (Mt. 25:45) One must love even his enemies and those who persecute him. He dare not restrict his concern merely to his friends and relatives. (Mt. 5:44–7)

Contrast this with the selfish individualism which the evangelists of the Far Right preach—each man for himself and each class, each race, each nation for itself. If a Christian suggests that his fellow believers are responsible for helping the poor to find a way out of their poverty or encouraging the members of a downtrodden race to assert their inherent rights to be human beings, he is immediately branded a "social gospeler" or a "communist." The person who labors to help slum dwellers find better housing, organizes migrant laborers to work for higher wages, or agitates for medical care for the aged is obviously a "do-gooder." Any attempt to use the vast resources of the United States to aid the economic development of backward countries is stoutly resisted as being a "give-away program." Is this a "Christian" message?

This type of behavior on the part of so-called Christians was magnificently demonstrated in a recent issue of the weekly newsletter of a Church of Christ in Murfreesboro, Tennessee. First, a newspaper article was photographically reproduced which described the ousting of Wendle Scott as director of a Church of Christ school in McAllen, Texas that trained Mexicans for the ministry. He was dismissed for participating in a march of striking Mexican-American farmers in the Rio Grande Valley to obtain higher wages and union recognition. Then, the minister of the Tennessee church, Evangelist Thomas G. O'Neal, offered some comments on the incident which clearly indicated his own level of spiritual comprehension. According to O'Neal, the Texas minister "has left the noble work of telling men and women what to do in order to be saved and has of late taken up the work of demonstrating for social reform." Moreover, he informed the readers that:

> Jesus Christ and his apostles were not found demonstrating in order to get the people's pay check raised twenty to forty-five cents per hour. It was Christ himself who said, "Go into all the world and preach the gospel to every creature. He that believeth and is baptized shall be saved; he that believeth not shall be damned." Mark 16:15–16. The results of obeying the gospel preached by the apostles was not a raise on the pay check but was salvation from sin. The consequences of not obeying Christ was damnation, not a failure to earn more. . . .
>
> This is but an evidence of the social gospel in action. Many will not go this far, but Scott was willing to travel down the road of the social gospel of modernism this far. Those who have given themselves and the Lord's Church to the building up of all kinds of social institutions supported by the church are on the same road of the social gospel that Scott is.[31]

Second, Christ taught not only love but also peace. The prophet Isaiah called him the "Prince of Peace," (Isa. 9:6) and his message of salvation was one of peace as well as rescue from eternal damnation. Vengeance belonged only to the Lord; therefore, the follower of Christ was expected to turn the other cheek and go the second mile. (Rom. 12:19; Mt. 5:39–41) When Peter precipitously struck the slave of the high priest with his sword, Jesus ordered him to replace the weapon in its sheath. (Jn. 18:10, 11) Paul recognized his God as the "God of love and peace," (II Cor. 13:11) and he urged the Christians in Rome to "live peaceably with all [men]." (Rom. 12:18)

The Radical Right falls far short of this standard; in fact, violence and intimidation are its hallmarks. Two instances illustrate the extremes to which the Right will go. On the night of February 1, 1962 while a forum was being held at a West Los Angeles synagogue on the topic "The Radical Right—Threat to Democracy?" terrorists exploded bombs and left anti-Semitic and anti-communist leaflets at the homes of the two speakers, the Rev. John G. Simmons and Brooks Walker, a Lutheran and a Unitarian minister. In its report of the incident *Christian Century* correctly commented that the extremist tries to win power by deception, fear, and finally by force, and these people "are ready to turn our country into another Algeria, where terror and anarchy place every life in daily danger."[32] At a "Faith and Freedom Rally" which was sponsored by Carl McIntire's American Council of Christian Churches in the San Fernando Valley of California on June 23, 1961, Lutheran minister L. W. Linnerson attempted to introduce a statement by J. Edgar Hoover that strongly disapproved of "self-styled experts on communism." After failing in his efforts, he walked out of the meeting and read the Hoover statement to a group of people gathered outside the entrance to the building. While he was reading it, two men told him: "You had better leave if you want to leave in one piece." In the next few days he received numerous harassing telephone calls during the night, several automobiles circled incessantly around the block and slowed down or stopped in front of his house, and men sat in a car parked across the street staring at the pastor and his family hour after hour.[33] Can a true Christian identify with a movement that is responsible for these kinds of actions?

A third fault of the Radical Right is its pharisaism. The great failing of the religious sect known as the Pharisees was that its members *used* religion to enhance themselves instead of serving as instruments of God. Christ's public condemnation of their hypocrisy pointed out this basic fact about them, and their self-seeking was at the root of their rejection of Jesus. If one substitutes "Christian Rightists" for Pharisees in a paraphrase of Christ's denunciation in Matthew 23 and Mark 12, it becomes amazingly clear how much they are alike. "You love the chief places at great anticommunist rallies and seminars. You love to be called 'experts' by those present at meetings. You devour widows' savings and pensions by obtaining contributions for your organizations while at the same time living in luxury yourselves. You traverse land and sea to find a convert for the cause and then he is more of a fanatic than you. You strain at minor points of doctrine and details of personal conduct and neglect the weightier matters of Christianity such as justice, mercy, and faith. Prophets and wise men are sent to call you back to a life of commitment and service to Jesus Christ, but you lash out against them with vile invective, make them the targets of smears and whisper campaigns, and threaten them with physical violence." With all fairness one can affirm that the self-righteous "Christian" prophets of the Radical Right are truly "American Pharisees."

A fourth concern is the problem of Christian unity, a matter which is discussed frequently in the Scriptures. Christ prayed that his disciples "may be one, even as we are one," (Jn. 17:11, 12) and Paul wrote: "You are all one in God" (Gal. 3:28) and "by one Spirit we were all baptized into one body." (I Cor. 12:13) The Apostle scolded the Corinthians for their jealousy and strife because they broke into factions and identified themselves with Paul, Apollos, Cephas, or even Christ. Paul said they were "men of the flesh" and "babes in Christ." (I Cor. 1:12; 3:1–3) Even the Psalmist David declared: "Behold, how good and pleasant it is when brothers dwell in unity!" (Ps. 133:1)

The Radical Right completely ignores the divine injunction for unity among Christian believers. The schismatic and atomizing factor in Rightist dogma and practice is epitomized in the activities of Carl McIntire, a New Jersey minister who was expelled from the Presbyterian Church in the U.S.A. in 1936. He formed his own church federation, the American Council of Christian Churches, to combat the "liberalism" and "modernism" of the Federal (later National) Council of Churches, established a small newspaper known as the *Christian Beacon* to alert people to the latest activities of the modernists and communists, and created a tax-exempt religious organization called the Twentieth Century Reformation Hour which is now bombarding the country with Right-wing propaganda via the medium of radio. McIntire continuously and vehemently lashes out against the National and World Council of Churches, the Revised Standard Version of the Bible, the United Nations, the seemingly timid American foreign policy, and the social and economic legislation of the last three decades. He spreads dissension among various churches by encouraging individual members to question the loyalty and integrity of their fellow Christians, pastors, and denominational leaders, and he urges his listeners and readers to abandon their churches or, if possible, to detach their congregations from their denominational affiliations. McIntire himself founded his own separate Presbyterian denomination and mission board, and he created the American Council (and its overseas counterpart, the International Council of Christian Churches) to coordinate the efforts of the separatist groups and to serve as a pipeline for Rightist and anti-National Council propaganda.

Although he has had almost no success in splitting the major denominations, he has done his share to arouse suspicions and spread falsehoods in the various churches about the patriotism of denominational leaders. This was plainly evident in the above mentioned Air Force Manual affair. It was American Council material about alleged communists in the Protestant clergy that had been included in the controversial manual, and McIntire's forces feverishly endeavored to exploit the incident for the purpose of discrediting the National Council.[34] Undoubtedly the Apostle Paul had such people as McIntire in mind when he declared: "I appeal to you, brethren, to take note of those who create dissensions and difficulties, in opposition to the doctrine which you have been taught; avoid them. For such persons do not serve our Lord Christ, but their own appetites, and by fair and flattering words they deceive the hearts of the simple-minded." (Rom. 16:17,18)

The fifth and most serious departure of the Radical Right from the Biblical faith, however, is to be found in its violation of the First Commandment. Robert McAfee Brown points out that a basic belief of Protestant Christianity is that no man-made scheme or system can be given final and uncritical devotion. All persons and all systems stand under the judgment of the Gospel, and any of them can be called into question when it makes unconditional claims for itself. The Radical Right, on the other hand, sets up certain gods which are not subject to the scrutiny of the Gospel. One of these is the idolatrous practice of *Christian Economics* in equating laissez-faire capitalism with Christianity. Another example is the idolatry of "law and order" as the ultimate criteria of moral action. This is allowing the laws of one's society to become the final definition of obedience to God and thus invalidating Peter's affirmation: "We must obey God rather than men." (Acts 5:29) A further form of idolatry is that of reducing God to a kindly accomplice to one's purposes, or in other words saying that "God is on our side." For instance, many of these people will designate a military venture in which their country is engaged (such as the Vietnam War) as a righteous cause and flippantly invoke the blessing of the Almighty upon it. At the same time they would never think of asking God to exercise his judgment upon their involvement in the endeavor, for this would be a tacit admission that their country might possibly be in the wrong.[35] Conservative Christians who identify closely with the Radical Right often fear the so-called "apostasy" of their liberal counterparts, but they are oblivious to their own even more serious sin of idolatry. This idea was explicitly stated by the Rev. Dr. Charles R. Ehrhardt in a widely acclaimed sermon delivered to his congregation at the First Presbyterian Church of Phoenix, Arizona on December 17, 1961. He said:

> Anticommunism has become a god in the lives of those who do not have the true God as their Lord. There are many who are now prepared to sacrifice time and money in the name of anticommunism, who are unwilling to sacrifice time and money to Jesus Christ through his Church.[36]

The Threat to American Democracy

The Radical Right, however, not only menaces the spiritual vigor of evangelical Christianity in the United States. For several reasons this ideological movement also poses a distinct threat to American democracy, and every person, regardless of his religious position, should be prepared to resist the prophets of the Far Right. For one thing, the Right-wing extremists have injected a dangerous element of hate and distrust into American life. They have turned citizens against their government, laymen against their ministers, and parents against their children's teachers.

Leading public figures have tried again and again to warn people about this danger. Governor Nelson Rockefeller of New York declared in a speech on July 14, 1963:

> These people have no program for . . . the American people except distrust, disunity and the ultimate destruction of the confidence of the people in themselves. They are purveyors of hate and distrust in a time when, as never before, the need of the world is for love and understanding.[37]

The Rt. Rev. John P. Craine, Episcopal Bishop of Indianapolis, contended that the Far Right had adopted the same tactics as the communists and further commented: "I can only say that if I were intent on destroying this great nation, I can think of no better way than to create distrust, hate and fear, as is being done today."[38] The Director of the Federal Bureau of Investigation, J. Edgar Hoover, cautioned that: "Today far too many self-styled experts on communism are plying the highways of America giving erroneous and distorted information. This causes hysteria, false alarms, [and] misplaced apprehension by many of our citizens."[39]

The seriousness of the hate and distrust generated by the Far Right was underlined at the time of the assassination of President John F. Kennedy in 1963. One week after this tragic event, Thomas G. Aaron resigned as chairman of the Kentucky Young Americans for Freedom (a fairly conservative youth organization) and issued a public statement which read: "I am now satisfied that the climate of political degeneracy and moral hysteria masquerading as 'true Americanism' bears substantial culpability for the murder of the President of the United States." He then called on the other members of the group to "re-examine their participation in organizations which in their zeal are destructive of American ideals of liberty, justice and peace with dignity for all."[40]

A second threat of the Radical Right is its anti-democratic stance, symbolized quite clearly in the familiar bumper sticker slogan: "This is a republic, not a democracy." The extreme Right, with its totalitarian, leader-dominated groups, has attacked the free institutions and civil liberties which comprise the American way of life. In a totally irresponsible manner the Rightists are trying to undermine the democratic process by fostering distrust of elected officials and are seeking to destroy the non-ideological two-party system with its hallmark of a "loyal opposition." Freedom is impossible in a society whose members distrust its leaders and institutions. In the name of anti-communism the extremists even wish to suppress the right of an individual person to think and say what he pleases. The irony of the matter is that in attempting to weaken communism, the adherents to the Radical Right actually weaken American democracy and liberty instead.

A number of prominent people have also spoken out against this peril. The eminent historian, Henry Steele Commager, pointed out that:

> By their conduct and their philosophy they [the Radical Rightists] lower the moral standards of the society they pretend to defend. Eager to put down imagined subversion, they are themselves the most subversive of all the elements in our society, for they subvert "that harmony and affection" without which a society cannot be a commonwealth.[41]

Senator Thomas H. Kuchel of California warned his colleagues in a Senate speech on February 2, 1962 that "the radical right in this country is as grave a danger to the security of our country and the faith of our people in the constitutional system of government as is the radical Communist left."[42] The most forceful statement, however, was made by Senator Stephen M. Young of Ohio, and every loyal and concerned American citizen should pay careful attention to his timely admonition:

> I believe the radical right today is an even deadlier threat to our democratic traditions and institutions than are the American adherents to communism. . . .
> Every picture of a race riot, North or South, fomented by right-

wing extremists, every American smeared by fellow Americans for his political beliefs, every reckless charge against responsible Government officials by the demagogues of the right do more to serve the aims of international Communism than 5000 American Communists could do.[43]

A third drawback of the Radical Right is its witting or unwitting tendency toward "patriotism for profit." This is best illustrated by an advertisement seen by this author in a Patrick Henry Bookstore which read: "Patriotism Pays." The Rightists are always selling something—books, recordings, magazines, pamphlets, films, bumper stickers, buttons, gummed seals, and gadgets of every description. At rallies and crusades protracted appeals for funds compare with the emotional efforts of old-fashioned revivalists. Also, participants in various "schools" and "seminars" willingly pay exhorbitant sums for "tuition," such as the $100 fee for a five day "Anti-Communist Leadership School" staged by Billy James Hargis in Tulsa in January 1962. Many of the Rightists are nothing more than pitchmen and professionals in the art of preying upon public fears and suspicions for the sake of financial gain.

Hargis and his Christian Crusade is an excellent example of patriotism for profit in action. His organization was a tax-exempt religious corporation until recently, and it has an annual income of approximately one million dollars. Hargis himself draws only a small "salary" (in five figures), but he does have a $7,500 automobile, a $44,000 "parsonage" (although he pastors no church), a $50,000 Greyhound bus which was reconditioned to make it a palace on wheels for use on his road trips, and a seven hundred acre ranch near Tulsa.[44] His fund-raising tactics are reminiscent of a snake oil peddler in a travelling medicine show. The *New York Times* report of his endeavors at his group's national convention in 1961 to secure funds to pay for network radio time for the Christian Crusade is a classic account of the huckster at work. He told his audience that he could place the program on the Mutual Broadcasting System network for six months "for only $38,870," and then embarked upon what the reporter appropriately described as a "prayer auction."

> "I pray to God for one man to sponsor this program for six months. I know that man exists in this audience. Will he stand up?"
> No one stood.
> "All right, then, we will divide this burden. I need four men who will accept God's challenge and give $10,000 each to sponsor this program."
> Two men stood up.

> "Give us four, Oh, God, who would give $5000 each. Quickly!
> . . . $2000?"
> One man stood.
> "$1000?"
> Three men stood up.
> And so it went, down from $500 through $100. At [the] end
> seventy-nine men and women had pledged a total of $38,870—the
> exact amount needed.[45]

Somewhat in the same vein has been the criticism directed at Schwarz's more moderate Christian Anti-Communism Crusade. For example, in an address over television station KTVU in Oakland, Attorney-General Stanley Mosk of California reported that the Schwarz organization in a Los Angeles crusade had made the impressive net profit of $214,757 in the months of July through September 1961. Moreover, Mosk noted that each person at the meeting had received a price list of materials that were available for purchase. If an individual were to buy one of each booklet and tape recording, it would have cost him $689.10. The attorney-general commented that there was "a presumption in the eyes of these promoters that anyone who fails to buy all this material is uninformed and perhaps unpatriotic."[46] A "student" at the five-day Mid-West School of Anti-Communism in Omaha, Nebraska in 1962 reported that the "tuition" charge for the entire week was $20.00. One could also obtain a set of tape recordings covering all the sessions for $75.00 which, in the words of Schwarz, was "a bargain!"[47]

An incredibly crass form of patriotism for profit has been practiced by some Right-leaning businessmen in California. Joe Crail, the president of Coast Federal Savings and Loan Association, established a "Free Enterprise Bureau" in his company and allocated four percent of the net revenue before taxes to support it. In 1961 this agency reportedly mailed out over two million pieces of conservative reading matter. In a speech to a group of fellow executives Crail declared: "Anti-communism builds sales and raises employee performance." The Free Enterprise Bureau is "our least expensive form of getting business."[48] The late D. B. Lewis, head of the Lewis Food Company, the producer of Dr. Ross Dod Food, uttered the following interesting remarks about a Rightist radio and television program, the Dan Smoot Report, which his company sponsored:

> We've sponsored everything from Hopalong Cassidy to Tarzan, but
> Dan [Smoot] is far and away the best seller. . . . I'm getting more
> for my advertising dollar than any businessman in America. . . .
> People get so excited over Dan's show they'd feed the dog food

to people if we'd let them. Thousands write us, and hundreds of thousands buy the product because they like the program.[49]

The tragedy of this commercialism is two-fold. For one thing, such an unabashed exploitation of one's sense of loyalty to his country cheapens patriotism. Furthermore, it victimizes people, especially those who can least afford it such as the elderly and widows. Many of these charlatans play upon the genuine fears and concerns of people in order that they might line their own pockets. At the same time, by offering panaceas instead of reasonable approaches toward finding solutions to the problems which alarm their followers, the apostles of the Far Right seldom render any genuine services to the people who are pouring funds into their coffers.

The fourth and probably most serious danger of the Radical Right is its excessive bellicoseness, a point which was touched upon earlier in this essay. In plain language the Right urges that the United States give no quarter to communism anywhere in the world. Mouthing the simplistic phrase, "There is no substitute for victory," the Rightist pressures the American government to carry on an adventurous and highly dangerous foreign policy. Thus he argues: why not invade Cuba, tear down the Berlin Wall, liberate the East European satellites of the Soviet Union, "unleash" Chiang Kai-shek, and reduce Hanoi and Haiphong to smoking ruins? Moreover, the Right-wing extremists suggest that control of military operations and strategy in the present Vietnam conflict be taken from the civilians and placed in the hands of military commanders in the field, an action which could lead to dire consequences. Obviously, one possible way of easing international tensions and obtaining peace in the world is the road of discussion, compromise, and seeking areas of mutual understanding. But, by urging American withdrawal from the United Nations, rejecting the idea of cultural exchanges with communist countries, and denouncing negotiations with communist leaders, the Radical Right is in essence asking that this country adopt the other alternative to solving international problems, namely, armed conflict. It is apparent that the chauvinistic policies of the extreme Right, if not checked by moderate and clear-thinking citizens, will eventually lead the United States down the path to World War III and the inevitable destruction of a nuclear holocaust.

A Positive Approach to the Problem

This essay has endeavored to show how and why the Radical Right is inimical to the principles of evangelical Christianity and American democracy. But, what should be done to help those people caught up in the ideology and to protect American society from its destructive effects?

Certainly blind counter-reaction is not the answer because the Rightist needs assistance, not condemnation. One thing that would help is a generous dose of friendship and reason. The Rightist should be confronted with quiet assertions of truth and gently shown the irrationality of his position, such as the inconsistency of fighting communist subversion at home but turning one's back on the civil rights struggle, thus enhancing the appeal of communism. His delusional system should be penetrated whenever possible, but in a kind and loving manner.

Another useful procedure would be to expose the activities of the Right-wing extremists. Firm stands should be taken against those who try to stir up suspicion against school teachers or local officials. Facts and figures should be published to show the true activities of extreme Right itinerant evangelists. Church groups particularly need to be informed about the risks of sponsoring or cooperating with various "Christian" anti-communist organizations and speakers. Infiltrators in clubs and churches should be pointed out and neutralized as diplomatically as possible.

Also, everything possible must be done to strengthen the "liberal-conservative" center of American society and prevent the formation of a great ideological cleavage. A program of political education should stress the value of the two-party system, freedom of speech and dissent, democratic procedures, and moderate, gradual changes within the American constitutional framework. The contrast between democracy and totalitarian systems of the right and left should be studied and understood. It is, however, not enough to be against totalitarianism in any form. Americans must also implement positive measures to eliminate the social, political, and economic frictions in this society which the adherents of totalitarian ideologies are so adroit at exploiting. The superiority of the values of freedom will only become apparent when those who believe in them are able to come to grips with the burning social problems of the day.

Evangelicals must be especially careful not to underestimate the threat of the Radical Right since extremism has infected the church and weakened its witness. Yet, if the evangelical church is to have any impact on American society, it will have to apply the medication of the Gospel to its own sores. This problem cannot be ignored because not only the future of Christianity is involved but also that of American democracy. The subversion that is occurring now is actually from the Far Right, and if Christians do nothing to counter it, they will awaken one day to find that the nihilism of the Right has replaced both democracy and Christianity. Senator Young of Ohio tells of an experience which ought to shock every complacent American out of his slumber. While the senator was at a dinner party in Washington, an ultra-conservative congressman unleashed a fiery denunciation of "home-grown Communists who chew away at the foundations of our republic." A veteran European diplomat turned to the senator and said: "One thing has always puzzled me about you Americans. You have nightmares about Communist demons burrowing from within. Yet for years American fascists have grown increasingly dangerous and nobody seems disturbed—least of all your congressmen."[50]

Fortunately, some of the main factors which contribute to fascism are still lacking in the American situation. The Radical Right does not have a single scapegoat on which it can pin the blame for all the alleged faults in this society. Communism is much too vague and unreal to bear such a responsibility. At present there is no dynamic, charismatic leader around whom Rightists can unite and who can lead an assault against the "decadent" political and social institutions of contemporary America. Also, the country is not suffering from the effects of some traumatic national disaster, such as the humiliation of a lost war or the dislocation of a total economic collapse. Nevertheless, the danger from the Far Right is too serious for concerned Americans to ignore, a fact which recently was graphically illustrated by a statement that a retired Air Force general made before a loudly applauding audience of American Legionnaires in California: "Military takeover is a dirty word in this country, but if the professional politicians cannot keep law and order it is time we do so, by devious or direct means."[51] Therefore, it behooves every thinking evangelical to give heed to the advice which President Lyndon B. Johnson gave in his first address to Congress:

> Let us put an end to the teaching and preaching of hate and evil and violence. Let us turn away from the fanatics of the far left and the far right, from the apostles of bitterness and bigotry, from those defiant of law, and those who pour venom into our Nation's bloodstream.[52]

NOTES

1. See the excellent discussions in Ira Rohter, "The Righteous Rightists," *Transaction,* IV (May 1967), 27; Victor C. Ferkiss, "Political and Intellectual Origins of American Radicalism, Right and Left," *Annals of the American Academy of Political and Social Science,* CCCLIX (Nov. 1962), p. 7; Daniel Bell, "The Dispossessed" in Daniel Bell, ed., *The Radical Right* (Garden City: Doubleday, 1963), pp. 7–12; Brooks R. Walker, *The Christian Fright Peddlers* (Garden City: Doubleday, 1964), pp. 14–15; and Arnold Forster and Benjamin R. Epstein, *Danger on the Right* (New York: Random House, 1964), pp. 7–8. Throughout this essay the words Rightist and Right will be capitalized whenever they refer to the Radical Right.

2. Forster and Epstein, *Danger on the Right,* pp. 6–7. This book contains useful descriptions of the activities of the principal Radical Right groups. Other treatments of Rightist organizations which are easily obtainable include Walker,

Christian Fright Peddlers; Harry and Bonaro Overstreet, *The Strange Tactics of Extremism* (New York: Norton, 1964); and Donald Janson and Bernard Eismann, *The Far Right* (New York: McGraw-Hill, 1963).

3. Forster and Epstein, *Danger on the Right*, Appendix.

4. *Ibid.*, xii; and George B. Leonard, "What Is an Extremist?" *Look*, XXVIII (Oct. 20, 1964), p. 37.

5. Eric Hoffer, *The True Believer* (New York: New American Library, 1958), pp. 75–76.

6. Edward V. Stern, "Galloping Paranoia," *Christian Century*, LXXIX (Mar. 14, 1962), p. 323. The paranoid tendencies of the Radical Right are treated extensively in the works of Richard Hofstadter, especially his essays "The Pseudo-Conservative Revolt—1955" and "Pseudo-Conservatism Revisited: A Postscript" in Bell, *The Radical Right*, and his book *The Paranoid Style in American Politics and Other Essays* (New York: Alfred A. Knopf, 1965).

7. Hofstadter, *Paranoid Style*, pp. 29–32.

8. Rohter, *Trans-action*, IV, pp. 27–28; Robert Lee, "Social Sources of the Radical Right," *Christian Century*, LXXIX (May 9, 1962), pp. 595–97.

9. These traits are spelled out in considerable detail in T. W. Adorno, *et. al.*, *The Authoritarian Personality* (New York: Harper, 1950).

10. Herbert McClosky, "Conservatism and Personality," *American Political Science Review*, LII (Mar. 1958), p. 37.

11. Overstreet, *Strange Tactics of Extremism*, pp. 224–25.

12. *Ibid.*, pp. 225, 228.

13. William S. White, "Public and Personal," *Harper's Magazine*, CCXXIII (Nov. 1961), p. 98.

14. Bell, *Radical Right*, p. 12.

15. Walker, *Christian Fright Peddlers*, pp. 229–30.

16. Benjamin R. Epstein and Arnold Forster, *Report on the John Birch Society 1966* (New York: Random House, 1966), p. 3.

17. *Ibid.*, pp. 43–44.

18. A detailed treatment of this is found in *Ibid.*, pp. 70–82.

19. Fred J. Cook, "The Right Has Nine Lives," *Nation*, CCIV (Mar. 13, 1967), pp. 333–34.

20. Overstreet, *Strange Tactics of Extremism*, pp. 272–73; Hofstadter, *Paranoid Style*, p. 37.

21. For a typical example of this kind of journalism see John A. Stormer, *None Dare Call It Treason* (Florissant, Mo.: Liberty Bell Press, 1964).

22. *Congressional Record*, 87th Cong., 2d Sess., 1962, CVIII, Part 3, p. 3676.

23. The findings of the investigation conducted by the editors of *Eternity* are reported in Donald Grey Barnhouse, "Communism and the National Council of Churches," *Eternity*, XI (Sep. 1960), p. 6ff.

24. Fred Schwarz, *You Can Trust the Communist (to be Communists)* (Englewood Cliffs, N. J.: Prentice-Hall, 1960), pp. 59–63.

25. *New York Times*, Feb. 3, 1962, p. 7; July 16, 1963, p. 23.

26. Walker, *Christian Fright Peddlers*, pp. 106, 185; *Christian Economics*, Sep. 26, 1950, p. 4.

27. Hofstadter, *Paranoid Style*, pp. 81–82.

28. Quoted in Fred J. Cook, "The Ultras," *Nation*, CXCIV (June 30, 1962), p. 573.

29. "Profiles: The Ultimate City—L.A.," *New Yorker*, XLII (Oct. 15, 1966), pp. 108, 110.

30. Overstreet, *Strange Tactics of Extremism*, pp. 144–45.

31. *Westvue Messenger* (Murfreesboro, Tenn.), Aug. 9, 1966. Copy in the possession of the author.

32. "Why Must Rightists Resort to Terror?" *Christian Century*, LXXIX (Feb. 14, 1962), pp. 187–88.

33. Walker, *Christian Fright Peddlers*, pp. 41–42.

34. Forster and Epstein, *Danger on the Right*, p. 110. Barnhouse, *Eternity*, XI, pp. 7ff. The author of the manual actually used literature from Billy James Hargis and the Circuit Riders. McIntire, however, firmly endorsed it and several National Council leaders charged publicly that he was really responsible for the anti-NCC statements. *New York Times*, Feb. 19, 1960, p. 8; Feb. 25, 1960, p. 13.

35. Robert McAfee Brown, " 'Christian Economics' and Theology," *Union Seminary Quarterly Review*, VII (June 1951), pp. 8–10; and Roger L. Shinn, "The Public Responsibility of Theology" in William A. Beardslee, ed., *America and the Future of Theology* (Philadelphia: Westminister, 1967), pp. 187–89.

36. Quoted in Louis Cassels, "The Rightist Crisis in Our Churches," *Look*, XXVI (Apr. 24, 1962), p. 42.

37. *New York Times*, July 15, 1963, p. 23.

38. Quoted in Walker, *Christian Fright Peddlers*, p. 55.

39. J. Edgar Hoover, "Shall It Be Law or Tyranny?" *American Bar Association Journal*, XLVIII (Feb. 1962), p. 120.

40. *New York Times*, Dec. 1, 1963, p. 50.

41. Henry S. Commager, "A Historian Looks at Our Political Morality," *Saturday Review*, XLVIII (July 10, 1965), p. 18.

42. *Congressional Record*, 87th Cong., 2d Sess., 1962, CVIII, Part 2, p. 1464.

43. Stephen M. Young, "Danger on the Right," *Saturday Evening Post*, CCXXXV (Jan. 13, 1962), pp. 6–7.

44. Harold H. Martin, "Doomsday Merchant on the Far, Far Right," *Saturday Evening Post*, CCXXXV (Apr. 28, 1962), p. 20; Forster and Epstein, *Danger on the Right*, pp. 69, 81. These observations are further reinforced in considerable detail in the excellent book by John H. Redekop, *The American Far Right: A Case Study of Billy James Hargis and Christian Crusade* (Grand Rapids: Eerdmans, 1968).

45. *New York Times*, Aug.7, 1961, p. 8.

46. Quoted in "Patriotism for Profit," *Christian Century*, LXXIX (Feb. 28, 1962), pp. 253–54.

47. Leola McKie, "I Went to a Schwarz 'School,' " *Ibid.*, LXXIX (July 4, 1962), p. 843.

48. Fletcher Knebel, "Rightist Revival: Who's on the Far Right?" *Look*, XXVI (Mar. 13, 1962), p. 22.

49. *Loc. cit.*

50. Stephen M. Young, "Speaking Out," *Saturday Evening Post*, CCXXXV, p. 6.

51. *Anaheim* (Calif.) *Bulletin*, Aug. 12, 1967, quoted in Hans J. Morgenthau, "What Ails America?" *New Republic*, CLVII (Oct. 28, 1967), p. 21.

52. *Congressional Record*, 88th Cong., 1st Sess., 1963, CIX, Part 17, p. 22839.

William W. Cuthbertson is Professor and Head of the Department of History at William Jewell College in Liberty, Missouri. He was born in St. Louis, Missouri on June 22, 1927 and studied at William Jewell College which awarded him the A.B. degree in 1952. He then earned a B.D. degree at the Southern Baptist Theological Seminary in 1955 and a Ph.D. degree in history at the University of Rochester in 1962. From 1955 until 1958 Mr. Cuthbertson was the recipient of a University Fellowship at the latter institution. In 1958 he joined the faculty of his alma mater, William Jewell College, and he was promoted to the rank of professor and appointed to the chairmanship of the Department of History in 1966. He was also a visiting lecturer in American history at the University of Missouri in Kansas City during the summer of 1964.

Mr. Cuthbertson is active in Missouri politics as a member of the Democratic Party and frequently contributes articles on community affairs to the local newspapers in his area. In addition to his academic duties, he occupies a number of positions of leadership in the Second Baptist Church of Liberty, Missouri.

Professor Cuthbertson was listed in *Who's Who in American Colleges* in 1952, and he was chosen as one of the "Outstanding Young Men in America" in 1965. He is a member of the American Historical Association, the Organization of American Historians, and the Clay County (Missouri) Museum Association. Mr. Cuthbertson serves as a director of the last named group. His fields of special interest include American diplomatic history, the Progressive movement, and the United States in the twentieth century.

WILLIAM W. CUTHBERTSON

The Christian, the American Military Establishment, and War

The present age has been marked by an awesome growth of militarism in America, and unless evangelical Christians shake off their apathy, a creeping fascism may soon become totalitarian statism clothed, to be sure, in the trappings of democracy. The Prussianization of the United States is proceeding apace. The Military Establishment is coming to dominate government councils, allocation of the budget, formulation of foreign policy, and the direction which scientific research takes. A widespread and well-financed propaganda machine dispenses the Pentagon's ideology and drums up support for its arms program. The military persistently seeks a universal conscription program to further inculcate Americans with the martial spirit, and from time to time it has come near to defying Congress and the president. Four hot wars and a cold war since 1914 together with a conscious drive for power by military leaders have nearly succeeded in destroying the civilian character of the nation's government and economy. The saddest part of the spectacle is that the American people, once intensely anti-militarist, are, for the most part, blissfully unaware of and apathetic about this development.

Dangerous Trends in the Military-Industrial Community

The country has not been without those who have protested against the growing power and influence of the military and its industrial allies. Several eminent Americans have pointed out that the generally pacific traditions and institutions of the United States are being undermined and that a people which increasingly accepts military analyses and solutions is in danger of exchanging its free society for the regimentation of a garrison state dominated by military messiahs and a warrior caste.

On January 17, 1961 President Dwight D. Eisenhower spoke out

67

against the perils inherent in a large and permanent armaments industry and an overgrown defense establishment. This popular President and respected military leader sounded a warning note against a relatively new danger to American democracy. He said:

> This conjunction of an immense military establishment and a large arms industry is new in the American experience. The total influence —economic, political, even spiritual—is felt in every city, every state house, every office of the Federal Government. We recognize the imperative need for this development. Yet we must not fail to comprehend its grave implications. Our toil, resources and livelihood are all involved; so is the very structure of our society.
>
> In the councils of Government, we must guard against the acquisition of unwarranted influence, whether sought or unsought, by the military-industrial complex. The potential for the disastrous rise of misplaced power exists and will persist.[1]

In the seven years since this warning there is little evidence that the American people or their elected leaders have taken heed. The strength of the armed forces has increased, the arms industry has grown mightier, and Congress has taken no steps to insure that American liberties and democratic processes will not be infringed by the military-industrial complex.

Ten years before President Eisenhower's speech, Senator Ralph Flanders of Vermont had uttered a similar warning: "We are being forced to shift the American way of life into the pattern of the garrison state. . . . Our wealth, our standard of living, the lives of our young people and our institutions are under the control of the military."[2] In 1964 Dr. John R. Swomley, noted opponent of universal military training, presented impressive documentation for the thesis that militarism had so infected the American value system that the Pentagon was able to exercise "decisive power" in the economy and over foreign policy, having usurped constitutional powers from civilian officials.[3] Former Senator Paul Douglas, Senator Stuart Symington, Charles E. Wilson (Eisenhower's Secretary of Defense), and other respected leaders have spoken out from time to time against the trend toward militarism but there has been no public discussion consonant with the magnitude of the danger.

The United States has a tradition of anti-militarism which dates back to President George Washington's admonition to guard against "overgrown military establishments which, under any form of government, are inauspicious to liberty, and which are to be regarded as particularly hostile to republican liberty."[4] Suspicion of standing armies and military strongmen remained a deeply ingrained habit of mind with Americans until the twentieth century; yet by the 1960's, this tradition appears to be so weakened that it can no longer be relied on as a bulwark against dominance by the Military Establishment.

Men of liberal sympathies have been disturbed by the evidence that a "fascist" element exists in the national heritage. The Americans have not been a pacific people at all times in their history. The expansive, two-fisted method of the frontiersman had its counterpart on the national level. Military solutions to certain national problems were chosen over other approaches time and again. Indians, Mexicans, Spaniards, and Filipinos could all testify of the American propensity to use force. Thus, it might not prove too difficult for a powerful military to convince the American people that the only solution to a major national challenge is the resort to armed force.

Pressing questions then face us. Just how far has the country moved in the direction of militarism? How decisive is the control exercised by the military-industrial complex, and how great is the danger to individual freedoms and to democratic processes? And last, to what extent do Americans accept the militarist ideology and military tutelage?

Some feel that militarism has progressed to a shocking degree. Others argue that nothing out of the ordinary has taken place, or nothing, at least, which has not been necessary for our security. Therefore, in order to have a meaningful discussion, one needs a working definition of "militarism." Alfred Vagts, a leading authority on military history, wrote some years ago:

> Militarism is thus not the opposite of pacifism; its true counterpart is civilianism. Love of war, bellicosity, is the counterpart of the love of peace, pacifism; but militarism is more, and sometimes less, than the love of war. It covers every system of thinking and valuing and every complex of feelings which rank military institutions and ways above the ways of civilian life, carrying military mentality and modes of acting and decision into the civilian sphere.[5]

Arthur Ekirch, Jr., has said more recently of modern militarism:

> In other words, military power is able to dominate civil authority to the point where the latter becomes a willing dupe of military men, overwhelmed by their prestige, and confused as to the validity of the experts' opinions on questions of larger policy.[6]

In the United States there has come into existence a military elite, a powerful and inbred officers' corps which draws its members primarily from among its own sons and those of the white middle class. Less than six per cent of this select group have come in the past from the working class. The 1962 West Point Class of 601 cadets included 123 men who were sons of officers.[7] There are other indications that the current leaders of the armed forces act in such a way as to perpetuate an elite caste. Military "brats," who have heard frequent derogatory remarks about civilians, are trained in military academies and receive something less than a liberal education. It is no wonder, then, that we have produced military leaders who chafe under civilian restraints and who doubt civilian adequacy. Some members of this group actively promote militarist dogma in the United States.

So far there have been few instances of open insubordination by the military and few examples of candid criticism of Congress or of the President. Nevertheless, there has been much covert censoriousness of the nation's civilian decision-makers. Informed observers report that a significantly large number of higher officers believe that civilian leaders are incompetent and inefficient, lack "guts," and are tainted with socialism or some "ism" other than "one hundred per cent Americanism," as defined by these same officers. Moreover, civilian directives often have been circumvented with impunity. A few disgruntled officers have gone so far as to suggest that they were bound not by the civil leaders but by a higher allegiance. For example, General Douglas MacArthur soon after his dismissal protested against:

> a new and heretofore unknown and dangerous concept that the members of our armed forces owe primary allegiance or loyalty to those who temporarily exercise the authority of the Executive Branch of the Government rather than to the country and to the Constitution which they are sworn to defend.[8]

No proposition could be more dangerous, for this has been the plea of dictators for centuries. "It is my duty to save the state by overthrowing the state." A cursory reading of Latin American history will indicate how poorly democracy fares when such thinking pervades the military.

Some American officers, believing that the military life is a higher and purer mode of existence, have persistently attempted to beg or browbeat Congress into passing a universal military training law. They want to draft American young men, habituate them to discipline, and imbue them with the proper military way of thinking. Since World War I, repeated calls for universal military training have been motivated as much by a desire to return a constant stream of "right-thinking" boys to civilian society as by a desire to build up a trained reserve.

Control of labor is not beyond the U.S. military's aspirations. A draft of workers was requested by Admiral E. J. King and General George C. Marshall in the closing months of World War II. A bill which would have permitted the armed forces to assign conscripted labor to jobs in designated factories was quickly drawn up in the House of Representatives. It is true that this was a wartime measure, but a similar action could be justified by the military mind in peacetime as a necessity for "preparedness." The military has sought to further its control and ideology by promoting R.O.T.C. programs in high schools and colleges. In some colleges all first- and second-year men are obliged to participate. Not even religious organizations are exempt from the conscious attempt to spread the military dogma. The armed forces often use the chaplaincy to propagandize the churches because after all, the churches might foster the "wrongheaded notion" that one cannot love one's enemy and bayonet him at the same time. It seems safe to suggest that a value system which ranks military institutions and attitudes above the ways of civilian life does indeed exist in the United States, and this situation is not restricted to the military.

The business community, allied by economic interest and political philosophy with the military leaders, has accepted many of the assumptions of militarism. In 1944 Charles E. Wilson, then president of General Electric, proposed "a permanent war economy" and a wedding of big business and the military. Author Fred J. Cook's comment was: "No German industrialist in the age of Hitler was ever more willing to embrace the military for benefits conferred."[9] In the past few months, the House Armed Services Subcommittee on Defense Spending has also revealed something of the magnitude of the collusion between strategically-located Pentagon officials and the business community. The fact of the military-industrial combination is too well established to need substantiation here. However, the complex's extent, its power, and the implications of its existence are matters of deep concern, for it has aggressively fostered the movement of America toward militarism.

During World War II a large and permanent arms industry came into existence in the United States. It hired the most talented scientists away from the universities, and it worked closely with the armed forces to develop new weapons and to produce the mountains of materiel needed to win the war. As weapons systems became increasingly more sophisticated and the technology to produce them more complicated while at the same time billions of dollars were spent on development and research, it was only natural that the military and business community meshed personnel. Civilian employees were assigned to work with units of the armed forces while military specialists advised the businessmen. At higher levels, industrial leaders and Pentagon "brass" conferred regularly over contracts and other matters of common interest. After the war, the great armaments industry was not dismantled but remained intact because of the challenge of international communism and a concomitant preparedness campaign. The connection between business and the military continued and grew stronger.

Retiring officers often found that a convenient and comfortable place would be made for them in industry. Big business has not been slow to perceive that former high-ranking officers are extremely useful in negotiating fat contracts with their erstwhile comrades. Officers who are nearing retirement sometimes use their influence to secure contracts for favored companies with which they have worked for years, with a view to future employment. Some posts are quite lucrative. For example, a former Air Force general received $300,000 in salary from an aircraft manufacturer in the first four years of his retirement. Companies with the most retired officers seem to get the most contracts. A special investigating subcommittee of the House Armed Services Committee, headed by Representative F. Edward Hebert of Louisiana, probed into this movement of upper echelon officers into positions in business. A 1960 report of the committee revealed that 261 retired generals and admirals and 485 other former high officers from the Army and Navy were employed by the concerns which supplied over seventy-five per cent of the government's arms. Earlier, in 1959, Senator Paul A. Douglas protested against the "potential and actual abuses" of the situation. The number of companies involved was small, but included about one hundred of the largest corporations. From 1957 through 1961 fifty defense suppliers were awarded about sixty-three per cent of the prime military contracts, worth nearly ninety billion dollars, which were let by the Department of Defense. General Dynamics, the most successful recipient, also had the highest number of retired officers, 187![10]

Growing Military Influence in American Life

The military-industrial complex has achieved vast and perhaps decisive power in the political arena. Through a huge and well-funded propaganda machine it seeks to persuade where it does not have direct control. The military side of the partnership spends millions of dollars annually on public relations. Professionals prepare news releases and articles while free liquor, air transportation, cruises, and room and board are supplied to journalists. The military branches operate international exchange programs, a broadcasting network, schools, seminars, newspapers, and various entertainments in order to improve its image, get its message across to the public, and put pressure on the government. In addition to this, millions of dollars worth of publicity are donated to the military by television, radio networks, and the press. The military point of view is spread further by associations of reserve officers and their civilian affiliates. Uniformed men make thousands of speeches before schools, churches, service clubs, and other local audiences. American Legion and Veterans of Foreign Wars organizations also utilize every opportunity to inculcate military ideas. The resources at the disposal of those who oppose a military program or militaristic ideas are pitifully small in comparison.

This colossal propaganda engine works quietly and ceaselessly to gain for the military the arms, men, and *policies* which it desires, and for industry the profits for which it hungers. However, the machine may be speeded up if private citizens or Congress become obstructive. On a number of occasions in the past when programs dear to the military-industrial complex were threatened by recalcitrant civilians, a tremendous propaganda campaign was mounted. One such instance was the fight over universal military training in 1948, another was the inter-service squabble over missiles in 1959, and a third was the hassle over the B–70 bomber in 1962.

It is nearly impossible for Capitol Hill and the White House to withstand the pressures generated by such a propaganda machine. Opposition to military demands is twisted by these people into opposition to the nation's security itself. Those who have the temerity to object to excessive spending for arms are pictured as senile, leftist, muddle-headed, or worse by the militarists. If this type of political blackmail does not work, a "scare" campaign may be instigated to make it appear that the nation is in the midst of a grave international crisis and that dire consequences will follow from any failure to grant the military's requests. This is based on the correct assumption that a fearful public (neurotic when it comes to communism) will deluge Congress and the President with requests to acquiesce.

A fear campaign was begun by Air Force General Thomas Power in January 1960, when Congress debated the question of whether to grant the Strategic Air Command money to obtain more bombers and increased funds to keep them constantly airborne. The general announced to the Economic Club of New York (note the audience) that there was a fearful "missile gap," that is, the Soviet Union was far ahead of the United States in building operational missiles. In the meantime, while the United States was catching up, his Strategic Air Command would protect the nation if it received its money and planes. The press took up the cry. When President Eisenhower attempted to refute the assertion, he was ignored. The "missile gap" even became a significant issue of the Kennedy-Nixon campaign. Anyone who opposed Power's request risked being charged with lunacy or even treason. It is quite interesting that in 1961 military intelligence revealed that the general's assessment was incorrect and that there had never been any missile gap!

Another instance of the use of the false crisis scare technique to overwhelm Congress was the attempt by some Army leaders to force universal military training on the country in 1948. John M. Swomley, who was intimately connected with the opposition to U.M.T., has recounted in his book, *The Military Establishment*, the extent of the Army's propaganda and the lengths to which it went to gain its militaristic ends. Swomley argues persuasively that Army leaders did not care about the reserve manpower aspects—they neglected the reserves which they had—but were more concerned with brainwashing the young men of America with militaristic ideals. In this supposed crisis, military leaders pictured Russia with its hordes poised at the gates of Western Europe ready to take over unless the bill for compulsory service was passed. Army spokesmen insisted that the voluntary program was not working. Yet those who probed deeper into the issue found that the Army was undercutting the voluntary programs by raising its physical and educational standards for inductees. At the same time, the Army was systematically weakening the reserves and mustering men out of service three to four months before their enlistments were up. There was no crisis. It was a piece of utter hypocrisy and cynical chicanery. Colonel William H. Neblett, the national president of the Reserve Officers Association at that time, testified, "I know from my own knowledge of the men who worked up the fear campaign that they do not believe what they say."[11]

One must ask, "To what lengths will the armed forces go?" He must ponder what would become of democracy if a group of chauvinistic officers were to become unduly frustrated with civilian control of the reins of government.

The military establishment applies pressure on Congress in both direct and indirect ways. Officers propagandize the enlisted men and urge them to write home to their parents and wives, hoping that they in turn will contact their representatives in Washington. No opponent is allowed the freedom of military bases to offer contrary information. Military men stationed in Washington lobby actively in the halls of Congress, in the offices of bureaucrats, and even in the White House. These men are highly paid, dedicated, articulate, persistent, and, in their own way, patriotic. Perhaps the fact that most Congressmen themselves are reserve officers or veterans accounts in part for the receptiveness of the legislature to military propaganda.

The civilian nature of the United States government has been further weakened and militarism strengthened by the penetration of the bureaucracy by military people and ex-servicemen. Federal law gives preference to veterans seeking civil service positions. Retired officers are appointed to head civilian agencies and bureaus while hundreds of officers serve on numerous government commissions. Perhaps the military exerts its power most crucially in the National Security Council and other contexts in which it has direct access to the President and cabinet members. Of the seven members of the Security Council, with the exception of the President, only the Secretary of State represents a purely non-military department or agency. The Secretary of Defense, although a civilian by law, must lean heavily on the advice of a group of forty to fifty military advisors in his department who not only formulate views on defense needs, but who also write policy papers on economic matters and foreign affairs. The total effect of this infiltration of the bureaucracy by the military has not been to incline the United States toward peace and civilianism.

Militarism has gained ground in other areas. The military has achieved a significant amount of economic control through "ownership" of vast properties and through its arrangements with industry. The Department of Defense has practical title to property worth over two hundred billion dollars. It secures raw materials, manufactures and distributes goods, and consumes the products of its industries. Its annual income through defense appropriations is greater than the individual gross national products of most countries in the world. The 1968 defense budget of the United States, roughly seventy billion dollars, represents about ten per cent of the total gross national product and over fifty-five per cent of the total annual expenditure. It is the largest defense authorization in the peacetime history of the United States. Economists estimate that defense spending in the past has generated twenty-five to thirty-five per cent of all economic activity in the country, and spending for the Vietnam war will drive this rate higher. Over one-tenth of the nation's work force of over seventy million people are enrolled in the military, employed as civilians by the Pentagon, or work in defense industries. Perhaps no nation in the past, except one threatened with extermination or one committed to aggression, has committed such a great proportion of its wealth and citizens to war making. The military's power over the economy may not be altogether accidental. Donald M. Nelson, head of the War Production Board (a World War II agency), has asserted: "From 1942 onward the Army people, in order to get control of our national economy, did their best to make an errand boy of the W.P.B."[12]

In addition to having achieved a disturbing level of power in the economy and government circles, military leaders in the United States have attained unusual influence in formulation of foreign policy. They show a disquieting ability to dominate or bypass the State Department, sometimes described as the "peace" department. The military presses its conception of the international situation on the executive branch of the government, Congress, its business allies, its employees, and the American people as a whole by all the powerful means it has built up over the years. Unfortunately, the Pentagon "brass" usually view the international situation through military-tinted glasses. Several observers of the military's climb to power have pointed out that after the end of the Second World War, military leaders could see no possible challenger to American might except Russia and immediately they began to speak *as if* the Soviet Union were indeed the next enemy to be destroyed. It is possible to argue that the openly hostile talk of war by army leaders has been the cause of, and not the result of, tensions between the United States and Russia.

Although the question of which side started the Cold War is a matter of some concern, of much greater importance is the question, "Who is to define the country's international goals, the civilian or the military?" The professional soldier tends to define the international situation in military terms and to see the nation's foreign policy objectives in the same way. This is not at all to argue that there are not men of broad vision and deep insight in the services, but the tendency is to weight the military aspects most heavily. If the challenge from an outside nation or nations is deemed sufficiently strong, then the military in all probability will argue that domestic goals must be subordinated to and perhaps even sacrificed for military goals. In the past, social, economic, educational, and peaceful international programs have all fallen victim to war or preparation for war. Since the mid-1930's, in every crisis the military and its industrial allies have consistently and heatedly urged Congress to suspend or terminate social welfare programs for the sake of national security. If in every international emergency the military's wishes become determinative in both domestic and foreign policy, then in a protracted period of continuing crises the military comes to acquire a monopoly of the right to determine national goals.

Although the military leaders of the United States do not now have control of this nation's foreign policy, they influence it strongly. The total effect of this influence has been the encouragement of militarism. The Pentagon has had considerable say about which countries are to receive military and economic aid. The individual services may declare military equipment to be "surplus" or "outdated" and dispose of it to "friendly" countries. The very presence of America's far-flung armed forces in dozens of countries allows the military an opportunity to converse with and influence the civilians and governments of host countries. These in turn may put pressure on Washington to accept policies that originated with the American high command. Especially fruitful, from the military's point of view, is the opportunity to collaborate with and do favors for their foreign counterparts. There is little doubt that American military aid in the past has fostered military hierarchies and regimes in other countries. Such an outcome of American aid has encouraged the notion that the United States is not interested so much in promoting democracy as in securing reliable allies, no matter what their politics. In many unstable areas of the world where there is no strong tradition of political democracy, providing the means of combatting external aggression *or internal subversion* is tantamount to asking the military to take over when any reform movement accompanied by the possibility of civil disturbance threatens the status quo. Since the United States almost automatically gives diplomatic recognition to these new governments, the image created is one of a militarist United States encouraging the creation of reactionary and militarist regimes abroad. One needs only to add a few examples of C.I.A. (Central Intelligence Agency) involvement in the politics of countries such as India or Singapore and its clandestine use of international student groups, and he begins to wonder how much of the militarist image is in fact reality.

The military-industrial complex climbed to its present high place of influence and power over a long period, but it accelerated its pace after World War II. Since the days of the Civil War, big business has been seated rather firmly in the government saddle, but the military's chance to "mount up" is more recent. Perhaps the international situation in the years after 1946 made this rise to unwarranted power inevitable. The nation became convinced after the defeat of the Axis powers that it needed to remain strong militarily and, therefore, the great war-swollen industries were kept largely intact in case they were needed again. Apart from the needs imposed by the Cold War, however, there was a conscious push for power by the military. Examining the motives behind this thrust, one soon discovers that the leaders of the armed forces sincerely believed that they were absolutely patriotic in their actions.

Several motivations have been suggested as underlying the military's conscious drive for power. First, after 1918 the American juggernaut was speedily dismantled, its military drivers were excluded from any important voice in the nation's councils and with little ceremony were bundled off to their preserves. The experience left a bitter aftertaste with many officers and a determination to avoid a recurrence in the future. Second, after the coming of the Cold War, there began to develop among certain officers a feeling of deep frustration over civilian handling of the counter-strategy and of great pessimism about America's chances of defeating the communist enemy unless radical changes were made. Some hinted rather openly that the correct course of action was known: the nation simply needed leaders with the courage to act. Some officers openly spoke their conviction that communist and socialist influences in the government, schools, and churches had already destroyed the will of the leaders to take the correct steps. Should a large minority of officers come to share these feelings of frustration and pessimism the stage would be set for a military coup. As it is, officers widely suspect the competency of the civilians to the point that they take and hold whatever power is available. The resultant move toward militarism has brought about a diminution of traditional freedoms. The forms of democracy have been observed, but there have been important departures from the normal functioning of democracy, and certain functions assigned by the Constitution to civilian authorities have been taken over by the military.

Congress seems to be losing hold of both its traditional control over the purse and its function as the chief decision-making body of the nation. In matters of national security and national defense it all too frequently defers to the military. It has not officially delegated its power of appropriation to the armed forces, but for all practical purposes this is the effect of passing multi-billion dollar defense budgets with a minimum of investigation and debate. Several Congressmen have admitted that they do not know whether some of the billions spent for defense are necessary or wise. A comment by *U.S. News and World Report* in 1948 points up the willingness of Congress to abdicate its responsibility in the matter of judging the real need of arms expenditures, especially in the midst of a "fright" campaign mounted by Pentagon leaders: "War scares, encouraged by high officials only a few weeks ago, so alarmed the 144,000,000 U. S. public that top planners now are having to struggle hard to keep Congress from pouring more money into national defense than the Joint Chiefs of Staff regard as wise or necessary. It is proving more difficult to turn off than to turn on a war psychology."[13] Congress deferred to the military again in 1948 on the matter of conscription—after an unparalleled propaganda effort by the Pentagon. Representative Dewey Short and four other members of the House Armed Services Committee, however, in a minority report made a scathing attack on the Army for its activities. Speaking before the House, Short said: "The Congress and not the Army is the policy-making body of this Nation, and we should never become a rubber stamp of certain officers who want to Prussianize the Nation."[14]

This country lost an important guarantee against militarism when the real power to decide for war or peace was moved from the Capitol to the Pentagon. As long as the nation faces devastation in seconds by enemy warheads on hurtling missiles, the chances that Congress and the Presi-

dent will be able to make the choice for or against war are greatly reduced. Only after disarmament has proceeded a very long way will the
war-making decision return to civilians; therefore those opposed to militarism ought to support some form of disarmament. This *de facto* delegation of the war-making power to the military is a departure from American democratic principles that could have far-reaching consequences.

Militarism will ultimately succeed or fail in this country on the basis
of its acceptability to the American people. To what extent, then, will the
public acquiesce in the moves toward military control? The American
people in the middle years of the twentieth century have continued to exhibit concern for their own freedom and that of others. They have sought,
perhaps grudgingly at times, to ensure and broaden the civil rights of all
citizens. They have undertaken with the help of other nations to bring
about freedom from want and fear for millions outside their borders. Still,
it is possible that these same Americans might in their search for military
and economic security take some rash step which will result in the loss of
their basic liberties. Perhaps unconcern, or a lack of vigilance, or a moment of faintheartedness brought on by international crisis might cause
them to give up their democratic inheritance and turn to militarism for
temporary succor. The prospect that they will firmly resist the military is
not hopeful, for many ordinary citizens indicate that in circumstances
where national security and military necessity are concerned they will allow infringements of their traditional rights.

The probability of a direct and overt take-over by the military is minimal—the idea is generally repugnant to Americans—but there has been
little opposition to covert manipulation and control built up over a period
of years, since democratic forms have been left undisturbed. It might be
in just this way that a full-blown fascism could develop. The militariza-
tion of the American mind is moving inexorably ahead because much of
the public is receptive to the militarist doctrines poured out by the vast
propaganda machine controlled from Washington. Veterans' organizations, which tend to be right-wing and ultra-conservative, accept in a
most uncritical way the propositions of the military leaders. A *Junker*
class of industrial barons and usually conservative farmers are willing
believers. The press, which as a whole has been politically conservative
and nourished by the millions of dollars which the military-industrial complex spends for advertising, is rather effectively muzzled. Eight million
American job holders are directly involved in defense. The economic
prosperity of additional millions of people is indirectly tied to military
spending. The total effect of all this is to encourage assent, not dissent.
One is led to believe that in a period of intense international tensions and

threat to the national security the American people would abdicate their right of judgment and defer to the military. Today, there is little opposition to militarist doctrines, and Professor John Swomley has noted that:

> In general the public is unaware that it is being deliberately propagandized by the military. Although Congressmen know what is happening, few take any steps either to expose or oppose the steady militarization of the American mind. In high places there seems to be a willingness to let the military-industrial complex continue to exercise power.[15]

The Dangers Posed By American Militarism

The dangers from militarism are real, present, and serious. Thus far an attempt has been made to show that militarism has made great gains in the United States in the past twenty-five years. It appears that if the present trends are not halted and reversed, the United States will eventually become a totalitarian state dominated by the military-industrial complex. Freedom of expression and perhaps even freedom of thought would become impossible. More and more of the economy would become slave to the needs of the warfare state. Military morals would displace the ethical teachings of Christianity and other humanitarian systems. Foreign policy would come under the full control of militarists, and the chance would be immeasurably greater that some military "expert" would risk everything in a preventive thermonuclear attack.

History provides a plethora of illustrations of the tendency for militaristic political units to become totalitarian. Americans have suspected the foreign demagogue chanting about national greatness and military might but have shown little apprehensiveness about the possibility that a homegrown oligarchy in United States uniforms and peddling a chauvinistic nationalism might decide to take over the reins of government. It is difficult to explain why Americans are oblivious to the danger of a military seizure of power in this country. The fact that the militaristic doctrine demands centralization of power and authority in fewer and fewer hands is, of course, in obvious contradiction to the principles of representative democracy and the American tradition.

Indeed, it seems reasonable to assume that if a military dictatorship were to come into existence in this country, the main forms of a civilian and representative system would be maintained, as they were in fascist Japan, Germany, and Italy prior to World War II. The political reality would be, however, an elite of military and industrial figures who made the final decisions. Perhaps the movement in this direction has progressed further than most Americans realize. In 1953 when the popular hero-politician Dwight Eisenhower attempted to reduce the Air Force's budget by five billion dollars, the chiefs of that service refused to accept a civilian executive's decision without a fight in Congress. Eisenhower found it an extremely difficult task to oppose the brass and keep down military spending. In the early months of Kennedy's administration when the new President showed some slowness in acceding to the military's requests, Pentagon sniping at the Commander-in-Chief became an open shame. Senator Stuart Symington, ordinarily known as a friend of the armed services, rose on the floor of the Senate to defend the young President and stormed: "The point to note is that military men of high rank . . . are now attacking the very core of the American system. . . . I for one do not intend to see this disloyal operation continue without the full knowledge of the American people."[16]

Militarism usually demands a one-party system or perhaps two parties of no significant difference. In the United States the military-industrial complex has shown a strong preference for staunch conservatives. Huge campaign chests are created by industrial leaders whose companies have fattened on billions in war contracts. Some large corporations employ men who go up and down the land making anti-communist, anti-liberal, anti-socialist, and anti-New Deal speeches. Since party labels in the United States mean little, the military-industrial complex has not found it necessary to build up one party with funds and propaganda while it destroys the other. The crucial point is that the militarists support most consistently and generously one political viewpoint. Only about five per cent of the Pentagon's officers admit that they are "liberals."[17]

Americans have assumed that their Military Establishment desires to retain democracy, yet this group consistently supports obvious military dictatorships in other countries. Let us imagine the occurrence of some fast-breaking international crisis. Would the dwellers in the Pentagon continue to support democracy, or even its forms, if the civilians offered opposition to actions felt necessary by the military? Public statements of not a few high officers indicate that they believe civilians are weaklings and only the military knows what is best for the country.

In the garrison state the citizen quickly loses most of his personal freedoms. Since militarism presupposes a dangerously hostile outside world, the citizen within the camp must hold himself ready to make any sacrifice —his money, his civil liberties, and yes, even his life. It has been the experience of the Western World that constitutional guarantees of political and civil rights gradually erode under authoritarian regimes. Free dissent is quickly banned. The free conscience is allowed only as long as it does not express opposition in word or act to the official line, and the government seeks through every means of propaganda and terror to insure "correct thinking."

Militarism in the United States poses a danger to the traditional freedom of information. Dictatorships in the twentieth century have sought to achieve thought control by censorship and by taking charge of the media of mass communications. How can the citizen form an independent judgment if he has available only information approved by the official organs of the state? Today military leaders classify certain reports as "secret" and even deny Congressmen access to them. The military has found ways to compromise the independence, and thus the reliability, of the press. Each of the three services is well-funded for public relations and the mass communication media of the nation tend to go along with, rather than oppose, the policies of the military. They also tend to accept briefings and background reports as reliable sources of information rather than recognizing them for what they are, namely, slanted propaganda and managed news. Some of the press is militaristic, "hawkish," and conservative by choice. For example, the positions of the widely-distributed *Reader's Digest* and *Time-Life* publications as well as dozens of metropolitan newspapers are clearly oriented in that direction. In fact, someone ought to do a study on the number of military officers who retire not into industry but to the staffs of major newspapers and magazines.

The last two presidential administrations have supplied us with examples of "managed news." The prestige and news-worthiness of any executive statement is so great and the presidential information-gathering sources so extensive that the individual citizen feels completely inadequate to evaluate or oppose an administration's pronouncements. Should the military take over the executive branch at some future date, or if some avowed militarist should be elected president, the citizen's chances of countering the doctrines or power of the Military Establishment would be practically nil. No real opposition to the military would be allowed, and yet a loyal opposition is desirable and even necessary to prevent fatal mistakes. For example, General MacArthur vigorously insisted that the movement of United Nations troops across the 38th Parallel would not draw the Chinese into the Korean War. His view was based on poor military intelligence and an even poorer assessment of the psychology of Communist China's leaders and their ability to field an army. There will be a continuing need for a sober and critical approach to decisions proposed by the leaders of the armed forces. Instead of this we have seen a growing tendency of people from the ordinary citizen to the President himself to rely on the military's expertise, regardless of whether it is in weaponry or the world situation.

President Eisenhower, in his farewell address, expressed a deep concern over the possible death of the "free university." He was afraid that these traditional centers of free scholarship might become little more than government workshops where federal employees who had lost the push of intellectual curiosity would labor over government-dictated projects. He was not speaking of some remote possibility. Already a large percentage of scientific research in the universities is done at government behest and with government subsidies. The institutions which get the most federal money are not necessarily those which have displayed the most originality but those which have showed the greatest ability to write a grant request acceptable to the government. Much of this research is military in nature.

In the Cold War situation, government subsidization of the universities has proved to be detrimental in several ways. Government contracts have brought a gradual form of control over science and scientists. Freedom among scientists to exchange information has been diminished, for projects and discoveries may be classified as "secret." Another injurious aspect is the arrangement whereby scientific research is preponderantly oriented in one direction, that is, to enable the government to solve its military-technological problems. Captive brains come more and more to serve the warfare state. This is the reverse side of the coin which President Eisenhower mentioned: "Public policy could itself become the captive of a scientific-technological elite."[18] It was the communist challenge, not a basic desire to increase knowledge, which motivated the federal government to engage in a feverish search for some grand mechanism, or an assortment of contrivances, which would neutralize the enemy.

It is precisely at this point that the weakness of the military mind is exposed, for these men conceive of the major challenges to the United States in terms of strategy, logistics and weapons. They assume that security lies in superiority in bombs and missiles, anti-missile missiles and shelters. What good would these be if the enemy should decide to fight with microbes instead of projectiles? Bacteria might be dropped from an orbiting satellite to infest wide areas of the United States or slipped into the nation's water supplies by foreign agents. Recent history suggests that the enemy will choose to attack with an unexpected weapon at an unexpected place. Who could determine with any accuracy the identity of the perpetrator? Yet the United States continues to commit more and more of its resources to weapons and to limit itself to *only one* response to the communist challenge. Arnold J. Toynbee, in his ponderous *Study of His-*

tory, has suggested that civilizations or nations which were unable to devise a variety of responses to outside challenges, especially those which depended almost solely on a military response, were destroyed, *usually by internal forces.*

In addition to its other injurious effects on higher education, Washington's subsidies have brought distortion to the balance of the university's disciplines and a serious problem of faculty morale. Huge quantities of money have been poured into science departments for buildings and equipment and to attract the brightest minds while little has been spent in other divisions. To the government's largesse, university trustees often have added more millions. Unduly impressed by shining new equipment and "that brilliant new professor in physics which we got away from Columbia," university administrators reflect the government's attitude that the natural sciences alone have the solution to the nation's problems.

The dangers of an economy in bondage to the warfare state have been pointed out by several noted men. Americans urgently need to give their attention to this problem and not allow the military-industrial complex to make the choice of their basic economic goals and priorities. The military has tried to achieve that control. The war chiefs have agitated for the country to commit an even greater part of its economic wealth and energy to fortifying the state against all comers. Great industrialists, who reap unjustifiable profits from bloated war budgets, concur with the military view. These allies are convinced that spending for defense—even billions for unneeded or outdated weapons and supplies—is preferable to government spending for social welfare programs. So, this is the choice: new "big-bang toys" for the military boys and fat profits for the capitalists on one hand, or more medical care, better housing, safer highways, more forest conservation, and a hundred other benefits for the common American on the other.

The military-industrial complex decries "socialistic" programs and seeks at every turn to convince the nation that in "this period" the country cannot afford them. Military men of high rank travel around the nation seeking to influence the choice of policies and lauding an economic system that has long since ceased to be a reality. Big business cries piteously for a return to unfettered free enterprise while it lobbies the government for tax write-offs, depletion allowances, subsidies, anti-union laws, and contracts which are let without competitive bidding. The military-industrial complex decided long ago where its economic interest lay and how to go about emptying the federal treasury.

Do the American people know where their true economic interests lie? Have they considered the real costs of a war economy? The dollars spent on one destroyer would build homes for eight thousand people while an additional hundred residences could be built for the price of one fighter plane. The aero-space budget for 1968 would provide adequate housing for nearly one million persons. (Consider the business activity and employment that a program on that scale would generate.) Furthermore, an economy geared to war production actually harms the consumer and small businessman by encouraging monopolistic concentrations of business power and inhibiting competition. A few companies grow rich and powerful from government contracts and thereby gain a competitive advantage over their rivals. They undercut their smaller competitors until they have driven them out of business, and then prices are stabilized at relatively high levels.

On the surface the worker may appear to gain advantages from the war economy, but these can be traced to other sources. The warlords would have us believe that prosperity, full employment, and better products are all "spill-over" or "spin-out" from defense activity. There is no reason to doubt that if the billions expended for war were allocated to peaceful projects, the same benefits would accrue to the American workingman. Up to this point the military-industrial complex has consented grudgingly to share a part of the war profits with labor. However, the leaders of the military-industrial complex lean greatly toward conservatism, a political viewpoint which has consistently opposed social and economic gains for the common people. The student of history will recall that the great militaristic states of the past have exploited and repressed the lower classes in their societies.

A dangerous by-product of militarism is likely to be the destruction of the strong humanitarian tradition in America. Already, flippant, professional iconoclasts are referring to this as "do-goodism," and the militaristic climate will not be conducive to the further flowering of a humane culture. A system which ignores the essential humanity of men and prepares to slaughter thousands and even millions cannot but brutalize its followers. In his novel *War and Peace* Leo Tolstoy many years ago laid bare the de-civilizing, de-humanizing aspects of war and the anguish it produced for those who were caught up in its processes. Therefore, a rationale must be found for wholesale homicide, since the long tradition of Christian humanism is not easily cast off. Tristram Coffin puts it this way in *The Armed Society*: "Manslaughter, while it is widely and honorably practiced, still has some psychological disadvantages, and to practice it professionally requires an elaborate rationalization."[19] One must hasten to point out, however, that the Nazis and Japanese warlords did not apparently suffer undue anguish over their bloodletting. Moreover, there are shocking illustrations that a few American soldiers have hardened themselves to the task of destroying their fellows. Major General William

M. Creasy, who once presided over the development of bio-chemical horror weapons for the U.S., reportedly deplored "this humanitarian fervor of ours."[20] If, as a consequence of the military ethic, there is an almost inevitable disappearance of humanitarianism, the evangelical Christian is obliged not only to declare that this is too high a price to pay but also to condemn the ethic and its adherents. A genuine Christian cannot abdicate his moral responsibility by offering the excuse that he is compelled to give his assent. He may have to pay with his life for opposing such immoral dictates of the state, but the Scriptures urge him to "Be faithful unto death, and I will give you the crown of life." (Rev. 2:10)

The ultimate danger posed by militarism in the United States is that of the absolute destruction of American society and of Western Civilization as we know it. If the militarists succeed in obtaining control of American foreign policy, they will bring only one point of view to its practice. If this happens, it is the author's firm belief that the nation's military guardians will in all probability seek a military solution to the communist challenge, that is, a preventive thermonuclear war. The long period of Cold War enmity for the Russians (and more recently for the Chinese) increases the possibility of such a fatal action. Professor Stanley Hoffman, a Harvard University political scientist, has written in his brilliant essay on war:

> *Among nations, conflict turns into war almost inevitably.* For the contest between groups that feel themselves intensely different from one another and whose highest loyalty is to themselves prepares the ground for violence, and war is there to serve as an available method of action and outlet of passion, as an instrument in the calculation of gains, a carrier of the dreams and delusions of the great, the fears and faiths of the many.[21]

If the inevitable result of militarism is war, then a humanitarian concern for mankind ought to demand in this thermonuclear age that the great power blocs negotiate a *detente*. However, the military in the United States has usually opposed any serious negotiations with the Russians or Chinese leading in that direction. The theme of the military-industrial complex and the Radical Right has been that the U. S. cannot negotiate, for the Communists can never be trusted to keep any agreement (a generalization not borne out by the facts of history). Further, those who are militarily inclined rarely miss an opportunity to downgrade the State Department and the arts of peaceful persuasion. Diplomats are characterized as "stuffed shirts in striped pants," as "sissies and cookie-pushers." The civilian desire to negotiate is regarded as a sign of weakness and there are repeated warnings from high officers of the dangers of "appeasement." Somewhere in the intellectual processes of these men "compromise" has become "appeasement."

The favorite historical illustration is Munich and pre-World War II diplomacy. This one example is supposed to teach conclusively that "aggressors" will not be satisfied by compromises and that the diplomat should confine himself to giving stern warnings and ultimata. The examples of hundreds of successful international compromises are ignored. Since the military has exhibited general opposition to negotiation, American Christians who desire peace and accommodation must endeavor to reduce the influence which the officer corps has on foreign policy and to convert those who encourage a militant, inflexible approach to international relations to a more reasonable policy position.

The aggressive, hand-on-gun stance is fraught with danger. There is too great a possibility in the militarized state that the professional soldier will tire of the patient diplomacy necessary in this era of the balance of terror. Seeing some supposed advantage, he may gamble all on a lucky throw of the military dice. It is apparent today that the American military could create at any time an "incident" to set off a thermonuclear war, or make use of a miscue by some member of the communist camp for the same purpose. One might note here that the Kremlin leaders could have used the admitted but accidental American bombing of a Soviet ship in a North Vietnamese harbor on June 2, 1967 as an excuse for war. The militarists on either side could take advantage of any such trifling incident to demand unreal concessions from the other side or to begin hostilities. There is at present the possibility that American political leaders, following the counsel of the military, may escalate the conflict in Vietnam once too often and bring on the nuclear holocaust. Heretofore military errors have brought upon man dreadful consequences; today they may bring the final ones.

Christianity and the Military Establishment

The threats posed to the individual Christian and to American society by the gains of militarism already have suggested the outlines of a rationale on which opposition to that system might be based. An interesting sidelight is the condemnation of war as policy by the British House of Commons in 1936: ". . . this House affirms its profound belief in the futility of war, [and] views with grave concern the world-wide preparations for war."[22] Much of American activity during the Cold War may very well be adjudged as having been useless by men in the future, for in spite of prodigious spending and the massive power of American military forces, communism has not been prevented from extending its influence or control over great areas of Europe and Asia. The opponents of militarism need not follow along with the Tolstoyites who have renounced every use for force by man on man. Instead, the Western humanist may plead, as did his Greek predecessors, for rational action. He may question whether war waged under modern conditions is reasonable at all. The ordinary citizen of the United States may take a pragmatic approach and insist that militarism will not bring him the satisfaction of his desires as a free individual in the free society. The ancient aspiration for justice under moral law can hardly be realized through militarism. Have not warring nations often destroyed as much as they have preserved? As one observer has noted: "Even if the end of the adventure were peace and freedom for all, the story would have been long and bloody enough to make of this final meaning a rather belated consolation."[23] The Christian, dedicated to compassion and love for all men, will question a system organized for the task of slaughter.

The course of action of the military-industrial complex in the United States seems to be leading almost inevitably toward thermonuclear war. The humanist will oppose this trend for humanity's sake. The early humanists re-emphasized in Western society the intrinsic value of every man. Each individual was of immeasurable worth for each person shared in humanity, a sovereignty not to be assaulted by the state, nor by the church, nor by another man. The consistent humanist cannot admit any ultimate demand by the state on man. Militarism and humanism are essential opposites for the martial ideology dehumanizes man. Militarism treats man as an object, the state's property, and places the enemy on the level of animals to be exterminated. The *Christian* humanist, in his most lucid moments, has always understood the universality of his religion and that his vocation must not be limited by national boundaries nor false calls to patriotic duty. The Christian is bound to suspect the national Military Establishment which asks him to obliterate one who is divinely loved without being morally certain that this action toward his human counterpart in unavoidable. The basic dilemma of the Christian at war will always be how to love one's enemy and kill him too.

The military-industrial complex in this country apparently has used and plans to use the ordinary citizen as a tool to create a monument to national self-glorification, the triumph of "democracy" and "capitalism" over other economic and political systems. The military speaks of the "duty" of American boys to die for the nation's ideals—to die before they have had a chance to distinguish between the verbalization of ideals and those actually practiced by the military-industrial complex. The military has sought for constant renewals of the draft and periodically called for universal military training. "Duty" becomes not an inner compulsion but the bowing to the superior force of the state. American boys become objects to be honed for warfare. They are taught to kill an enemy they may never see, a foe visualized only as a stereotype implanted by the propaganda of the military-industrial complex and not a fellow creature with warm blood, human loves, and simple hopes and fears. No action could be more uncharacteristic of the divine Son of God whom Christians claim to imitate than this depersonalization of one's relation to his fellow man.

All of this suggests that militarism poses a threat to civilization and that the long-continued jostling for the high seats of power by nations armed with thermonuclear weapons assures more than ever that the next conflict will most likely be the last war. Almost any modern war, even without the use of those terrible weapons, would be worse than the evils it was designed to ward off, but a nuclear contest will only destroy what man has labored so mightily to create, his civilization. The unthinking mouth the slogan, "Better dead than Red," not realizing that war and militarism may be more destructive of their goals than communism. There is a fate worse than death—life without meaning. As Professor Hoffman so ably sums it up in his study of war:

> The social scientist can hardly fail to see history as a graveyard of men, buried after having killed and been killed for an incredible number of causes. Retrospectively, it is hard to find a meaning here —and easy to lament with so many poets the absurdity of the whole story.[24]

Thermonuclear war is not likely to usher in a period of utopian peace for the victor, but it may very well preclude the possibility of history having any further meaning.

The Christian citizen will discover that the garrison state destroys his ability to function as a free individual in a free society. He has already found that as militarism has grown in America there has been a reciprocal reduction in his ability to take a meaningful part in the government. Basic decisions come not as a result of consensus, but are imposed from above by a power elite. When the militarists are finished, only a hollow mockery of democracy will remain. Civil rights will be unprotected by tradition or a yellowing scrap of paper and raw power will prevail. The free citizen ought to oppose militarism in order that he may retain his freedom to act—to go here or there without an official pass, to enter whatever vocation he wishes without permission, to assume or refuse employment without a government penalty. Americans have generally enjoyed the freedom to act but certainly will lose this liberty in a militaristic, totalitarian society.

The individual of sensitive mind eagerly longs for freedom of expression and the right to become his best possible self without restrictions or encumbrances except those to which he has freely assented. Perhaps no man living with other men can attain this ideal but it can be more nearly achieved in a free society than in a militarized state. Basic to the free individual is his right to freedom of thought, but how can he think if his mind is constantly barraged with propaganda? If the press is prohibited from functioning freely, if sources of information are distorted, if access to some types of information is prohibited, if free experimentation and the exchange of ideas is forbidden, there is no freedom of thought. The militaristic state restricts a man in these ways and many more as well. The free individual finds himself compelled to stand against any person or system which would treat his mind as a magnetic tape to be programmed at will.

The evangelical Christian finds a rationale for opposing militarism in his faith—he opposes it for conscience's sake. Contrary to the assertion of Ernst Troeltsch that the state and all questions relating to it were ignored by Jesus, the state was a part of the mundane scene and was so affirmed in the Messiah's teachings. Followers of the Way were not urged to ignore the present age but to redeem it. There is no loophole here whereby the citizen may escape the obligations of the Christian ethic by positing a separate civil ethic. A dual standard of morality with one code to guide the Christian's action in the religious area and another code for the secular realm has been proposed, but the evangelical Christian must insist on one consistent ethical norm for all men in all conditions. Scholars have uniformly agreed that the Jews did not compartmentalize life into secular and sacred divisions. Men were to live their *whole* lives before God according to his will revealed in commandments and instructions. This characteristic of Jewish thought was basic to the thinking of Jesus also. The Christian citizen, thus, must resolve any apparent conflicts between the demands of the state and his duty toward God within the bounds of one ethical system—that of Jesus of Nazareth.

Those who believe that war may be justified have often quoted the verses in Romans 13 which begin "Let every person be subject to the governing authorities." This Pauline statement in no way endorses the unbridled use of force by the state. Indeed, it comes immediately after a passage in which the apostle exhorts his readers to live a life of nonviolence, blessing their persecutors, seeking no vengeance, feeding their enemies, and overcoming evil with good (Rom. 12:14–21). The statement of Jesus that one ought to "Render therefore to Caesar the things that are Caesar's" is quoted also to imply the heavy obligation of the Christian citizen to the state. This single, rather oracular statement is less convincing than the fact that Jesus refused to concern himself with the national aspirations of the Jews. His energies were devoted to the Kingdom of God, a spiritual realm. He chose for himself the role of a spiritual leader and refused resolutely to become a military messiah, even though there were Old Testament precedents. If the "Caesar" statement does indicate an obligation to the state, that debt should not be thought to have the same absolute character as the debt to God. The Christian sees his first and highest duty to God, as did Jesus. Therefore, one may never in the name of serving Caesar act contrary to the ethical principles of Christ. One might add concerning the passage in Romans that Paul admittedly put more stress than did Jesus on obeying the civil authorities, perhaps because he feared that unnecessary violations of the law might stir up persecutions worse than the local ones already being experienced by Christians. Never did the apostle imply that one's allegiance to the state justified an immoral act.

The American Christian, living in a country moving toward militarism and engaged in periodic wars abroad, is faced with a pressing question: "Is the Christian ever justified in using force, and may he with a clear conscience become a participant?" Here is not the place for an extended discussion of pacifism, a subject upon which so many words have already been penned. This writer has found the most thorough and concise discussion of the relevant Biblical passages to be that of the English theologian G. H. C. Macgregor in his volume *The New Testament Basis of Pacifism*. This lucid little book makes the point that a Christian does not need to, and perhaps cannot, stand on an absolute prohibition of the use of force between men or groups of men. Professor Macgregor maintains, instead, that the Christian's choice is "between moral and non-moral use of *force*" in many situations. There is an absolute ban on *war* because it trangresses the New Testament ethic.[25] After a thorough examination of the Scriptures, Macgregor concludes that the Gospels, with two doubtful exceptions, show Jesus consistently living by the principle of non-resistance. If Christ's life is one that is well-pleasing to the Heavenly Father, must the Christian not seriously consider the possibility that he himself is to forego the use of force and also shun war?

The history of the early church indicates that it understood the life of the Way to be one of peace. "Blessed are the peacemakers, for they shall be called sons of God." (Mt. 5:9). For nearly two centuries the church was almost wholly pacifist. Scholars can find no examples of Christians becoming soldiers *after baptism* until about 170 A. D. The early church fathers—Justin Martyr, Clement of Alexandria, Tertullian, Origen—insisted that Christians were pacifists. Origen, writing perhaps as late as 230 A. D., declared: "We Christians no longer take up sword against nation nor do we learn to make war any more, having become children of peace, for the sake of Jesus who is our leader."[26]

Yet, in spite of the consistent witness of the early church, the question still remains: may a war be justified on certain occasions and under certain circumstances? Perhaps so, if war, as a means, and the end which it seeks do not transgress the ethics of Christ. Another relevant question, however, is: "Does not war always contradict the goals of the Kingdom, and the redemption of man, and does not modern total war inevitably involve every participant in immoral means?" One noted scholar recently concluded: "In modern total war, where murder without risks, slaughter in anonymity, and the denial of the humanity of the foe prevail, the sacrifices of conscience which national loyalty demands have reached a new high."[27] It is perhaps too high.

The evangelical Christian, however far he may wish to walk with the humanists, knows that there is a higher reason for him to question the whole idea of modern war toward which the militarists are leading him. The heart of the New Testament ethic is the injunction to love. Christians are instructed to love God, one another, their neighbor, *and their enemy*. Loving one's enemy is not an optional matter: "But I say to you, love your enemies . . . so that you may be sons of your Father who is in heaven" (Mt. 5:44–45. There is a lengthy passage in Matthew (5:38–48) which sets forth the Christian way of meeting evil. It is the way of non-violence and love for the adversary. One is to overcome evil not by greater evil but by good. Perhaps such actions in the face of an armed foe are foolishness. It led the Galilean to the cross, but it was the redemptive way. If force is to be used, surely it must not be for punitive measures or merely to save our own lives. Rather, it must have redemption as its end. Given the ambiguities of the international situation and the awful efficiency of modern devices for killing, and faced with the threat that man may end his history with a final and fiery act of sin, it seems crystal-clear that the Christian ought to expend every possible effort to resist those pressures which militate for the use of force in international affairs. If a thermonuclear debacle is avoided, we may have time to go about our Father's business.

NOTES

1. *Public Papers of the Presidents of the United States: Dwight D. Eisenhower, 1960–61* (Washington: Government Printing Office, 1961), p. 1038.

2. Quoted in John R. Swomley, Jr., *The Military Establishment* (Boston: Beacon Press, 1964), p. 1.

3. *Ibid., passim.* Dr. Swomley is Associate Professor of Social Ethics and Philosophy at the St. Paul School of Theology (Methodist) in Kansas City, Missouri. He was from 1947 to 1955 a director of the National Council against Conscription.

4. James D. Richardson, ed., *A Compilation of the Messages and Papers of the Presidents* (Washington: Bureau of National Literature, 1897), I, 208.

5. Alfred Vagts, *A History of Militarism* (New York: Meridian, 1959), p. 17.

6. Arthur A. Ekirch, Jr., *The Civilian and the Military* (New York: Oxford University Press, 1956), x.

7. Figures taken from Tristram Coffin, *The Armed Society, Militarism in Modern America* (Baltimore: Penguin Books, 1964), p. 63.

8. Quoted in *Ibid.*, p. 105.

9. Fred J. Cook, *The Warfare State* (New York: Macmillan, 1962), p. 67.

10. U.S., Congress, House, Committee on Armed Services, *Employment of Retired Commissioned Officers by Contractors of the Department of Defense and the Armed Forces*, 86th Cong., 2d Sess., 1960, H.R. 1408.

11. William H. Neblett, *Pentagon Politics* (New York: Pageant Press, 1953), pp. 44–46.

12. Donald M. Nelson, *Arsenal of Democracy* (New York: Harcourt, Brace, 1946), p. 363.

13. *U.S. News and World Report*, XXIV (May 14, 1948), 68.

14. *Congressional Record*, 80th Cong., 2d Sess., 1948, XCIV, Part 7, 8379.

15. Swomley, *The Military Establishment*, pp. 127–28.

16. *Congressional Record*, 87th Cong., 1st Sess., 1961, CVII, Part 7, 9103.

17. Coffin, *The Armed Society*, p. 82.

18. Dwight D. Eisenhower in *Public Papers of the Presidents*, p. 1039.

19. Coffin, *The Armed Society*, p. 64.

20. *Ibid.*, p. 71.

21. Stanley Hoffmann, *The State of War* (New York: Frederick A. Praeger, 1965), p. 255. Italics mine.

22. Great Britain, *Parliamentary Debates* (Commons), CCCVIII (1936), 208.

23. Hoffmann, *The State of War*, p. 261.

24. *Loc. cit.*

25. G. H. C. Macgregor, *The New Testament Basis of Pacifism* (New York: Fellowship of Reconciliation, 1947), p. 11.

26. *Contra Celsum*, v, p. 33.

27. Hoffmann, *The State of War*, pp. 262–63.

James E. Johnson is Professor of History at Bethel College, St. Paul, Minnesota. He was born in Johnson City, New York on March 26, 1927 and attended the public schools of that city. Mr. Johnson was a student at the Triple Cities College of Syracuse University where he received the B.A. degree in 1950. He obtained the M.A. degree in 1953 from the University of Buffalo and the Ph.D. degree in history in 1959 from Syracuse University.

Mr. Johnson was a teaching assistant in the Department of History at Syracuse University for two years and was an instructor there during the summer session of 1959. He has subsequently returned to that institution on two different occasions to serve as a visiting professor in the Department of History. He joined the faculty of Youngstown University in 1959 as an assistant professor and was promoted to associate professor in 1961. He has been a member of the Department of History at Bethel College since 1961. His primary areas of concern lie in the fields of American social and intellectual history, particularly with reference to the influence of religion on American culture. He is also deeply interested in the evolving social welfare program in the United States of the twentieth century.

Designed for use by high school American history students, two books by Professor Johnson on the history of immigration have recently appeared: *The Irish in America* and *The Scots and Scotch-Irish in America* (Minneapolis: Lerner Publications, 1966). He also published a series of articles on Charles G. Finney in the *Journal of Presbyterian History*. He belongs to a number of professional organizations, including the American Historical Association, Organization of American Historians, National Social Science Honorary Society, and Minnesota Historical Society. In addition, he is a member of a Baptist General Conference church and considers himself a political independent.

JAMES E. JOHNSON

The Christian and the Emergence of the Welfare State

Colonial America

The philosophy of rugged individualism has been woven into the fabric of American life from the earliest days. Since the majority of the early settlers were Protestants, they easily incorporated this philosophy into their religious beliefs. The resulting "Protestant ethic" as interpreted by Max Weber represented the blend of religion and capitalism. This "gospel of work" had a prescription for success which followed the individualistic line. The Puritans and Pilgrims of the New England colonies introduced another version with their doctrine of election and the divine calling. God became identified with the interests of those who were successful in life. The man who was diligent in his calling, thrifty with his goods, and upright in character was assumed to be basking in the favor of the Almighty. The more he accumulated goods and multiplied his fortune, the more his peers were convinced that he was following the divine prescription for success.

Conversely, the poor, whether lazy or unfortunate, were treated with varying degrees of contempt. Since the Puritans could not really conceive that an impoverished person was one of God's elect, they ruled out any mercy toward the poor and reduced them to an inferior class socially and morally. Any relief or aid extended to them was kept to the barest minimum so as not to discourage any efforts on their part to help themselves. There is little historical evidence that the compassion which Jesus showed toward the needy was present in colonial America. There is no indication that the poor were treated charitably because they might be fallen creatures due to original sin. The prevalent view was that they could be regarded as social outcasts since God had by-passed them in his calling.

These views were not confined to colonial New England but were present in all the colonies. The position of the Anglican Church regarding poverty was quite similar and perhaps a case can be made that the Protestant establishment in colonial America had a middle-class orientation from the very beginning. In the Middle colonies, where a greater degree of tolerance might be expected, persons obtaining relief were publicly identified. In New Jersey the pauper was required to wear a badge on the right sleeve with a blue or red "P" along with the first letter of the name of the city or county in which he resided.[1]

There was, to be sure, abundant opportunity in colonial America for an individual to make a living. A person could acquire land rather easily and establish a farm which would provide most of the necessities of life. The person in need of aid would most likely have been the victim of some misfortune like the loss of his crop, the destruction of his home by fire, or a prolonged illness. In the towns the situation was somewhat different, but the opportunities were still quite good. Therefore, it can be said that rugged individualism did yield dividends to those who practiced it, even if the dividends were rather meager at times.

Nineteenth Century America

Early nineteenth century America was rural-agrarian oriented and still evidenced confidence in the philosophy of individualism. With so much frontier left to conquer and with abundant opportunities, the Protestant ethic could be applied by many individuals in a meaningful way. There were rumbles of discontent, however, as mill workers in the towns of New England felt themselves being squeezed by economic forces they neither understood nor controlled. Others also protested, but the sparks of discontent merely smouldered; seldom did they break out into open flames.

The Civil War is used as a dividing line by many textbook writers to mark the emergence of modern America. Whether this line be accepted or not, the forces which emerged after that war were those that have a bearing on the problem of the church and the welfare state today. The rural-agrarian viewpoint of the antebellum period was subjected to disintegrative pressures, and the philosophy of rugged individualism was also challenged.

Four forces in post-Civil War America which affected the Protestant church were Darwinism, Marxism, higher criticism, and an acceleration of industrialism-urbanism. The Darwinian idea posed a problem to some Protestants since it challenged the story of creation as given in the Book of Genesis. If evolution were true, then these Christians believed that their faith was threatened because it was grounded in the literal Biblical account. Marxism challenged the usefulness of the church, especially to the urban proletariat who felt they were being exploited by their employers. Religion, according to Marx, was nothing more than an opiate to dull the senses of the exploited so that they would not protest their wretched condition. Higher criticism also challenged the authenticity of the Scriptures. Theological students who returned from graduate studies in Germany had very disturbing ideas. They claimed that the stories of the flood and Noah's Ark were borrowed from Mesopotamian literature, and that internal evidence showed the Pentateuch was a composite of writings from different authors representing widely separated eras. In addition, the higher critics challenged the Biblical accounts of miracles as well as the historicity of many events. In spite of all these disturbing phenomena, in the long run it was industrialism and urbanism which had the most profound effect on American Protestant churches.

Reaction of the Protestant Church

The church reacted to the movements described above in a variety of ways. Darwinism caused a deep cleavage, with one group attempting to accommodate it while the other rejected its ideas completely. The branch that accepted Darwinism was called liberal Protestantism. This group also sought to incorporate into their theology the evidences of scholarship by the higher critics. Consequently, the liberals altered their views on some basic doctrines. The other branch came to be known as fundamentalism and adopted a stand which opposed the evolutionary hypothesis as well as most of the writings of the higher critics. Fundamentalists adopted a creed that stressed certain areas which they considered vital to their theology. These included belief in the inerrancy of the Scriptures, the deity of Christ, the virgin birth, the substitutionary atonement, and the second coming of Christ. The fundamentalist stand against evolution was articulated by William Jennings Bryan at the Scopes trial in Dayton, Tennessee, in July 1925.

The previous adjustments and splits were serious, to be sure, but the larger society was not involved in the debates within the church except for the Scopes trial which attracted national attention. The growth of industrialism, however, and the phenomenal increase in urban centers were issues vital to all of society. The reaction of the church to these matters would concern a larger audience.

The period between the end of the Civil War and the start of the twentieth century was one of change and transition. The laissez-faire approach was that state intervention should be kept to an absolute minimum in order to attain the maximum economic growth possible under the free enterprise system. The rugged individualism of colonial America continued to be reinforced by the "hands off" policy of the government.

A school of thought emerged during the period which defended the laissez-faire doctrine in a rather sophisticated manner. The ideas entered this country through the writings of Herbert Spencer, an English author, and were further developed by William Graham Sumner. This group came to be known as Social Darwinists since they applied the evolutionary hypothesis to society in general. Sumner joined together for his generation three lines of thought: the Protestant ethic, Darwin's theory of natural selection, and the ideas of the classical economists. Social Darwinism provided a rationale for the laissez-faire doctrine which fortified the position of the industrial capitalists. In Sumner's view, the man who was on top got there by struggling and the process of natural selection justified his superior position. "The millionaires," he said, ". . . get high wages and live in luxury, but the bargain is a good one for society."[2]

The doctrine of laissez-faire came under attack in the later stages of the Gilded Age. Jane Addams, Edward Bellamy, Henry George, and other social reformers raised their voices in protest as did the sociologist, Lester Frank Ward. These people opposed the doctrine of self-interest which characterized laissez-faire philosophy, as well as that of untrammeled competition. They declared that they could not remain passive in the face of so much suffering and want and support a theory which claimed that the state should not intervene to help the needy.

Since people were attracted to the areas where the factories located, urbanism with its concomitant problems emerged on the scene. Slums inevitably developed and individuals like Jane Addams tried to improve living and housing conditions, particularly for poor immigrant families. Social reformers called the attention of city councils and state legislatures to overcrowded slum areas where wretched living conditions prevailed on every hand. Robert Hunter said that: "The men, women, and children turn out of bed or rise from mattresses on the floor, gulp down some handfuls of food, and leave the home for the mills. . . . [They] hurry along in crowds to be in time to begin their twelve or more hours of continuous work."[3] Jacob Riis reported that in one city block of New York City the Tenement House Commission counted 155 deaths of children in a single year (1882). He felt that the infant mortality rate could be taken as a good barometer of the general sanitary condition of an area and said: "Here, in this tenement, No. 59 1/2, next to Bandit's Roost, fourteen persons died that year, and eleven of them were children. . . ."[4] A writer for one of the muckraking journals saw equally bad conditions in Chicago:

> In the center of Chicago are now two small cities of savages— self-regulating and self-protecting. In one of these there are thirty-

five thousand people; in the other, thirty thousand. . . . The inhabitants neither labor regularly nor marry. Half of the men are beggars, criminals, or floating laborers; a quarter are engaged in the sale of dissipation; and a third of the women are prostitutes."[5]

The critics of the laissez-faire doctrine maintained that it may have been an adequate philosophy for an agricultural society, but that it was a dangerous policy to pursue in the complex industrial society which was emerging. One writer stated, "I have long been convinced that, while the laissez-faire theory rendered good service by clearing the modern world of the worst . . . system of the last century, it is utterly inadequate as regards the great problems now pressing upon the world."[6] Articulated by various reformers, the view began to gain ground that the state could be employed to deal with the situation. In other words, the state was the one agency capable of handling the problems of monopolies, slums and tenements, and public health. Consequently, with respect to the function of the state, a struggle began to develop between those who wanted to cling to the laissez-faire doctrine and those who wanted to use the powers of government to solve some of society's problems.

The churches were also divided on the issue of laissez-faire economics. Some churchmen applauded the achievements of industrial giants such as Andrew Carnegie and John D. Rockefeller. Russell Conwell, a Baptist clergyman in Philadelphia, repeated a lecture entitled "Acres of Diamonds" over five thousand times. In this lecture he stated that it was not only permissible from a religious standpoint to become rich, but also a moral obligation for every man. "I say that you ought to get rich," he said, "and it is your duty to get rich."[7] Bishop Lawrence of the Methodist Church piously stated that "Godliness is in league with riches," and the clergyman Henry Ward Beecher said that any workingman worth his salt could support a family on a dollar a day, providing he did not drink or smoke. If Beecher's income was in excess of twenty thousand dollars a year as was rumored, he can hardly be commended for berating the poor for being poor! The church, at least on one side of the fence, had little to offer the suffering masses huddling in the slums of the large cities except the traditional Protestant ethic of colonial America.

Twentieth Century America

At the turn of the century when the industrial development of the country was accelerating, the migration to the larger cities likewise increased in tempo. In the rural areas and small towns of the nineteenth century the kind help of a friendly neighbor was usually available in time of trouble. The growing cities of the twentieth century, however, were characterized by an almost vicious impersonality. The individual often became lost in this complex maze of lonely people living together. The philosophy of rugged individualism was an inadequate answer to the problems at hand.

There was a growing realization on the part of some that the rural-agrarian standards of the previous century might not work in the new era. Rugged individualism did not usually provide answers to the new problems of society and it was realized that a new system of ethics was needed. This new system would have to pinpoint problems caused by factors not under the control of the individual and offer help through the media of social agencies. Hence, a group of reformers emerged who stressed the need for the welfare state.

Fundamentalist Protestants had been little concerned with these questions. The fundamentalist continued to emphasize individual regeneration and gave little attention to the need for social reform. A small group of Protestant clergymen did attempt to find a solution by applying the gospel to the new social situations. The historian of this movement states that "their attempts to reorient the historic faith of America to an industrial society comprised the social gospel."[8]

The social gospel movement was a reaction against the pietistic individualism of fundamentalist Protestantism. Its aim was to awaken the churches to their responsibility for the societal needs around them. Many respected clergymen joined the ranks of this new movement, among whom were Lyman Abbott, Washington Gladden, Shailer Mathews, and Walter Rauschenbusch. Rauschenbusch had been pastor of a church in the "Hell's Kitchen" area of New York City and had been sickened at the disgusting conditions under which some of his fellow citizens were forced to live.

Rauschenbusch and his colleagues formulated a theory that called for the conversion of society. He was convinced that individuals would benefit enormously as soon as progress could be made in obtaining a better social order. The social gospel advocates adopted a very optimistic view of human nature and of the ability of men to solve their problems wisely. In contrast to the Puritan view of original sin and the bleak future of society, they assumed that the Kingdom of God could and would become a reality in human history. This Kingdom could be understood as the fulfillment of social progress through the adoption of programs to solve social problems.

The rock on which the social gospel foundered was World War I. The fundamentalists had taken issue with the social gospel at several points. One of the most obvious sources of disagreement was the idea of the perfectibility of man and the inevitability of progress. World War I seemed to vindicate the fundamentalist view. One writer has stated that "even the wildest millennialist apocalypses, after the horrors of the First World War, seemed more plausible to some than the liberal faith in automatic and inevitable progress."[9] Consequently, the experiment in finding a gospel ethic to fit social problems had to be set aside during the decade of the 1920's in America. This does not mean that humanitarian concerns ceased during this period,[10] but merely that those who advocated a social gospel became less active for a brief interlude.

The Great Depression

The crash of the stock market on October 24, 1929 merely capped a process that had been building for some time. It soon became apparent that the nation was facing a crisis much more serious than the Wall Street crash. Factories shut down, debtors were unable to meet their obligations, banks failed, and the lists of unemployed grew to ominous lengths. There are no accurate statistics concerning the number who were out of work, but estimates range from ten million up to fifteen million. These individuals saw their savings disappear as they searched hopelessly day after day for any kind of work. The *New York Times* reported that fifty-four men were fortunate enough to be arrested in time for a free meal and shelter just when a sudden change in the weather took place.[11] All areas of the economy were affected. Miners in the coal fields of Kentucky and West Virginia, for instance, were "permitted to spend as much time underground as they wanted. . . . And all this increased effort . . . produced only more trouble, for the product swelled the glut and forced the prices still lower."[12]

It was becoming increasingly clear that the state was the only logical agency left to carry on the task of administering welfare to those in need. Rugged individualism had little to offer for such harsh times but President Herbert Hoover still faithfully adhered to it as he indicated in this speech in 1932:

> No governmental action, no economic plan or project can replace that God-imposed responsibility of the individual man and woman to their neighbors. . . . If we shall gain in this spirit from this painful time, we shall have created a greater and more glorious America. The trial of it is here now. It is a trial of the heart and conscience, of individual men and women.[13]

What Hoover did not realize was that the churches and private agencies could not cope with the huge task of relief that was emerging. Voluntarism was becoming increasingly ineffective. Stating that the task was too large for them, the Red Cross refused to accept twenty-five million dollars that the President wished to make available.

The depression idled millions of individuals who could not arbitrarily be considered lazy or lacking in moral fiber, and those individuals were forced to ask for help to resolve their predicament. The continuation of the depression caused voluntary contributions to diminish, and city, county, and state governments found themselves approaching bankruptcy in their efforts to provide needed relief funds. In 1932 the Congress passed the Emergency Relief and Construction Act authorizing $300 million for loans to states, counties, and cities on an emergency basis.

The churches were obviously affected by the new developments and budgets began to be tightened as church boards took a long look at their programs. Pastors found themselves spending more and more of their time finding work for members of their congregations who were unemployed and the calls for aid that were coming into the churches could no longer be met with the limited resources which were available. These events caused some churchmen to reevaluate their whole attitude toward the problem of need. A Baptist journal which had suggested in the 1920's that the solution to the high cost of living was consumer belt tightening, now struck a different note. In an article entitled "Charity or Federal Aid," the *Baptist* commented: "We can be . . . sure that in any fair conflict between rich and poor, Jesus could be found on the side of the poor." The same journal continued: "Called by any name, federal aid . . . to . . . the unemployed could not possibly be so destructive to the self-respect of the recipient as . . . what we are now doing."[14] The Northern Baptist Convention passed a resolution in 1932 stating that: "Civil government is the sovereign agency for the promotion of the general welfare."[15]

Churches, reacting to their traditional fears of blurring the distinction between church and state, were afraid to take government money. Yet the depression caused the church to examine its position toward social welfare, to assume an empathic attitude, and to say: "There, but for the grace of God, go I." The depression heightened man's understanding both of his own vulnerability and of the fact that the world could be cruel and unfair. Consequently, it helped him to turn to law and justice as the source of his welfare judgments. All injustice did not disappear because of this changing attitude, however, and there were still some fifteen states during that era that denied paupers the right to vote.[16]

The New Deal

Although the expression "Welfare State" was commonly heard during the Fair Deal presidency of Harry Truman, it should be understood that our country is not presently in such a category. Social welfare received a trial run during the presidency of Franklin D. Roosevelt in that attempts were made to alleviate the problems facing human beings. The objective of social welfare is to secure for each human being basic economic necessities, equal opportunities with his fellow citizens, and a milieu in which he can achieve self-respect and enjoy freedom of thought and action. An authority in the field states that social welfare is "the organized system of social services and institutions, designed to aid individuals and groups to attain satisfying standards of life and health."[17] Social welfare programs can be in existence without the presence of a welfare state.

The term "welfare state" includes another dimension beyond social welfare programs. It includes social action, not only social welfare programs, but also attempts to achieve the reform of basic conditions through political or other processes. Aiding flood victims is an illustration of social welfare, but seeking for laws that promote conservation practices to prevent future floods is social action.[18] Great Britain and Sweden are well advanced toward the attainment of a welfare state, but our country does not yet begin to match most of their programs. From one point of view, such a state is "a society with a government that is benevolent rather than malevolent. This is hardly something to be cringed at."[19] Our present democratic system in the United States is involved in the process of assuming authority and responsibility commensurate with the demands of an expanding industrialized and urbanized society. We have inaugurated a number of commendable social welfare programs and have taken social action when and where the need is evident, but we do not have a welfare state.

In some aspects and objectives the New Deal was reminiscent of earlier reform efforts in the United States, particularly the Populist and Progressive movements. Nevertheless, the New Deal was also a departure from the past in that the laissez-faire or "hands off" policy was abandoned. President Franklin D. Roosevelt illustrated this break when he said that, "the Government itself was going to use affirmative action to bring about its avowed objectives rather than stand by and hope that general economic laws alone would attain them."[20] Although many inconsistencies can be found in the New Deal program, it was consistent in its objective to help people attain some measure of social justice. Frances Perkins, Secretary of Labor, reflected this concern when she said that "all the political and practical forces of the community should and could be directed to making life better for ordinary people."[21] It was also a break with the past because the government intervened to require that those in need be treated with dignity. The rule was that no one should hold individuals receiving aid up to public shame and demand of them behavior that was not expected of the populace as a whole. The Federal Emergency Relief Act of May 12, 1933 repudiated the old poor relief philosophy and candidly recognized that in a complex industrial society the individual was no longer in complete control of his economic destiny. The emergency loan program of the Hoover administration was replaced by a system of direct grants to the states for relief purposes.

The churches naturally spoke out and their church legislative gatherings took on a new tone. The editor of the *Yearbook of American Churches* wrote that "an unusually large number of official and national meetings were scheduled for 1934, [and] nearly every body found its agenda concerned with discussions of the social implications of religion."[22] The Northern Baptist Convention followed this trend by appointing a Commission on Social Action.

The New Deal introduced a new outlook into American economic life. It intervened extensively in the economic arena by underwriting mortgages, insuring bank deposits, giving aid to the unemployed and aged, and introducing programs to stimulate employment such as the Works Progress Administration, Public Works Administration, and the Civilian Conservation Corps. Moreover, the state promoted economic activity through such devices as National Recovery Administration and the Tennessee Valley Authority.

Since the Roosevelt administration assumed power when the appalling results of the lack of a social security program were apparent for all to see, the New Dealers came to believe that the government must provide not only opportunity for its citizens but also a measure of economic and social security. The Social Security Act of 1935 constituted the most obvious and important legislative recognition of this view, but one can also note the Railroad Retirement Acts, the Farm Security Administration, and similar measures. So much progress was made in these areas that by 1954 over fifty-eight million persons were covered by the retirement programs.[23]

President Roosevelt emphasized even further steps in his State of the Union message of 1944. Since most of the important New Deal reforms were in operation, he outlined a domestic reform program for postwar America which contained an economic "Bill of Rights." The President included in this proposal the right to a useful and remunerative job; the right to earn enough to provide adequate food and clothing and recreation; the right of every farmer to raise and sell his products at a return which will give him and his family a decent living; the right of every businessman to trade in an atmosphere of freedom from unfair competition; the right of every family to a decent home; the right to adequate medical care; the right to adequate protection from the economic fears of old age, sickness, accidents, and unemployment; and the right to a good education.

Individual New Dealers were influenced by the teachings of social Christianity. President Roosevelt, for example, when queried by a reporter as to his philosophy stated: "I am a Christian and a Democrat—that's all." Harry Hopkins was particularly impressed by a course in Applied Christianity at Grinnell College, and Henry Wallace stated that the reforms of the New Deal would fail unless inspired by a larger vision than "hard driving profit-motives of the past."[24]

Of course, not all churchmen were enthusiastic about the New Deal. J. Franklin Norris, a noted Baptist, told a crowd in Carnegie Hall that Roosevelt was a dictator seeking to regiment the people. J. Gresham Machen, a Presbyterian, stated that the New Deal could only lead to slavery under a centralized bureaucracy. A New York minister said that aid to the unemployed was un-Christian because it robbed people of their responsibility and opportunity to give aid to the needy.[25] Another critic believed that the government was punishing the hard-working citizens by the "passing of their hard-earned savings over to mendicants and deadbeats, who never worked when they had work and who won't work after the administrative socialistic schemes finish squandering the money of the taxpayers upon them."[26] One clergyman complained that the government hand-outs would cause a situation where it would be years before the "lazy, dole-seeking laborer will again honestly 'look' for work." "Thank God," he said, "there are some folks left who know that real happiness comes from earning one's own bread by the sweat of the brow."[27]

It was evident that sincere church people were on both sides of the fence regarding the social welfare programs of the New Deal. Undoubtedly many millions had received aid of some sort from one or more of these programs whether they wholly approved of them or not. Much of the concern seemed to center on the fear that social welfare programs would usher in some kind of socialism. There is no evidence, however, that Franklin Roosevelt or his "Brain Trust" took issue with capitalism *per se*. They disagreed with the laissez-faire philosophy and wanted to use the power of the state to meet human needs. They did not, with the possible exception of the Tennessee Valley Authority, introduce any schemes that should be called socialism.

The Situation Today

The New Deal program was supplemented by the Fair Deal of President Harry Truman. Among other things, Truman recommended a higher minimum wage law, wider social security, tougher antitrust laws, expanded federal aid to education, and a federal medical insurance program. The New Deal and Fair Deal naturally resulted in much more extensive government regulation than in the past, but the originators of these programs regarded their reforms as attempts to strengthen capitalism rather than destroy it and as logical alternatives to the socialist route. In his final annual economic report, President Truman rejected the view of the laissez-faire economists that "We are the victims of unchangeable economic laws, that we are powerless to do more than forecast what will happen to us under the operations of such laws." He asserted rather "that our economy within reasonable limits will be what we make it," and that "intelligent human action will shape our future."[28]

The Eisenhower administration adopted a similar view. In an address of October 19, 1954, Arthur F. Burns, the chairman of the Council of Economic Advisers, said that "it is no longer a matter of serious controversy whether the Government should play a positive role in helping to maintain a high level of economic activity. What we debate nowadays is not the need for controlling business cycles, but rather the nature of governmental action, its timing and its extent."[29]

As a result of the reform movements previously described, the welfare-state is becoming a reality in our country today. The scope of government activity has been greatly enlarged. There obviously are individuals who would like to curb federal power, repeal some of the legislation on the books, and return to the "good old days." Our political campaigns are often filled with dogmatic assertions about changes that ought to be made, but the fact remains that very few Americans seriously propose any really wholesale renovations in our evolving system. The government has acknowledged at least two great responsibilities: to help those individuals who have needs, and to see that the economic system as a whole does not break down.[30]

The movement toward a welfare state continues in many areas of life today, this movement reflects aspirations rather than desperation. These aspirations constitute a level below which no one should be allowed to fall. As our productivity increases, we raise the minimum level of aid for those in need.[31] It should be noted that not all of the focus is on the national government. The states, through the grant-in-aid programs, are performing important functions in the area of welfare. Welfare costs rank second only to education in local expenditures.

Today, society has come to accept the view that the sick ought to receive adequate medical care, handicapped persons need help to enable them to lead useful and productive lives, and children should have a chance to grow up and become useful members of society. Actually, the government gives assistance to those in need and sponsors insurance programs for protection from unforeseen circumstances. Old age payments to senior citizens and medicare provisions have extended needed coverage in the latter categories. Government-sponsored programs which serve to lighten the burden of insecurity on American families are recognized by the community as a good thing which actually adds to the real wealth of the country.

Role Of The Churches

In spite of the fact that society has accepted responsibility for meeting the needs of distressed persons, the Protestant churches have not kept pace. No major Protestant denomination has yet demonstrated its capability to minister effectively to the throngs that are crowding America's inner cities. The hesitancy of church groups to grapple with this problem has caused one person to remark that "not one has done a really admirable job of assimilating depressed minority racial groups, and hardly one can be found that is not gradually losing effective contact with the lower income, working classes."[32]

The traditional reaction of the Protestant churches has been to flee from the inner city and its problems. The urbanization process of the late nineteenth century caused large segments of the working classes to be estranged from Protestantism because the orientation of the church was rural-agrarian, and because many of the urban working people were immigrants from Catholic areas of Europe. "Between 1868 and 1888," states one historian, ". . . although nearly 200,000 people moved into the part of New York City below 14th Street, seventeen Protestant churches moved out, their places being taken by only two Roman Catholic churches and a single synagogue."[33]

There were exceptions to this trend, however. St. Bartholomew's Church in New York City built an elaborate parish house in 1891 at a cost of $400,000, and there were other Episcopal churches that did likewise. The institutional church offered a wide variety of athletic, literary, and benevolent activities. St. George's Episcopal Church in New York City organized vocational classes, established a cooperative grocery, and provided wholesome recreational activities for every age group. The Congregational Church at Elmira, New York, pastored by the Rev. Thomas K. Beecher (brother of Henry Ward Beecher) amazed Mark Twain with its library, lecture halls, and gymnasium. The Salvation Army also performed the function of an institutional church in adapting Christianity to the new conditions of the city. These were exceptions, however, and even today many Protestant churches are abandoning the demoralized transi-

tional areas of the inner city in order to follow a select constituency to
the more attractive residential suburbs.

The slums of the inner city vividly demonstrate the need for something other than a reliance on rugged individualism. The people living
there have experienced a progressive deterioration in their economic and
personal standards. These slums present a hazard because of the high
incidence of disease, crime, juvenile delinquency, prostitution, and other
forms of anti-social behavior. Consequently, they present a "social problem requiring the joint effort of many individuals working through responsible channels in terms commensurate with the demands of the
situation."[34] The church can aid in such a situation in a variety of ways.
Obviously, it can support open-occupancy covenants offering an individual
a choice of housing that is not limited arbitrarily by one's race, national
origin, or religion. The Quakers of Philadelphia initiated a program of
"self-help" housing in which they helped to buy and renovate old homes
for families willing to do part of the work. "Neighbors, Inc.," a community organization in Washington, D. C. related to an integrated Methodist Church, has sought to maintain high community standards in housing for both white and Negro residents.[35]

The most practical approach to the problem of slums today is through
the urban renewal programs of the federal government. The rehabilita-
tion of existing houses and neighborhoods as well as the demolition of
wornout structures is part of the program. An urban renewal program
has many of the elements necessary to make the city a pleasant and
desirable place in which to live, work, and play. Since the church cannot
possibly provide the funds to accomplish this, it seems logical that the
church should lend a supporting role to the government in such a worthy
task.

The elimination of slums through urban renewal or any other reasonable program should be helpful to the ministry of the church. Since it is
concerned about the problem of juvenile delinquency, the church should
encourage any program which shows promise of cutting down the incidence of such behavior. The enormous needs of urban renewal and other
massive programs has caused some Protestant churches to recognize the
necessity for government-financed programs.

Actually, the church should be thankful that resources are at hand to
meet the needs in today's society. The church should accept with enthusiasm its opportunity and responsibility to help lead the community
in a united quest for the better environment which is becoming increasingly possible. Too frequently, according to one author, the church has
had a "reputation for rummage sales, soft-touch handouts, morbidly senti-
mental holiday distribution of food baskets, and charity as bait on

sectarian hooks. . . ."[36] Instead of losing out because of massive governmental welfare programs, the church is today in the unique position to command influence as it never has before. "One may even venture to say," declares one writer, "that only Protestant Christianity stands in position to give the great secular programs of social welfare which are currently emerging the spiritual depth and perspective which they must have if they are to do the most good."[37]

The argument that the church is being bankrupted by government competition in the welfare field is nonsense. The church can work with hospitals, orphanages, schools, homes for the aged, assistance programs for migrants and other under-privileged groups, and similar agencies and programs. The church can fulfill its mission by appealing to its members to enter vocations which involve helping others. Christian people should have a particular aptitude and motivation in this area and could thus influence the direction in which the state moves in social action.

In 1957 the National Council of Churches held a Conference on Policy and Strategy in Social Welfare at Atlantic City, New Jersey. The areas discussed included housing, racial and intergroup relations, family life, world order, services for the aging, educational opportunities, and mental health. The viewpoint that emerged from this conference and others is that the government should be used by the people as a means of making maximum provision for the common welfare and that the church should carry on its mission within such a context.

Those Christians who become concerned about the amounts of money being spent by the federal government for social welfare programs would do well to compare such expenditures with those for our missile program, federal aid for highways, and the military. Millions of our citizens are living perilously close to the margin of bare existence while billions of dollars are being spent for missiles, the space program, and the defense effort. Realizing that the role of the state is not going to diminish in the near future, some religious leaders are viewing their former policies concerning church and state relations as obsolete. "Practically speaking," says a Jesuit author, ". . . cooperation with the state means that the church uses the tax power of the state for sectarian welfare programs."[38]

To be sure, many Christians oppose state-supported welfare programs. They see the church as the last area for individual rather than collective action. They are uneasy because there is seemingly no longer room for the individual act of love towards the other person. Actually, the welfare programs have the potential to expand the act of love fairly and to a greater range of people. What these individuals have overlooked is the fact that this is a fallen world. One Christian writer has pointed out the fact that the "reason . . . we have . . . compulsory Social Security, welfare

taxes, and a legally established 'right to assistance' for those in need is
that personal giving has proved in the past to be both inadequate and far
too capricious to meet the needs of the people."[39] All too often, personal
giving by church members for charity has meant giving to satisfy personal
desires or to accommodate petty loyalties and prejudices.

The fact remains that a secular program for society cannot meet the
most basic human needs. The physical and economic securities which
the welfare state satisfies are important, but psychological and spiritual
insecurities are perhaps even more harmful if left unfulfilled. Churches
should actually rejoice because they are now free to concentrate their
efforts where the more basic needs are evident. As the state assumes
increasing responsibility for material assistance, churches can devote more
of their efforts to non-material needs. "To the rough frontiers of modern
man's desperate need in the realms of personality, social adjustment,
values, and faith," writes H. S. Miller, "they [the churches] are being
more insistently called."[40] The ministry of the churches can give the
individual comfort, purpose in life, confidence, and encouragement. This
role for the church is as old as the church itself, and Protestant theologians
have encouraged this involvement for some time. Reinhold Niebuhr has
distinguished between justice and charity: in his scheme of things, justice
is assigned to the state and charity to the churches.[41]

Protestantism in America has been quite slow in taking on any responsibility for societal sin. Its churches have remained in the tradition of
Wesley, who was, according to Richard Niebuhr, "more offended by
blasphemous use of the name of God than by a blasphemous use of his
creatures."[42] Of course, if it is true that many of the Protestant churches
are dominated by a middle-class psychology, they are unable or unwilling
to see the needs of society. A smug middle-class orientation can cause
blindness toward the needs of persons who fall into less privileged
categories.

Many churches do care for fatherless children, provide family counseling, maintain homes for unmarried mothers, and recently have entered the
field of helping the aging. The larger portion of today's poor and troubled
turn, however, not to the church but to the state or to a community-
sponsored agency for help. This is significant because the church was the
primary welfare agency in society for over a thousand years. Too frequently, however, the church lapsed into the habit of caring only for its
own. Consequently, "modern welfare was . . . born of the church's failure
and of the failure of the small community. . . ."[43]

In many churches ministers face difficulties if they take a stand on
social issues. One minister, who was himself a casualty of this kind of
situation, said that the church should address itself to the needs of its

community, "but the ministers who attempt to lead their churches in such a program will do well to save some of their energy with which to look for another job."[44] Since Protestantism in the United States has been a middle-class oriented movement, church boards which have responsibility for the financing and organization of the church have often kept a close watch on the social views of their minister. "In short," according to one writer, "the clergyman [is] financially dependent upon those 'men in the community who are least likely to approve [of a minister's] . . . criticism of the existing economic order.' "[45]

The church also does not have extensive competence in the area of social welfare because it is a complex field involving economics, psychology, sociology, and the science of politics. It is unrealistic to assume that the average church member or minister can attain the expertise necessary to understand the needs in this area. It is quite possible that naive and impulsive judgments are often made by church members who lack an understanding of the whole picture.[46]

Christian people who are troubled by the welfare picture today often draw hasty conclusions regarding vast, expensive tax-supported programs which seem to put a premium on shiftlessness and immorality. Should the church be concerned with what is happening to children in foster homes or those receiving AFDC payments? Others question whether the church should be involved in the matter of the adequacy of Social Security payments or aid given to migrants. Some would have the church stay clear of social issues: "We have political parties, chambers of commerce, labor unions, parent-teacher associations, service clubs, and many organizations through which we can work for the improvement of society. We need not desecrate and degrade the church for that purpose."[47]

When the church is concerned, it is often with such matters as whether those receiving old-age assistance should be permitted to own a television set, or whether the government program of AFDC payments is encouraging illegitimacy. Perhaps a more Christian approach would be to admit that welfare programs have to be broad enough so as not to punish the sick and the needy just because a few chiselers get through in the process. Many churches have not condemned the sins of avarice, envy, and pride as readily as they have those of immorality, sloth, and drunkenness.

Perhaps a legitimate function of the church is to minister to those to whom no one else will minister and to experiment with innovative approaches which might be assumed by government if useful. Christianity is not a religion of escapism, but it includes a practical system of ethics that has much to say to individuals and social groups about their responsibilities to one another. The church must relate vitally to the mentally retarded, the blind, the sick, and the morally reprehensible. It should accept the hard task of loving those whom men consider the least lovable or appealing. Helping the lovable child is fine, but would it not be much more commendable to render aid to the dull, awkward child for whom the complexities of ordinary life and the competition of school are too much?

There is a place for constructive reform in a free society and the church should not be indifferent to it. This is not to say that the church will condone evil by the state or any other institution. Christianity demands justice and love, not indulgence. The church need not call for a program that maintains the unfortunate individual in luxury, nor should it attempt to remove moral responsibility from him. "The problem is not to eliminate judgment," writes one author, "but to discover in this fallen world, the way to make it most nearly in accord with a Christian view of man's relationship to his fellows."[48]

The church often opposes the welfare state and sees its position threatened because the church has so often conceived its functions in very narrow terms. Many churches and pastors see their job in terms of intra-ecclesiastical work; that is, building new buildings, inviting outsiders, developing more closely knit congregations, encouraging missionary endeavor, and providing inspiration for the faithful. Any outside activities consist of such programs as day camps, homes for orphans, and provisions for the elderly. These are concerns which have been recognized by society for some time, but some feel that it may be seriously questioned "whether Christian congregations ought to spend time, energy, and money to create church institutions of this type."[49] Rather, some feel that the church should assume a role in which it must work courageously and without thanks, namely, that of caring for the needs neglected by welfare programs.

A Christian view of society incorporates the idea that "none of us lives to himself, and none of us dies to himself." (Rom. 14:7) Rather we are "members one of another", (Eph. 4:25) or persons created for fellowship with one another and with God. It can be said that these verses refer only to Christian fellowship, but a broader outlook recognizes each person as a member of an interdependent community. It is true that the members of American Protestant churches have sent millions of dollars in relief supplies to needy areas overseas and have engaged in other worthy humanitarian activities. There are times, therefore, when each person is called upon to transcend his own private concerns in the interest of the common welfare. "Because man is endowed with certain distinctive talents great or small," in the opinion of one person, "he is responsible for making to the community the contribution which only he can make, and without which something will be lacking."[50] Since all men, Christian or otherwise, must make political choices in such matters, the Christian can seek for ways to counteract the evil in the political choices which he must make. Because of this, the Christian church, with all its shortcomings, "is the only school in which we are trained for this dual citizenship."[51] Of course, it is inevitable that the church will include people of different views concerning most public questions. Any heterogeneous group will experience differences of opinion. These divergent views should be welcomed and discussed because this is the way to pursue truth.

Many evangelical Protestants fear the loss of individual freedom that could accompany centralization of responsibility in government. They realize that a welfare state can become authoritarian, paternalistic, or oppressive. This group would rather see a maximum amount of responsibility shouldered by each individual in caring for his own welfare. An editorial in a well-known evangelical journal voiced just such fears. "The state's substantial control of human welfare," said the editor, "means that in time government action will progressively narrow the role of the churches. . . ." Further, the writer pointed out that the "socialist state" subtly transforms human "wants" into human "rights." "Instead of hailing state welfare programs as an extension of Christian social ethics," he said, "it is high time Christian clergy and laymen consider the premise that state welfare programs are inherently anti-Christian."[52]

The church surely has a mission to point the way for men who are searching the road to salvation and deliverance from their sins. Can it honestly be said, on the other hand, that a churchman who sees good in government social welfare programs is participating in something which is inherently anti-Christian? If so, this would mean that the Christians in Great Britain or Sweden who support their socialistic state are involved in an anti-Christian activity. It would also imply that working for the "general welfare" in support of the Constitution of the United States is wrong when the means to that end is a social welfare program at the national, state, or local level. Surely our Lord had great compassion for the sick and needy. Can we then seriously say that it is wrong to help them unless it is done through church-related or private channels? Why are private means superior to those of government agencies established for the specific purpose of alleviating suffering?

The church can use the law, for example, as one basis for achieving social justice, not because the law is holy, or the lawyers superior people, but because the law applies equally and impartially to all men. If the state can establish clear, honest, and fair legal criteria for relief, the church would do well to recognize the value of such rules in a democratic society. Such a diligent application of the law would aid in preserving the dignity of the individual, a goal to which evangelical Protestantism can fully subscribe.

Conclusion

The freedom of the individual is an inherent value in our democratic society. The role of the government was less in an age when life was less complex and the laissez-faire philosophy seemed acceptable to a majority of the citizens. In recent years there has been a steady increase in the use of the power of the state to achieve social welfare goals. The dilemma in our democratic republic is how we can utilize this growing power of the state to achieve social goals and yet allow the individual the measure of freedom he needs for the democratic system to survive. The trend, it has been observed, is that "modern society is of necessity cast in a state-welfare mold, which diminishes individual responsibility and extends government authority."[53]

This increase in the power and functions of the state should not be looked upon as an evil development. Only the state has the power and resources to care for the many human needs and to do the necessary planning in a complicated technological society. It is presumptuous for any group, including evangelical Protestants, to assume that humanitarianism is an exclusively Christian virtue. The history of mankind demonstrates that humanitarianism has always existed outside the church and certain non-Christian groups today demonstrate high levels of concern for the needs of mankind. There is no reason to assume that all individuals serving in government today lack humanitarian goals. Obviously many have high ideals and the church should be thankful for them and cooperate with them whenever possible. The welfare programs of the government often are aimed at the equalization of opportunity. Such a goal is not only one of the fundamental purposes of democracy, but also an objective to which evangelical Protestants can subscribe.

Churches have not been able to meet the welfare needs of society in America, and it does not seem likely that they ever will be able to do so. One reason is that they are too divided, and in a city of many churches, no single one can inaugurate a community-wide service without antagonizing some of the others. The very complexity of urban society demands that an agency such as the state direct the welfare program in the interest of harmony and order. This is not to say that the actions of the state are always right, but unless the churches can present a program to meet human needs which is comparable in scope and consistency to the one run by the state, they are in no reasonable position to oppose the welfare program of the state.

As a matter of fact, the technology of the urban society contains the promise or provision for true social security for those who need help. The factories and farms, aided by computerization and other developments, have increased the potential productive capacity of our society to fantastic levels. It could well be that "Christians and other religious persons may . . . feel . . . that now, for the first time, men have available, . . . the resources for implementing the religious ideals of humanitarianism in a reasonably adequate manner."[54] The history of social legislation in some European countries offers a rather impressive record of man's achievements in self-help. America should be able to exceed all these records by utilizing its entire resource base for the common good.

The ministers who stressed the social gospel, by broadening the definition of Christianity to include justice for all members of society, "made it possible to harness the long religious heritage of the people in behalf of the realization of the American Dream of justice, equality, and opportunity."[55] The powerful force of this dream, fortified by the success of capitalism, has insured the failure of socialism in this country. The ideals which the nation has stressed and the concepts such as democracy, liberty, and opportunity are things to which "the American adheres rationalistically much as a socialist adheres to his socialism—because it does him good, because it gives him work, because, so he thinks, it guarantees him happiness."[56]

Evangelical Protestants are rising in the class structure and have become basically content with the existing social system. Since social reforms might affect their comfortable position, they often oppose them. Consequently, evangelicals often identify themselves with the interests of wealth and power in society. Moreover, "Middle-class Christians tend to make Biblical passages about 'the poor' and 'the sick' apply only figuratively to 'the spiritually poor' and 'the spiritually ill.' This distorts the literal message of God's word and may even contribute to a denial of the historical activity of Jesus Christ."[57] The compassionate work of Jesus was oriented very closely to the needs of the material world. As one minister who has so clearly comprehended this truth put it: "You cannot live the Gospel without getting involved in the dirty business of politics, economics, and social issues, because this is where men live their lives."[58]

It would be a sad development indeed if evangelical Protestantism were to become identified with a rigid opposition to the developing welfare situation in America. This kind of negativism would mean that evangelicals would be excluded from involvement in one of the most

powerful movements in American history. It is not suggested that evangelicals should support government welfare programs merely because
they are popular, but rather because there are no live options available
in today's complex society for meeting economic needs. Until other means
are developed, the state can and should be used for this purpose. David
Moberg has aptly observed: "Welfare activities demonstrate love. . . .
The church teaches by doing; its involvement in social welfare tells
people of the world that it shares God's love for all men."[59]

Billy Graham, the world-renowned evangelist, recently spoke in the
nation's capital and declared that he had become a "convert" to the
anti-poverty program. He stated that when the war on poverty was first
inaugurated: "I was against it, but now I am for it."[60] According to Graham, his change of position was due to a careful consideration of the
Biblical teaching on this subject and a study of the program of the
Office of Economic Opportunity. The evangelist further explained that
there were numerous Bible passages which call for the care of the poor
and needy, making anti-poverty efforts a major teaching of the Bible.

Society is not going to remain static. Cities will continue to grow and
to pack more people into giant living complexes in order to save space.
The individual becomes increasingly depersonalized by this process and
seeks for someone or something to identify with in order to maintain a
sense of purpose in life. The church should help in whatever way that it
can. Big business and big labor will also continue to expand. Big government is not only an established fact; it is the only way that the gigantic
power of corporations and labor organizations can be neutralized. Evangelicals should take note of these changes and adjust to them. Tired
arguments about "creeping socialism" will not suffice when it is recognized that nearly all of the means of production in this country are pri-
vately owned and operated. We are not becoming "just like Russia!" Her
economy and political system is vastly different from ours. We still
operate in a free and open society where the citizens vote for delegates
of their own choice to represent them. We have nothing to fear from
"the government" as long as it continues to represent "we, the people."
If the time ever comes when this is no longer true, there will be issues
to be dealt with which will be far more serious than government-sponsored
welfare programs. Meanwhile, evangelicals must be advised to catch up
with the twentieth century before the world enters the twenty-first!

NOTES

1. Richard B. Morris, *Government and Labor in Early America* (New York:
Columbia University Press, 1946), p. 16.
2. W. G. Sumner, "Consolidation of Wealth: Economic Aspects," *Independent,*
LIV (May 1, 1902), p. 1040.

3. Robert Hunter, *Poverty* (New York: Harper & Row, 1965), pp. 231–32.

4. Jacob Riis, *How the Other Half Lives* (New York: Hill and Wang, 1957), pp. 46–47.

5. George Kibbe Turner, "The City of Chicago—A Study of the Great Immoralities," *McClure's Magazine*, XXVIII (April 1907), p. 587.

6. Sidney Fine, *Laissez-Faire and the General-Welfare State* (Ann Arbor: University of Michigan Press, 1956), p. 374.

7. Russell H. Conwell, *Acres of Diamonds* (New York: Harper, 1915), p. 18.

8. C. H. Hopkins, *The Rise of the Social Gospel in American Protestantism 1865–1915* (New Haven: Yale University Press, 1940), p. 12.

9. Paul A. Carter, *The Decline and Revival of the Social Gospel: Social and Political Liberalism in American Protestant Churches, 1920–1940* (Ithaca: Cornell University Press, 1954), p. 56.

10. Clarke A. Chambers, *Seedtime of Reform* (Ann Arbor: University of Michigan Press, 1967) offers an interesting discussion of a secularized social gospel.

11. *New York Times*, Oct. 7, 1932, p. 2.

12. Harry M. Caudill, *Night Comes to the Cumberlands* (Boston: Little, Brown, 1963), pp. 170–71.

13. Vaughn D. Bornet, *Welfare in America* (Norman: University of Oklahoma Press, 1960), p. 14.

14. Quoted in Carter, *Decline and Revival of the Social Gospel*, p. 145.

15. *Ibid.*, p. 151.

16. Alan Keith-Lucas, *The Church and Social Welfare* (Philadelphia: Westminister, 1962), p. 35.

17. Walter A. Friedlander, *Introduction to Social Welfare* (2nd ed., Englewood Cliffs, N.J.: Prentice-Hall, 1961), p. 4.

18. David O. Moberg, *Inasmuch* (Grand Rapids: Eerdmans, 1965), p. 24.

19. Bornet, *Welfare in America*, p. 43.

20. Fine, *Laissez-Faire*, p. 393.

21. *Loc. cit.*

22. Carter, *Decline and Revival of the Social Gospel*, p. 175.

23. Fine, *Laissez-Faire*, p. 397. The figure is obviously higher today.

24. *Ibid.*, p. 381.

25. Robert M. Miller, *American Protestantism and Social Issues, 1919–1939* (Chapel Hill: University of North Carolina Press, 1958), p. 123.

26. *Ibid.*, pp. 122–23.

27. *Ibid.*, p. 123.

28. Fine, *Laissez-Faire*, p. 399.

29. *New York Times*, Oct. 19, 1954, p. 17.

30. Frederick L. Allen, *The Big Change* (New York: Bantam Books, 1961), pp. 251–52.

31. Wayne Vasey, *Government and Social Welfare* (New York: Holt, Rinehart, and Winston, 1958), p. 37.

32. Haskell M. Miller, *Compassion and Community: an Appraisal of the Church's Changing Role in Social Welfare* (New York: Association Press, 1961), p. 270.

33. Carl N. Degler, *Out of Our Past* (New York: Harper & Row, 1959), pp. 339–40.

34. J. Richard Spann, ed., *The Church and Social Responsibility* (Nashville: Abingdon Press, 1953), p. 237.

35. Miller, *Compassion and Community*, pp. 225–26.

36. *Ibid.*, p. 183.

37. *Ibid.*, p. 260.

38. Bernard J. Coughlin, *Church and State in Social Welfare* (New York: Columbia University Press, 1965), p. 104.

39. Keith-Lucas, *The Church and Social Welfare*, p. 8.

40. Miller, *Compassion and Community*, p. 141.

41. Coughlin, *Church and State*, pp. 20–21.
42. Keith-Lucas, *The Church and Social Welfare*, p. 28.
43. *Ibid.*, pp. 15–16.
44. Carter, *Decline and Revival of the Social Gospel*, p. 64.
45. *Ibid.*, p. 65.
46. David O. Moberg, *The Church as a Social Institution* (Englewood Cliffs, N. J.: Prentice-Hall, 1962), pp. 152–53, 385–86.
47. Howard E. Kershner, "The Role of the Church in Social Problems," *Christian Economics*, Dec. 1965.
48. Keith-Lucas, *The Church and Social Welfare*, pp. 30–31.
49. Horst Symanowski, *The Christian Witness in an Industrial Society* (Philadelphia: Westminister, 1964), pp. 78–79.
50. Spann, *The Church and Social Responsibility*, p. 21.
51. John C. Bennett, *Christian Ethics and Social Policy* (New York: Scribners, 1946), pp. 90–91.
52. "The State in Welfare Work," *Christianity Today*, IV (Jan. 18, 1960), 23.
53. Coughlin, *Church and State*, pp. 127–28.
54. Miller, *Compassion and Community*, p. 92.
55. Degler, *Out of Our Past*, p. 349.
56. *Ibid.*, p. 271.
57. Moberg, *Inasmuch*, p. 96.
58. Statement by the Rev. Wayne C. Hartmire in "Grapes of Wrath," *Time*, LXXXVI (Dec. 10, 1965), 96.
59. Moberg, *Inasmuch*, pp. 50–51.
60. Mimeographed press release of the Baptist Joint Committee on Public Affairs, Washington, D.C., June 16, 1967. Graham is also featured in a motion picture entitled "Beyond These Hills" which was produced by the Office of Economic Opportunity. This film demonstrates the accomplishments of the people of Avery County, North Carolina made through Community Action.

Robert D. Linder is Associate Professor of History at Kansas State University where he teaches courses in Renaissance, Reformation, and Christian History. Born in Salina, Kansas on October 6, 1933, Professor Linder earned a B.S. degree from Kansas State Teachers College in 1956, B.D. and M.R.E. degrees from Central Baptist Theological Seminary in 1958, and the M.A. and Ph.D. degrees in history in 1960 and 1963 from the University of Iowa. Here in 1962–63 he was a University Fellow. He also has taken advanced work at the University of Geneva in Switzerland in 1961 and has engaged in extensive travel and research in Europe in 1965 and 1967.

Mr. Linder has served as an officer in the United States Army. He taught briefly at the University of Iowa before assuming an assistant professorship at William Jewell College in 1963. He joined the faculty of Kansas State University in 1965 and was promoted to associate professor in 1967. He is active not only in his local Baptist church but also in the Republican Party in Kansas. He has worked with various civic organizations and non-partisan study groups, including the Municipal Charter Study Committee in Liberty, Missouri from 1963 to 1965. He is a member of many professional organizations, including the American Historical Association, American Society for Reformation Research, Renaissance Society of America, American Society of Church History, Rocky Mountain Social Science Association, Kansas Historical Society, and American Association of University Professors.

Professor Linder published a book, *The Political Ideas of Pierre Viret* (Geneva, 1964), and he has contributed articles to *Church History*, *The Journal of Modern History*, the *Archiv fur Reformationsgeschichte*, and the *Bulletin of the Foundation for Reformation Research*. He is also a contributing editor to *The Westminister Dictionary of Church History*. He is deeply interested in the history of religious and political ideas and specializes in the Reformation in Western Europe. In 1968 he was the recipient of the first annual Distinguished Teaching Award at his school.

ROBERT D. LINDER

A Christian Approach to the Contemporary Civil Rights Movement

A great deal of racial hate and bigotry has spewed forth from the lips of individuals in this country during the last decade. Much of it has come from white people during the course of the present-day movement to give the Negro citizens of the United States the civil rights to which they have been entitled for over a hundred years. During the so-called Albany Movement of 1961–1963, some of this vitriolic racism was recorded for posterity:

> You, Albany Nigger, are black, your hair is kinky, you smell like greens and side pork, you shuffle after white men, lust for his women folk, you live in Harlem town and you are getting damned uppity with your demonstrations and your prayer meetings. Your demands are an outrage—to worship in a white man's church, to sit next to white women at the movies, to eat with white folks and to go to school with white children. Nigger, you are making revolution! You and your agitator friends from the North with your sit-ins, registration drives, and praying! Nigger, didn't you hear them tell that black boy of yours "Go Home, Freedom?"[1]

This kind of language and feeling has been all too typical of the reaction of white people, North and South, to the desire of many citizens, black and white, to see Negro Americans receive their civil rights. In Albany, Georgia, in 1961–1963 there were sit-ins, pray-ins, and a voter registration drive. There was also violence, the beating of civil rights workers by law enforcement officials, and a stiffening of white resistance to any kind of meaningful change. In fact, the story of the Albany Movement is in many ways still being written.

In a penetrating analysis of contemporary America in a recent *Saturday Evening Post*, the distinguished author and social critic John Stein-

121

beck discussed the current drive for civil rights in this country. To demonstrate the mentality of many Negro Americans and to illustrate the realities of the current situation he related the story of a very intelligent Negro man who once worked for him in New York. He said that one winter afternoon he looked out his window and saw this man coming home from the store. As he rounded the corner, a very drunk, fat white woman came staggering out of a lounge, slipped on the icy pavement, and fell sprawling on the sidewalk. Instantly the man turned away from the woman and crossed the street, making certain that he stayed as far away from the shouting, cursing woman as he could. When he came into the house, Steinbeck said in a puzzled tone, "I saw that. Why did you do it?"

The Negro man responded, "Oh, that. Well, I guess I thought if I went to help her she was so drunk and mad she might start yelling 'rape'."

"That was a pretty quick reaction," Steinbeck replied. The Negro answered, "Maybe. But I've been practicing to be a Negro for a long time."[2]

Christianity Today reported in its January 6, 1967 issue that the problem of racial integration had split another Baptist church in the American South. A new Baptist congregation formed in Macon, Georgia, after the Tatnall Square Baptist Church had ousted its ministers because they favored racially integrated worship. Many of the members could not in good conscience abide by this decision and left to form the new church.[3] During 1964, thirty-eight churches in the state of Mississippi were destroyed by fire and dynamite. Why? Because they had become the centers for intensive civil rights activity among the Negro population.[4]

Moreover, the Negro response to white terrorism has been increasingly that of violent retaliation. The outbreak of rioting following the cowardly assassination of Martin Luther King, Jr. in April 1968 was all too typical of this kind of reaction.[5] Thus in the vicious circle, emotion begets emotion, bitterness leads to more bitterness, and hate promotes more hate.

All of the incidents cited above are aspects of the present-day drive for civil rights. In this decade civil rights has become the single most important domestic political issue in the United States as well as one of the burning moral and social issues confronting American Christians. The tragedy is that a cause so obviously righteous in both the political and religious sense should have become an issue at all for most Americans and/or Christians. But it has, and the complexities of the present situation need to be discussed and Christians need to be brought to grips with their political, social, and spiritual responsibilities in this matter. This will be the primary purpose of this essay.

What are civil rights? The meaning should be obvious; the term is almost self-explanatory. Civil rights are simply those rights and liberties possessed by the individual citizen as a member of the state. In the case of the United States, they are those rights guaranteed to *all* Americans by the Bill of Rights and certain other amendments to the Constitution. Positive legislation by the Congress also seeks to guarantee certain liberties to the individual against encroachment by other individuals or groups or even the central government. An example of this would be recent national and state laws in which individuals or groups are forbidden to discriminate against other individuals or groups because of their race, color, religion, or membership in labor unions. In short, civil rights are those political, economic, and social rights guaranteed to all Americans by the Constitution and local, state, and federal legislation.

The issue of civil rights in the United States is far from static. Even within the context of the current problem of racial discrimination, the focus of attention shifts constantly. It is virtually impossible to write about current issues in civil rights without excluding questions which are not only timely but vitally important. What is attempted in this essay is not to survey every ramification of the civil rights movement today nor even to explore every currently live issue. Rather attention will be directed toward the struggle of American Negroes for their civil rights. Also, some observations will be made concerning the need to extend these rights to other minority groups such as the American Indians, Chinese-Americans, Spanish-Americans, and even the underprivileged poor whites of America. For the most part, however, the focus will be on the Negro drive for civil rights since this seems to be the domestic political issue which most concerns American Christians at the moment.

A large segment of American Christendom appears to be divided, confused, and somewhat perplexed concerning the current civil rights movement. Many who consider themselves within the historic Christian tradition have either shunned the civil rights movement altogether or supported it only half-heartedly. Others have supported the quest for civil rights but decried the use of economic boycotts, public demonstrations, and other similar techniques for gaining meaningful results and securing concrete concessions. Some influential Christian periodicals have condemned ministers and other church leaders for taking part in civil rights' marches and joining picket lines. A few so-called "Bible-believers" have rejected the civil rights movement altogether, some condemning it from a states' rights point of view, others alleging that the movement is inspired or even directed by Communists. On the other hand, there are large numbers of evangelical Christians from every denomination who support the drive for civil rights for all Americans, regardless of their color, race, or creed. But the fact remains that there is a considerable amount of confusion among Bible-believing Christians concerning the nature and extent of the movement for civil rights, and this means that there is a need for a fresh evaluation of the entire matter.

Furthermore, as the quotation illustrating the hatred aroused by the Albany Movement clearly points out, religious and moral language is sometimes used to denounce the civil rights movement, often in a contradictory manner. Thus, in a curious bit of mental gymnastics, the Negro in Albany was castigated because he lusts after both the white man's woman and his church pew. And in the same account, it is interesting to note that a member of a society supposedly permeated by Biblical values has no compunctions about snarling obscenities at Negroes who pray for divine guidance in the matter of civil rights. One wonders why all the Christians suddenly seem to disappear during moments of racial crisis.

A Brief History of the Civil Rights Movement

The problem of civil liberties and the effort to secure the rights of the minorities are struggles as old as man himself. The American civil rights movement in its most important sense is as old as the first confrontation between European settlers and American Indians and the introduction of human slavery into the New World. From the beginning, the essential conflict of the civil rights movement was inherent in the contradiction between the practical economic and status advantages associated with slavery and racial oppression, and the Christian ideals of justice and love and their translation into the democratic ideology of liberty, equality before the law, and brotherhood. The shabby treatment of the Indians and the presence of African slaves which were visibly different in culture and color intensified this conflict and demanded resolution.

The early history of English America was an attempt to resolve this contradiction by combining both; that is, by continuing to treat the Indians and Negroes in an unchristian manner while making grudging concessions to religious and democratic ideas. In all this it is well to remember that of these two non-white groups, one was in America first and the other did not ask to go there. A second point to keep in mind is that most of the men who were part of the system which made all of this possible were professing Christians.

Thus the problem of securing civil rights for minorities in America is deeply rooted in the history of this land. Furthermore, it is complicated by the traditional concept of the division of powers between the central and local governments, and it is made more complex by the mores and customs of several centuries of slavery. In addition, there are modern complications such as ever-increasing urbanization which is changing the character of the American people and their way of life, and the closing of the former melting pot of the frontier. Finally, all of these problems are compounded by the demands of those who want everything overnight, those who refuse to do anything to earn their rights as citizens, and those who are simply ignorant of the existing problems.

The United States Constitution is basically a states' rights document. There is nothing in it about protecting the personal liberties of the people. It was the Bill of Rights and other later amendments to the Constitution which secured to the individual an immunity against certain arbitrary actions of the central government and guaranteed him certain basic rights as a citizen of the United States. Thus, very early in American history, the founding fathers took up the struggle to see that the civil rights of American citizens were embodied in written form as part of the law of the land.

Before the Civil War (1861–65), there were approximately four million Negroes in the United States. Of these, only about a quarter of a million were free and theoretically enjoyed the individual rights guaranteed by the Constitution. The remainder of the Negroes in the U. S. were slaves and not considered legally to be "people." Pre-Civil War freedmen were generally the more able Negroes. They had been emancipated for various reasons, many times because of the Christian scruples of a slave owner. Not a few earned their freedom by hard labor and purchased their emancipation from sympathetic masters. There were some Christian groups such as the Quakers, Mennonites, and Moravians who disapproved of slavery and prohibited slaveholding by their members. Many people do not realize that major denominations like the Methodists, Baptists, and Presbyterians attacked slavery as an institution long before the Civil War, even in the South. In 1780, the General Conference of the Methodist Church declared that slavery was contrary to the laws of God and required all of its itinerant preachers to free their slaves. In 1789 the Virginia Baptists urged their local missions "to extirpate this horrid evil (*i. e.* slavery) from the land." Many Baptist churches on the frontier forbade their members to own slaves. Presbyterians in New York and Pennsylvania both spoke out against slavery in the years following the American Revolution.[6]

However, as the cotton economy fastened itself on the South, slaveowners became more defensive about the institution which made possible their way of life. In many places, Southern Christianity was accommodated to the institution rather than the institution being destroyed by Christian values. As tensions between North and South mounted and the Civil War approached, Baptists, Methodists, and Presbyterians split along regional lines over the question of whether or not slavery was a sin. When the war came, Protestants of the North rallied to the Union and those of the South defended the Confederacy. The morality of slavery was only one of several issues leading to the Civil War, but for the churches it was the fundamental question. The scars of the great conflict of the last century are yet visible in American Protestantism and the basic question of whether it is sinful and immoral to deny other human beings their basic rights lingers on to the present.

The nearly four million Negro slaves were ill-prepared for freedom when it came in 1865. Most of them barely knew English, had seldom if ever left the plantation before 1865, and were schooled to obedience and the performance of tasks laid out for them. The freedmen quickly realized that there was a new order of things, but they were not prepared to fathom its significance or to participate effectively in society. Freedom, rights, privileges, duties, obligations, and responsibilities, even in the matter of family relationships, were all foreign to them. It was extremely difficult for most newly-emancipated Negroes to make any kind of genuine and meaningful adjustment in the years immediately following 1865.

If it was hard for the former slaves, it was far from easy for the former masters to adjust to the new order after the war. In fact, it was extremely difficult for the ex-slaveholders to accept as equals these whom until very recently they had considered to be their property. It was a traumatic experience for many white Southerners to give up all direction and control of their ex-servants and lose their former superior position in society. When one considers the relative positions of the whites and the blacks for two hundred and forty years prior to emancipation, it should not be surprising that it has taken nearly one hundred years to make fissures in the walls of mores and customs of so many people. When all of this became complicated by political, social, and prestige factors following the war, the way to understanding and reconciliation became even more elusive. And, of course, there was the continuing problem of changing the hearts of men, for at the root of the difficulties which have been experienced in gaining for all Americans their constitutional rights is the cold, hard fact of human perversity. The real obstacles to civil rights are usually not material but mental and spiritual, that is, they relate to what the Christian would call *sin.*

After the Civil War the Fourteenth and Fifteenth Amendments were passed, by which the Congress intended to make the Negro citizen the ward of the central government and the government the guardian of the Negro. Neither of these amendments was fully implemented in the years immediately following the war. Most of the nation actually repudiated the Fourteenth and the Supreme Court circumscribed both the Fourteenth and Fifteenth Amendments for more than half a century. The Fifteenth Amendment conferred suffrage on no one. At the time, the right to vote was not considered one of the necessary attributes of national citizenship, but exception from discrimination regarding voting because of race, color, or previous condition of servitude was. The right of suffrage in the states came from the states.

Thus, up until World War I the Supreme Court made the national government responsible for life, liberty, property, and equal protection against interference by the states. But it left to the states the power they had always had of protecting these rights from impairment by individuals. During this period of narrow interpretation of the Constitution by the high court, the South worked out an accommodation of race that was not known in other parts of the country, mostly because there were very few Negroes in the rest of the nation. Jim Crow law dominated the American South for nearly a century following the end of the Civil War.[7]

World War I brought significant shifts in population and in attitudes in the country. More and more Negroes moved out of the South. The Supreme Court gradually changed its temperament and began to interpret the Constitution more and more broadly. Decisions by the Court struck down white primaries, outlawed segregation in interstate commerce, and killed restrictive real estate covenants. World War II and the Korean conflict saw the end of segregation in the armed forces. Not content to settle for less in civilian life, the Negroes and their allies pushed for desegregation of the public schools, a struggle which culminated in the historic May 17, 1954 *Brown* v. *Topeka* decision of the Supreme court which declared the old concept of "separate but equal" facilities illegal. More recently, the civil rights' bills of 1957, 1960, 1964, 1965, and 1968 have converted the Fourteenth Amendment into an engine of positive action. It is no longer in any sense of the word a mere curb on actions of the state.

Much has been achieved, especially by the Negro American, but much remains to be done. In the case of the American Indian, virtually no one has appeared to champion his cause. In the colonial period and well into the nineteenth century only Quakers, some Baptists, and a few other smaller denominations had attitudes toward the Indians which today would be considered enlightened. It was only in the late nineteenth and early twentieth centuries that Americans began to experience pangs of conscience over the manner in which the native Americans were treated by European settlers.

Even today Indian migrants to urban areas often face discrimination in Christian churches as well as many other places. For one thing, they are usually from the lower socio-economic classes and cannot dress well enough to suit the average middle class church. Mission chapels and schools established especially for them help perpetuate segregation. In many ways, the past and present treatment of the American Indian represents a greater indictment of American democracy than does the history of the Negro in the United States.

There are still gigantic problems to be solved if Negroes, Indians, and other American minorities are to enjoy the full benefits of citizenship. Some of these are peculiar to the Negro community, others are shared by a larger number of other Americans as well.

There are at least five significant factors which will deeply affect the future of the civil rights movement in the United States. First, there is the fact that Southern Negroes and Northern Negroes are in many ways very different. The variations between Negroes in the North and South are at least as pronounced as those between Northern and Southern whites. And the body politic, economic and social in which the Southern Negro is to participate, is in a number of respects different in the South and in the North. And, of course, the American Indian and other minorities are in many ways quite different from Negroes in any part of the country.

Second, the technological revolution is hurting the Negro working man economically. This is especially true in the cotton, dairy, and other rural-oriented industries of the South where the economic dislocation of Negroes is becoming common. This is being caused by an industrialization of the cotton culture which will release almost two of every three people involved, a shift in dairy farming which will free four of every ten, and a conversion to beef cattle raising which will release seven of every ten. It may not be that Negro workers especially want to leave the South, but the economic push there is fully as strong as the economic pull from another region. In the North, the accelerated pace of automation in most industries is working hardships on the laboring man, skilled and unskilled, black and white, and creating tremendous economic problems which still have to be solved.

Third, the mass media is breaking into the Negro world and allowing him to see what he is *supposed* to be enjoying in the way of civil liberties and economic prosperity. The fact that he often is not raises the question of "why not" in his mind and causes further unrest. Also, the fact that television and Hollywood often distort real life makes it even more difficult to cope with this problem.

Fourth, the Negro churches are losing their place of dominance in Negro life. For years the churches have been the social as well as the religious centers for the Negro community. To their credit, Negro Baptist and Methodist churches have taken the lead in the civil rights movement in the South. However, this has hurt these churches when they have forgotten their spiritual mission in their enthusiasm for civil rights. Many devout Negro Christians have been alienated from their churches either because they did not do enough or because they did too much for the civil rights movement. It seems difficult to strike a happy medium between proper concern for the spiritual welfare of the individual and honest involvement in the drive for the rights of mankind. Most Negroes are still Baptists and Methodists, but there is a general attrition in the ranks of the faithful as the churches continue to wrestle with the problems of civil rights.

Fifth and last, there is the complicating factor of the war in Vietnam. Billions of dollars and immeasurable amounts of human energy are being funneled into the war in Southeast Asia while worthy projects designed to make civil rights a reality for all Americans go begging. Many Christian civil rights leaders are becoming extremely impatient and frustrated because so much is being spent in an undeclared war in Vietnam while Americans at home are forced to stand and wait for needed help in expediting current civil rights projects.

At this juncture it might be well to assess the total picture so far as the desires of the minorities are concerned. This will not only help clarify the objectives of the current civil rights movement but also further refine our definition of "civil rights" itself. Rights in the American context involve three levels, all of which are intertwined and all influenced by emotions, subjective thinking, and *too little Christian spirit!* These levels are: (1) the legal; (2) the social and cultural, where the most stubborn set of values is encountered; and (3) the technical and material, where there has been the most noticeable progress recently.

At present, the legal level is the object of primary concern by most civil rights leaders. However, it should be kept in mind that objectives on this level affect and impinge upon goals sought at other levels. What is being sought at the legal level? What does the Negro want? A leading authority on the history of the civil rights movement, Professor Chase C. Mooney of Indiana University, answers this question and gets to the crux of the matter:

> First of all, he seeks security of person: freedom from lynching, police brutality, and involuntary servitude, with the privilege of jury duty and a guarantee of equal administration of justice. Secondly, he wants to exercise the right to vote without poll taxes, party pledges, complicated and discriminatory registration, unevenly administered literacy tests, violence, intimidation, and mass purging of the voter lists. Thirdly, he desires freedom of conscience and expression unintimidated by labor groups, newspapers, hate sheets, and any other responsible or irresponsible forces. And fourthly, he

aspires to equality of opportunity where he will know no discrimination in regard to employment, education, housing, health services, and public services and accommodations.[8]

In other words, the Negro wants what every American wants and supposedly is guaranteed under the Constitution. Would not each of us want the same thing? What can evangelical Christians do to help this legitimate drive by Negro and other minority groups to attain full American citizenship?

Evangelical Christianity and the Civil Rights Movement

Perhaps the first step in coming to grips with the problem of the relationship between the civil rights movement and evangelical Christianity today is to admit past failures. This failure has been most pronounced among Southern Baptists, Methodists, Presbyterians, and a number of other Protestant groups, especially during the nineteenth and early twentieth centuries. Among these denominations during this period there was a propensity to defend Negro servitude on Biblical grounds. A number of churchmen actually found passages in the Scriptures to justify the South's peculiar institution, some not only defending slavery but declaring it to be a positive good. Great figures of the Old Testament who happened to own slaves, such as Abraham, were trotted out as examples of God's sanction of slaveholding. (Strangely enough, parallel passages concerning polygamy went unmentioned and unexplained.) The curse of Ham, the supposed ancestor of the Negro, was another major prop of the Biblical defense of slavery. All of these preposterous attempts to justify slavery on Biblical grounds are still being expounded in some extremist circles.[9]

Another source of failure has been a kind of traditional massive indifference on the part of great numbers of Protestants to the plight of many Americans wallowing in the mire of second-class citizenship. Many churchmen, past and present, have evaded the issue by insisting that it was a secular matter, not a spiritual one. For example, before the Civil War many Southern ministers preached that a Christian's duty ended with providing for the physical and religious welfare of his slaves. In more recent years economic considerations, such as the fear of being fired from a high-salaried pastorate, have kept many religious leaders who have doubts about the ethical position of segregation from raising their voices in any kind of righteous protest.[10]

Another failure in the past has been a great reluctance on the part of most fundamentalists and many conservative Christians to support social reforms because of an over-reaction against the so-called "social gospel" popularized in the early twentieth century by theological liberals. The fundamentalists and liberals have tended to go to the extremes, the former stoutly maintaining orthodox theology while ignoring or de-emphasizing Christian social ethics, the latter jettisoning historical Christian doctrine while embracing social action as a *raison d'etre*. Only recently, with the decline of theological liberalism and a renaissance of orthodoxy in various forms has there been a trend toward returning to the more balanced approach of the New Testament which emphasized both correct theology and Christian social concern.

One final obvious failure on the part of evangelical Christianity has been the lack of communication and exchange of ideas between white and Negro Christians. Exchanging pastors and choirs once a year on "Race Relations Sunday" is only a feeble step in the right direction. Too often in the past white Christians have been content to live in their cozy middle class suburbs and forget about their fellow-Christians in the urban ghettos and slums. And in too many cases, Negro Christians have been reluctant to take advantage of situations created by fellow-Christians of another color who earnestly want to know what Negroes think and feel about issues like civil rights.

In addition to the failures of the past, several of which have continuing significance in some circles, evangelical Protestant Christianity has been plagued with internal problems which have hindered many congregations from taking a vigorous, clear-cut stand favoring full civil rights for all Americans. One of these obstacles has been the recurring phenomenon of right-wing political and religious extremists using old-fashioned revivalist techniques to agitate against Jews and Negroes. These political radicals and religious bigots select certain elements of the historic Christian faith to buttress their own positions and give some kind of holy sanction to their often anti-Christian statements. Professor David O. Moberg, a distinguished Christian sociologist, does a sound job of analyzing this in his recent book *The Church as a Social Institution*. In this work Dr. Moberg points out that these extremists of the Radical Right attempt to identify basic Christian tenets with anti-Semitic, anti-Negro, anti-Catholic, anti-civil rights, anti-internationalist, and other negative doctrines in efforts to make the religious community accept the rest of their message. Naming names (*e.g.*, Kenneth Goff, Gerald L. K. Smith, Gerald Winrod, Harvey Springer) and calling dirty spades what they are, Professor Moberg concludes on a more positive note:

> But only a minority on the fringes of Christianity engage in actions designed to promote intergroup prejudice. The majority try to pro-

mote love and tolerance. This is evident from analysis of materials published for use in Sunday schools as well as from the numerous church projects aimed at developing high principles of motivation.[11]

Still, the extremists remain, and they appeal to well-meaning people in nearly every major Protestant denomination, often undermining much of what numerous evangelical Christians are doing for human rights.

A second internal problem facing socially concerned evangelicals is the fact that many fellow-believers have genuine fears concerning the growing powers of the federal government in every area of life. This makes them very reluctant to support any kind of civil rights legislation which places more authority in the hands of Washington bureaucrats.

Furthermore, older cultural patterns are still strong in many parts of the nation. As has been pointed out, regional mores often militate against Negro equality, factors of social prestige many times are involved, and some Christians still identify the culture of certain other centuries with the central doctrines of Christianity. Feeling often overrules reason, resulting in a state of emotional drunkenness from which many Christians later emerge filled with regret and a sense of sin. It is one of the less attractive of human traits that many people want to look down on someone else. This kind of attitude has become part of the culture in many areas of the United States.

Finally, there is a great deal of petty internal bickering constantly going on in many evangelical circles over such matters as the validity of the pre-tribulation rapture, the pastor's personality, or which version of the Bible should be used in the pulpit. Such bickering diverts attention from important doctrinal matters and urgent social issues, and at the same time saps the energy of Christians who might be using their talents in more worthwhile enterprises.

Another area which badly needs attention among evangelical Christians is the matter of what public relations experts call the "public image." Evangelicals have had a very bad press concerning the civil rights movement in recent years. Some of this is deserved, much of it is not. The point here is that because of the reluctance or refusal of some evangelical Christians to endorse the current drive for equal rights for all Americans, all Christians who might be described as fundamentalist, conservative, or neo-orthodox are getting a bad name. As historian David M. Reimers has noted, "Whites Only" was never carved over the doors of any white Protestant church in America, but in many places it may as well have been.[12] Others have pointed out, with growing monotony, that "the most segregated hour of the week is perhaps still 11:00 A.M.," the traditional time for Protestant worship.[13] One historian of considerable reputation recently has gone so far as to conclude that the "new evangelicals are the spiritual hard-core of the radical right."[14] This is simply not true, but there is enough substance to the charge to cause evangelical Christians to pause and think. Because of the intransigence of some professing Christians, it is becoming increasingly difficult for the majority of believers to talk about Jesus Christ and the validity of the Gospel message to their fellowmen.

Perhaps even more important to those today who claim to stand in the historic Christian tradition is the question of the future of Christianity among the Negro people of America and the world. Here three questions need to be raised: (1) What effect will the spectacle of white Christian foot-dragging on the issue of support for civil rights have on Negro Christians? How will they react? (2) What impact will white Christian reluctance to back what is an obviously righteous cause like the Negro quest for civil liberties have on the non-Christians in the Negro community? Will this turn them *en masse* against any consideration of the option of Christian commitment? (3) And finally, if white society becomes increasingly secular because Christians fail in their appointed task of preaching the Gospel, and if black society becomes increasingly secular for the same reason (in addition to the fact of white Christian indifference to Negro needs), then what will happen someday when a thoroughly secularized white society and a thoroughly secularized black society clash at full tilt over some future misunderstanding? If Christians, black and white, fail to be "the salt of the earth," what hope is there for the rest of mankind?

The Rev. Howard O. Jones, noted Negro minister and associate of Evangelist Billy Graham, makes the following observation from first-hand experience concerning the problems which discrimination and racial antagonism create for Christian missionaries in other countries:

> Discrimination against Negroes in America has a serious effect on the followers of non-Christian religions and African extremists. The Muslims use the racial problem in America to advance their cause in Africa. Muslims preach and teach that Christianity is a white man's religion, that Jesus Christ is the white man's Saviour, that the Bible is the white man's Bible. Muslims contend that Christianity offers no valid salvation or redemption for the black man. Using the race issue to prove that Christianity is inferior to Islam, Muslims continue to make great progress in their untiring efforts to win Africa.
>
> Communists also take full advantage of America's racial problem for their own purpose in Africa. Currently Russians and Red

Chinese are competing to conquer and control the continent. Communists capitalize on the unrest, strife, turmoil, and chaos among the African people to promote their own ideology.[15]

The overwhelming majority of American Negroes still claim to be Protestant according to a 1963 Harris opinion poll. Ninety percent said they were Protestants of various sorts, seven percent were adherents of the Roman Catholic Church, and only three percent had no religious preference. Fifty-five percent of all Negroes claim to be Baptists while Methodists are the second largest group with eighteen percent.[16] However, the same opinion survey asked Negro Americans to indicate which white institutions they considered "most helpful" and which they felt to be "most harmful" in securing for the Negro his constitutional rights. Fifty percent responded that they felt the Kennedy Administration was "most helpful" while only one percent said it was "most harmful." The U. S. Supreme Court received the second greatest vote of confidence as it garnered thirty-two percent of the "most helpful" votes and only one percent of the "most harmful." Far down the list of "most helpful" were the white churches. Only five percent of all Negroes felt that the white churches fell into this category. At the same time, eight percent of the Negroes polled felt that the white churches were "most harmful" to the cause of civil rights.[17]

These figures should jolt evangelical Christians out of their complacency concerning the civil rights movement. Obviously Negro Baptists and Methodists have a very dim view of the sincerity and authenticity of the Christianity of their white counterparts. This could indicate a tragic future for both evangelical Christianity and for race relations in the United States if something is not done about it at once. Most white Baptists and Methodists are not racists but many are culture-bound; most are not bigots but many are blinded by emotion. The opportunities and possibilities are far too great to allow the gulf between Negro and white Christians to continue to exist. In this matter, white evangelicals must begin to mend their spiritual fences.

At this juncture, the issues confronting evangelical Christians concerning the present-day civil rights movement should be relatively clear. Their responsibilities spring from their dual role as citizens and Christians. Their concern for their fellow-Americans should be of a twofold nature, social and spiritual. All Baptists, Methodists, Presbyterians, Lutherans, Mennonites, Quakers, Disciples, and other Protestants who consider themselves in the mainstream of the historic Christian faith should take seriously their moral responsibility to their fellowmen. If one American is being denied his constitutional rights, this affects all Americans.

Discrimination, segregation, racial hatred and other social evils all stem from the disposition of the human heart. Any solution to the civil rights problem or any other similar issue with moral and spiritual overtones must take into consideration the foibles of human nature. Politically speaking, the words of the late Supreme Court Justice Robert H. Jackson are particularly fitting: ". . . the attitude of a society and its organized political forces rather than its legal machinery, is the controlling force in the character of free institutions."[18] Religiously speaking, the great concern of Howard O. Jones, the late Martin Luther King, Jr., and many others for the spiritual needs of the Negro people must be kept in mind.[19] Furthermore, the spiritual transformation of more white people would go a long way toward creating an atmosphere of tolerance and love to replace the present climate of tension and hate. Christians of all races and colors would do well to heed the words of the Apostle Peter in the New Testament:

> Finally, all of you, have unity of spirit, sympathy, love of the brethren, a tender heart and a humble mind. Do not return evil for evil or reviling for reviling; but on the contrary bless, for to this you have been called, that you may obtain a blessing. For "He that would love life and see good days, let him keep his tongue from evil and his lips from speaking guile; let him turn away from evil and do right; let him seek peace and pursue it. For the eyes of the Lord are upon the righteous, and his ears are open to their prayer. But the face of the Lord is against those that do evil." (I Pet. 3:8–12)

Alternatives for Evangelicals

What are the alternative courses of action open to individual Christians, local churches, and organized denominations and fellowships? How can Christians meet the challenge of the present-day civil rights movement? There seem to be four basic paths which Christians can follow individually or collectively. First, evangelicals can defend the old order. That is, Christians can join the forces of political and social reaction and do their best to retain as much of the past as possible. Second, Christian believers can choose to do nothing or simply ignore the whole issue. This seems to be the line advocated at the present by a number of leading evangelical churchmen. This course might be labeled "social inaction" and would be in keeping with the emphasis by some upon doctrinaire conservatism: theological, political, and social. A third alternative might be to do a little, not enough to be identified with the New Left, socialism, or even political liberalism, but enough to soothe troubled consciences. In this manner, the evangelical could assume a "moderate" stance while learning to bend with the prevailing political winds.

The fourth possible response might be to adopt a thoroughly progressive attitude aimed at doing whatever is Christian, right, and possible to help all Americans achieve their civil rights. This approach would include making a concerted effort to wipe out every vestige of discrimination and racial hatred in Christian circles. It also would entail supporting demonstrably just demands for social and political reform. It would mean joining with others in an attempt to attain the twin goals of democracy in citizenship and integrity in Christianity, and it would require all professing Christians to start acting like Christians.

Adopting this last course of action would be the most difficult of the four which have been mentioned. It would require much prayer, a great deal of soul-searching, consistent Christian living, and a deep commitment to Jesus Christ. It also would call for some constructive thinking on the subject of civil rights. It would demand that Christians use common sense in approaching the matter, realizing that there are in all races the perverse and evil as well as the upright and good. It would involve renouncing the concept held by many people today that because one segment of our society has committed an injustice against another segment, it is proper that the first group should suffer at the hands of the second. Rejection of this kind of primitive philosophy is prerequisite to any basic understanding of, or any tentative solution to, the problems at hand. Finally, for the Christian believer this last approach to the civil rights movement would require the correct motivation. Speaking on the subject of the role of the church in racial integration, Dr. Charles E. Boddie, a distinguished Negro Baptist educator, put it this way: "The Protestant church has too long left such matters to the Brooklyn Dodgers and the CIO. It should integrate not because the Roman Catholics are doing so, but because it is the Christian thing to do."[20]

The Application of Christian Principles to the Issue of Civil Rights

No discussion of the relationship of the historic Christian faith to the current civil rights movement would be complete without some attempt to establish a few principles to serve as guidelines for those Christians who feel that they should be involved in political and social issues. These are only suggestions which hopefully will stimulate not only fruitful dialogue among evangelical Christians but also some constructive action as well.

First, Christians should keep in mind what the Bible has to say about the nature of man. This will help in getting down to the root of the problem of human perversity rather than merely trimming the branches only to have them grow back again. The Bible teaches and observation confirms that man is basically sinful. (See Psalm 51 and Romans 3.) This goes a long way toward explaining why some men resist a movement like that for civil rights and it makes clear that the spiritual disease of sin has political and social implications. The evangelical Christian should not be surprised when men act in an egocentric manner to maintain vested interests or keep other men downtrodden to serve their own selfish ends. The Christian also should be aware of his own shortcomings and ask himself if the stand which he has taken against civil rights might not be the product of his own lower nature rather than an outgrowth of his commitment to Jesus Christ.

A second Christian principle applicable to civil rights is the fact that God is "no respecter of persons" and that all men are equal in the sight of God. (Acts 10:34–48; Rom. 3:21–31; Col. 3:5–11.) The Christian faith either abolishes or transcends those human barriers which set man against his fellowman: "There is neither Jew nor Greek, there is neither slave nor free, there is neither male nor female; for you are all one in Christ Jesus." (Gal. 3:28.) This concept is beautifully illustrated by an incident in the early 1920s when Charles Evans Hughes, then Secretary of State, was welcomed into the membership of the Calvary Baptist Church in Washington, D. C. A little-known Chinese laundryman was received into membership at the same service. As Dr. Samuel Harrison Green, the pastor at the time, welcomed both men into the church, he is said to have remarked, "The ground is level at the foot of the cross."[21] God takes no more notice of the color of a man's skin than he does of the new clothes in which some people strut to church on Easter Sunday morning. Politically, this egalitarian concept was expressed by Abraham Lincoln more than a century ago:

> Let us then turn this government back into the channel in which the framers of the Constitution originally placed it. . . . Let us discard all this quibbling about this man and the other man, this race and that race and the other race being inferior. . . , and unite as one people throughout this land, until we shall once more stand up declaring that all men are created equal.[22]

A third Christian principle which needs to be brought to bear on the question of the civil rights movement is that of the validity of the salvation experience in Jesus Christ. It matters little how this experience is described: being saved, trusting Jesus, committing one's life to Christ, making a profession of faith, conversion, or encounter with God through

Christ. The main point is that it is an act in which God works through Christ to change men's lives, thus relating theology to men's actions. This is the key to Christian living. Man cries for the church to be more relevant; God seeks for it to be more Christian! "Therefore, if any one is in Christ, he is a new creation; the old has passed away, behold, the new has come." (II Cor. 5:17, cf. I. Pet. 2:9–12) The basic nature and will of individuals must be changed before society can be changed.

Fourth, the Christian principle of being honest and genuine in all of life's relationships should be mentioned. The Christian is an authentic person, not artificial or phony. Christ reigns in the life of the believer, even in the matter of civil rights. A Christian can afford to be himself, and he will grant others the same right. Regardless of race, creed, or color, the Christian believer will treat all people as human beings. (see Jn. 3, Gal. 2.)

Fifth, the most frequently mentioned but least practiced principle which is applicable to the civil rights movement is Christian love and brotherhood.[23] Admittedly, this is a difficult principle to implement in a world full of hate and war. However, there still seems to be something incongruous about the fact that some Christians can teach their youngsters the chorus "Jesus Loves the Little Children" in Sunday School and then voice racial prejudice around the dinner table after church. Others, by implication, twist the words of Jesus to read, "Suffer the little *middle class* children to come unto me" or act as if the Bible spoke of "the communion of the *white* saints." The faithful sing hymns and recite creeds about the universal brotherhood of all believers, yet as often as not they remain aloof from brothers of another nationality or skin color.

Yet the Bible is full of the teaching of love for God and others. (See I. Cor. 13; Col. 3:12–17; I Jn. 2 and 3.) Probably the most dramatic commandment given to Christian believers is the one emphasizing love and compassion: "You shall love your neighbor as yourself. Love does no wrong to a neighbor, therefore love is the fulfilling of the law." (Rom. 13:9–10.) Obviously, anyone who loves his neighbor as he loves himself will not hate that neighbor, take advantage of him, or try to deny him his God-given and constitutionally-guaranteed rights.

Finally, there is the Biblical principle of respect for human life, the corollary of which is a sensitivity to the needs of others. This includes the concept of moral responsibility as a disciple of Jesus Christ and a citizen of the United States. The Bible teaches that immorality, hatred, strife, jealousy, anger, selfishness, dissension, and the like are to be expected from non-Christians. On the other hand, the fruits of the Spirit as expressed through the lives of believers are listed as love, joy, peace, patience, kindness, goodness, faithfulness, gentleness, and self-control.

(Gal. 5:13–24.) An individual governed by these principles could never shoot a Medgar Evers from ambush, bomb a church full of little Negro children, or brutally club defenseless civilians no matter what their color.

An unknown poet, inspired by the words of Matthew 5:40, penned these words:

I sought my soul, but my soul I could not see.
I sought my God, but my God eluded me.
I sought my brother, and I found all three.

This kind of attitude found expression in the life of a distinguished Christian statesman, Brooks Hays from Arkansas, who lost his seat in the United States House of Representatives in 1958 because he dared take a stand against racial discrimination and for desegregation. A year after his defeat at the polls, he wrote the following in his book *A Southern Moderate Speaks*:

I have emphasized the role of the Southern Baptists in the field of race relations because of my personal identification with that faith, not because I intended to slight the work of any other faith. Many faiths showed that willingness to communicate urged by Paul in I Timothy 6:18 when the Richmond Ministers Association issued, early in 1957, an outstanding statement of the moral responsibilities of Virginians, dealing with all aspects of the segregation problem. One point that especially appealed to me was this: We believe that until a final satisfactory solution is achieved, every effort should be made to make available to both white and colored people the finest in educational and cultural advantages; that wherever possible, and as rapidly as possible, social custom violating the dignity of the Negro should be eradicated. The passing away of these irritating customs does not involve intermarriage or amalgamation of the races; it declares a wholesome respect for all people and evidences common courtesy.[24]

This is the kind of spirit which a vibrant evangelical Christianity should and does produce. Here is a man who was willing to sacrifice a promising career in the House of Representatives for the sake of Christian principles. Many other politicians who call themselves "Christian" have done less.

A Practical Program for Evangelical Christians Interested in Civil Rights

The foregoing principles should enable evangelical Christians to formulate a program of action relating to civil rights. The preparations need not be elaborate but theory and theology ought to be put into practice. The main consideration is a willingness to do something constructive and to render concrete assistance. Practical goals need to be pursued and tangible results achieved in order for the theoretical rights of the individual American to become realities. As a recent "working paper" of the National Council of Churches has stated: "The equal rights that have been couched in law are now being sought in life as practical social and economic matters."[25]

Nearly every denomination from the Southern Baptists to the United Presbyterians as well as the National Council of Churches now has some kind of formal program or agency designed to promote the cause of civil rights in their respective constituencies. By 1956, all major religious bodies in both the North and South had made pronouncements officially sanctioning the principle of desegregation. In spite of all their shortcomings and past failures, the concepts of social justice which are so basic in the present struggle for Negro rights have come largely from the religious people of America. To be sure, guidelines for desegregation handed down from national offices are often opposed or ignored at the congregational level. Still, more and more church members are challenging discrimination and segregation on moral and spiritual grounds. As Sociologist David O. Moberg observed in 1962:

> Integration within church congregations, as well as in church-related colleges, theological seminaries, and hospitals, also has progressed significantly during the past decade. Christians on the whole are somewhat more favorable toward abolition of the American "caste system" than secularists in the same community. Preachers in general have been more positive and articulate on the issue of race than laymen: many nevertheless uphold the status quo rather than work to reduce racial discrimination.[26]

Although there has been increasing soul-searching and a concomitant build-up of interest in the civil rights movement in evangelical churches, Professor Moberg's assessment is still basically applicable to the current situation. Much has been done, much remains to be done. Some groups, congregations, and individuals still live in the past, and in so doing bring reproach to the name of Christ by supporting political and social reaction. What can be done by concerned evangelical Christians who wish to offset this negative attitude and serve Christ in the matter of civil rights? The following six suggestions are offered to the reader as possible courses of action. They are not meant to be a substitute for well-thought-out programs sponsored by denominational agencies or to take the place of worthy projects already underway in many local churches.

However, they may prove stimulating and helpful to Bible-believing Christians who are looking for a way to put their Christian faith to work.

First, Christians need to develop the right attitude. White Christians must avoid the attitude of pity or condescension toward their fellow-believers of other racial and ethnic groups in particular and toward all other people in general. There is nothing so harmful as a charity that pauperizes, but needless to say, there has been too much of this in the name of race relations. No man of dignity and worth wants pity; rather he prefers and needs good will, sympathetic respect, and acceptance as an equal in the meaningful relationships of life.[27]

In this same vein, anti-Negro attitudes need to be rooted out of the very word and thought patterns of white Protestant Christians. Often such attitudes are fostered indirectly by identifying righteousness with the color white and sin with black. The so-called "Wordless Book" used by many fundamentalists in child evangelism is a good example of this. Moreover, this idea is conveyed by several popular fundamentalist ditties called choruses which depict the heart as "black with sin" until the Savior comes in, cleans it up, and makes it "white as snow." Actually, though white is often associated with purity in Biblical symbolism, sin is usually referred to as scarlet and not black. (Isa. 1:18.) At any rate, the unwitting usage of "fundamentalist lingo" can sometimes be detrimental toward taking even the first step in establishing good relations between white and Negro Christians.

Second, Christians need to become personally involved in the struggle for civil rights. This does not necessarily mean that evangelical Christians need to take part in picketing and civil rights demonstrations, but it may! Peacefully demonstrating for a good cause is in the best American tradition, and there may be cases when it would be immoral for a Christian believer not to do so. Christian believers in other nations have had to use the technique in behalf of their own civil rights under the law.[28]

The matter of becoming personally involved entails the application of Christian principles to every area of one's life including civil rights. For example, this application of Christian principles would include the concept of egalitarianism on which our nation was founded. This doctrine did not come from political liberalism but from Christian humanitarianism. The concept that all men are equal before the law comes from the Old Testament and was recognized by Jesus when he gave the golden rule and affirmed the principle that you should "love your neighbor as yourself." According to the Christian Gospel: ". . . in Christ Jesus you are all sons of God, through faith. . . . There is neither Jew nor Greek, there is neither slave nor free, there is neither male nor female; for you are all one in Christ Jesus." (Gal. 3:26–28.)

Personal involvement also will mean educating oneself about different aspects of the civil rights movement. The individual Christian needs to think and pray about civil rights, and seek God's leading in choosing a course of action to follow. The Christian will have to learn to approach this matter as maturely as possible in order to see the drive for civil rights in the context of other political, social, and economic problems. But most of all, he must learn to see civil rights from the point of view of the Negro community and other minority groups, look at things as they look at them, and take their complaints seriously. This will entail reading what they are writing, listening to what they are saying, and even thinking what they are thinking. Then one can honestly examine himself and confess his own inner prejudices and hostilities. This is actually the necessary first step in any kind of meaningful personal Christian involvement in the civil rights movement.

One final matter concerning personal involvement needs to be mentioned, and this really relates to the larger concept of Christian participation in politics in general. More evangelical Christians need to become active in political parties and run for public office. Many Christian politicians such as Senator Mark O. Hatfield of Oregon and Governor Warren Hearnes of Missouri have urged their fellow-believers to consider careers as public servants in government at all levels. Certainly this would be a means of practical implementation of many of the present social concerns of all Christians. Men of conviction, character, and integrity are needed in public life. If Christians do not take the initiative and participate in the American political system, they may some day forfeit their right to do so. No Christian can afford the luxury of criticizing his government and his country until he is first willing to work for them through the traditional political structure. At this point it should be noted that according to the religious census of the Ninetieth Congress, 272 of the 535 members of the House and Senate claim affiliation with denominations or groups which claim to be in the evangelical Christian tradition. Furthermore, twenty-six of the fifty governors associate themselves with basically evangelical denominations.[29] Even granting the present-day malady of religious affiliation without commitment, there still must be enough genuine Christians in the current Congress and the various statehouses across the country to ensure a sympathetic consideration of needed civil rights legislation and programs.

Third, evangelical Christians need to work diligently to establish lines of communication with fellow-believers of other races and colors. There is a need for more person to person contact between Christians of various racial and national backgrounds. The best way to develop an understanding of another person's problems, hopes, and aspirations is to get to know him better. It is more difficult to remain aloof from the civil rights movement when one personally is acquainted with some person who is being discriminated against or taken advantage of by another. White Christians need to have more of their Negro friends into their homes and Negro Christians need to invite more of their white Christian acquaintances to share in some of their experiences. If Christ cannot break down the wall of suspicion, prejudice, and hate, then perhaps no one can.

Fourth, Christians need to promote civil rights in the local churches. As a number of evangelical Christian leaders have pointed out in the past, segregation would have ended long ago at the local and every other level if the individual churches had led the way. The distinguished Baptist layman Brooks Hays took note of the crucial role played by local organizations, especially the churches, in the quest for civil rights for all Americans. In 1959 he wrote: "In the last analysis, it will be the churches and the local community organizations that will provide solutions to the problem of civil rights."[30] Certainly, as long as local congregations remain segregated, whether it be by simply employing bouncers to eject Negroes from the services or through more subtle techniques, they give moral sanction to discrimination in every other area of social life. The continued existence of Jim Crow worship is an open, running sore in the life of any church and repudiates the central thrust of the gospel that in Christ all men are reunited with God and with one another. As has been rightly pointed out by concerned evangelicals, there is no such thing as half-way reconciliation. It is impossible for a Christian to be reconciled with God but not with his neighbors for this would be a perversion of the Gospel. According to the Scriptures, the body of Christ is not divided into black and white but is one.

The tragic shame of the last decade of civil rights activity in the United States is that when the churches should have been leading, they have been following, and consequently and understandably many Negroes are looking elsewhere for help. The argument that the clergy should not meddle in politics by espousing civil rights is meaningless to the Negro who meets immoral discrimination on every hand. It is true that for many ministers, especially in the South, a Christian and humanitarian stand on the issue of civil rights would mean either preaching to empty pews or loss of financial support. It is also true that since the churches are made up of persons who comprise society itself, it has in recent years in middle class America seldom taken the lead in social reform. But these arguments in no way abrogate the responsibility of the individual believer for his fellow man. If New Testament Christians had acted like the majority of church members today, there would be no Christianity since it would have been neither economically sound nor socially acceptable to declare oneself for Christ and follow him in those early days.

On the other hand, there is a great deal of hope in the present situation, both in the North and the South. The action taken by denominations as a whole supports progressive congregations and pastors who wish to initiate change. Also, the concern of many Christians contributes to an uneasiness among believers elsewhere and thus indirectly encourages gradual revisions of culturalisms, non-Christian folkways, and even local laws. And of course, since the most effective sermons about race relations and against discrimination are preached by example and not words, many evangelical Christians are beginning to make an impact on their more spiritually lethargic brethren.

Ideally, local congregations should take the lead in every legitimate enterprise on behalf of civil rights. They can help mobilize public opinion on behalf of equal opportunity programs or fair housing practices. More important, the local churches need to be the first places in the community, not the last, to become desegregated. Naturally, not every church will become interracial overnight for a variety of reasons, largely because of location in a totally white or a totally Negro area. But every church can publicly announce that it will receive members from any racial group if the individual meets the theological and ethical standards expected from any other member. Furthermore, every evangelical Christian congregation should become a center of reconciliation by softening prejudice and exclusiveness with the unlimited resources of Christian love and understanding. This ministry of reconciliation is desperately needed in many localities recently rocked by destructive riots and senseless civil strife. In many situations, only the local church can step in to bring peace and stop violence. One cannot over-emphasize the extremely important place which the local congregation occupies in the current test of American democracy, American character, and American Christianity.

Fifth, the leadership of the evangelical denominations and churches needs energetically to promote civil rights. The lay leaders of many churches are often the most enlightened people in the community on the issue of civil rights. These Christian leaders need to speak out and make their witness count in this particular area of Christian social concern. Too many have remained silent for various reasons—social, economic, or practical. Some have rationalized away any responsibility for civil rights with the unscriptural argument that Christians should only be concerned with "getting people saved." There is a great need for evangelical lay leaders to follow out-spoken Christians like Brooks Hays, Mark O. Hatfield, Frank Carlson, and William P. Thompson in vigorously supporting measures to end the present abridgment of the fundamental rights of many Americans.

Another area in which Christian leaders can make their influence felt in civil rights is that of education of church members. As Franklin H. Littell points out in his book *From State Church to Pluralism*, one of the basic problems of many American Protestants today is that they are theologically illiterate. Most newly-inducted church members understand neither their commitment to Christ nor its relationship to their everyday living. Most of this is the fault of the leadership of the local congregations, both clerical and lay, in the context of the present preoccupation of the churches with statistical rather than spiritual growth. As Professor Littell puts it:

> Inadequately trained for membership, admitted without preparatory training, without the proper instruments of voluntary discipline, many members never have had the discontinuity between life in Christ and life in the world brought home to them. Here the ordinary members are less at fault than the leadership of the churches, who—though sworn to uphold the form of sound words and doctrine—neglect catechetical instruction and concentrate solely on the acquisition of more new members at any price.[31]

If evangelical Christians clearly understood what Christ expected of them in every area of their lives, they probably would be either more concerned with the needs of others or dissociate themselves from Christianity. Either course of action would help elevate the low quality of present-day church membership.

Sixth and last, concerned evangelical Christians need to promote and support civil rights at the national level. This can be done through both the denominations and the federal government. It is true that decisions made at the highest level of any organization or group are largely ineffectual and often wrongly motivated. It is also true that laws and court decisions will not produce a change of heart. However, pronouncements, enactments, and decisions made by denominations and the government do help to hasten change as well as make it easier for Christians to present their case and make their point. Furthermore, the law of the land is that all Americans *are* guaranteed their basic civil rights. What could be more Christian than to obey laws which are both constitutionally and morally sound?

Conclusion

Obviously not everyone who calls himself a Christian will agree with the basic thesis of this essay: that support of the present-day civil rights movement is both morally and spiritually right. However, it is hoped that evangelicals will at least face up to problems which have moral and spiritual as well as social and political implications and make an honest effort to determine what Jesus Christ would have them do. Also, it would be a major accomplishment if this essay would help people to avoid stereotyping Negroes (*e.g.*, they are all like Stokely Carmichael), white people (*e.g.*, they are all like Eugene "Bull" Conner), and evangelical Christians (*e.g.*, they are all like the people who run Bob Jones University).

Furthermore, the point should be made that those Christians who have reservations about supporting the civil rights movement because of their genuine fear of the rapidly increasing power of the central government are obliged to propose alternate solutions which *will work* at the state and local levels. In most instances, the federal government has intervened to correct abuses and right wrongs only after the state governments have failed to act on their own to insure enforcement of the "law of the land."

In a recent speech Dr. Ross Coggins, Director of Communications for the Christian Life Commission of the Southern Baptist Convention, eloquently placed before his constituency the issue of relating Christian evangelism to civil rights squarely. Speaking of the moral dimensions of the forthcoming Baptist-sponsored "Crusade of the Americas," Dr. Coggins remarked:

> President Johnson has submitted to the Congress a bill which would, over a three-year period, eliminate racial discrimination in housing. The coincidental timing of this major civil rights effort and our own massive evangelistic preparations has profound significance. What an opportunity to translate our evangelistic proclamations of life into a practical demonstration of love! Will Southern Baptists at the grassroots level give this legislation the massive support it deserves, or will we retreat into familiar postures of evasion, pious rationalization, or outright obstruction? The latter option will, in the thinking of thoughtful observers throughout this hemisphere, make the Crusade of the Americas seem a hollow mockery.[32]

The key to real understanding between the races and to ending senseless racial discrimination in the United States is the individual Christian and how he acts in secular society. As he demonstrates his transformed "life in Christ," others will want to embrace the Christian Gospel. They in turn will experience the power of Christ to change lives, even to the abolishing of racial hatred and antagonisms. The local church is the key to working out Christian answers to problems involving civil rights on the local level for it is the visible microcosm of a Christian society in the community. In many cases, it can provide both the example and the leadership necessary to weather the many stormy days ahead in the realm of race relations in the United States and elsewhere in the world.

The day of reckoning may be near at hand for the Christians of America. Never have churches been materially more powerful and spiritually less effective. A crowded world balancing perilously on the precipice of disaster needs the kind of spiritual and moral leadership which only genuine Christianity can give. There is no longer any room in our churches for bigotry and discrimination nor for those who practice these things in their lives. The task before the churches is difficult, the challenge is immediate.

The best way to conclude an essay of this nature is not with pious phrases, thundering condemnations, or false vows. Rather, let evangelical Christians of all races wrestle with the hard-hitting challenge thrown out by Negro minister Howard O. Jones in the conclusion of his book *Shall We Overcome?*

> The Christian church therefore must become the light of the world and the salt of the earth in every area of life. Only as Christians who are cleansed of attitudes of segregation and discrimination and who are baptized with the love of God and love for one another can we stem the rising tide of violence, hatred, and bloodshed now confronting us. We must quit evading the issue and making excuses. We must stop being overcome with race prejudice and bitterness. As Negro and white Christians let us allow Christ to settle the problem once and for all. Let us not be satisfied until we have overcome.[33]

NOTES

1. Cited in H. Frank Way, Jr., *Liberty in the Balance: Current Issues in Civil Liberties* (New York: McGraw-Hill, 1964), pp. 1–2.

2. John Steinbeck, "America and the Americans," *Saturday Evening Post,* CCXXXIX (July 2, 1966), p. 38.

3. *Christianity Today,* XI (Jan. 6, 1967), p. 43.

4. From the files of the American Civil Liberties Union. Also see Howard O. Jones, *Shall We Overcome?* (Westwood, N.J.: Fleming H. Revell, 1966), pp. 18–19.

5. For example, see the reactions to stories of civil rights workers and their detractors in the "Letters to the Editor" column of various magazines and newspapers. Frequently both Christianity and the American system are strongly denounced in these letters because so often the resistance to the drive for civil rights is couched in religious and patriotic language.

6. David M. Reimers, *White Protestantism and the Negro* (New York: Oxford University Press, 1965), pp. 3–24; and Owen D. Pelt and Ralph L. Smith, *The Story of the National Baptists* (New York: Vantage Press, 1960), pp. 27–28.

7. See C. Vann Woodward, *The Strange Career of Jim Crow* (New York: Oxford University Press, 1955).

8. Chase C. Mooney, *Civil Rights: Retrospect and Prospects* (Washington: Service Center for Teachers of History, 1961), pp. 12–13.

9. Reimers, *White Protestantism and the Negro*, pp. 5–6; and Eric L. McKitrick, ed., *Slavery Defended* (Englewood Cliffs, N.J.: Prentice-Hall, 1963), p. 94.

10. Reimers, *White Protestantism and the Negro*, pp. 6–10; and William Jenkins, *Pro-slavery Thought in the Old South* (Chapel Hill: University of North Carolina Press, 1935), chap. 5. A recent admission of past failures by the leadership of the gigantic and dynamic Southern Baptist Convention is a heartening and spectacular example of that of which I speak. In a document released on May 20, 1968, seventy-one denominational leaders of major stature declared themselves guilty of condoning racial prejudice in the past. They further stated that "judgment begins at the house of God" and "we therefore acknowledge our share of responsibility for the injustice, disorder and wickedness of our land." The manifesto called for the creation of a Baptist task force to assist in dealing with the nation's social problems. *Manhattan* (Kan.) *Mercury*, May 21, 1968.

11. David O. Moberg, *The Church as a Social Institution* (Englewood Cliffs, N.J.: Prentice-Hall, 1962), p. 448.

12. Reimers, *White Protestantism and the Negro*, p. 158.

13. Moberg, *The Church as a Social Institution*, pp. 451–52.

14. William G. McLoughlin, "Is There a Third Force in Christendom?" *Daedalus*, (Winter 1967), p. 61.

15. Jones, *Shall We Overcome?* p. 115.

16. William Brink and Louis Harris, *The Negro Revolution in America* (New York: Simon and Schuster, 1964), p. 220 .

17. *Ibid.*, pp. 232–34.

18. Quoted in Way, *Liberty in the Balance*, preface.

19. Jones, *Shall We Overcome?* p. 19, and Martin Luther King, Jr., "A Challenge to the Churches and Synagogues," in *Race: Challenge to Religion*, edited by Mathew Ahmann, (Chicago: Henry Regnery, 1963), pp. 155–69.

20. Quoted in Bernice Cofer, ed., *Racial Integration in the Church* (New York: American Baptist Home Mission Societies, 1957), p. 4.

21. *Ibid.*, p. 42.

22. Speech of July 10, 1858 in John G. Nicolay and John Hay, eds., *Complete Works of Abraham Lincoln* (New York: Tandy-Thomas Co., 1905), III, p. 51.

23. All of the many Negro Christians whom the author queried on the problem of how best to relate the Christian faith to the movement for civil rights emphasized the point that a generous outpouring of Christian love by professing believers would go far in creating a world in which civil rights would be no issue at all. As one of these persons wrote: "If this theme [Love] was carried to its fullest extent in our teachings and in our lives seven days a week, twenty-four hours a day, there would be no problems on this globe and certainly not when it comes to dealing with human beings and their civil rights."

24. Brooks Hays, *A Southern Moderate Speaks* (Chapel Hill: University of North Carolina Press, 1959), p. 214.

25. Benjamin F. Payton, *A Strategy for the Next Stage in Equal Rights: Metropolitan-Rural Development for Equal Opportunity* (New York: National Council of Churches, 1966), p. 4.

26. Moberg, *The Church as a Social Institution*, pp. 451–52.

27. Kyle Haselden, *The Racial Problem in Christian Perspective* (New York: Harper & Row, 1959), pp. 137–52.

28. *Christianity Today*, XI (Jan. 6, 1967), p. 43.

29. *Ibid.*, XI (Dec. 9, 1966), pp. 36–37.

30. Hays, *A Southern Moderate Speaks*, p. 195.

31. Franklin H. Littell, *From State Church to Pluralism* (Garden City, N.Y.: Doubleday, 1962), p. 134.

32. Ross Coggins, "Moral Dimensions of the Crusade of the Americas," a

speech delivered March 8, 1967 at the annual meeting of the Christian Life Commission of the Southern Baptist Convention, Miami Beach, Florida. The bill in question finally was passed in April of 1968, following the tragic assassination of Dr. Martin Luther King, Jr. on April 4, in Memphis, Tennessee.

33. Jones, *Shall We Overcome?* p. 144. For a striking example of the Christian attitude that shall "overcome," see the courageous magazine *Freedom Now* (edited and published by Fred A. Alexander, Savannah, Ohio).

Donald E. Pitzer is Assistant Professor of History at Indiana State University, Evansville Campus. He was born in Springfield, Ohio on May 6, 1936, attended Messiah College and Wittenberg University, receiving the A.B. degree from the latter in 1958. He did graduate work at Pennsylvania State University and then at The Ohio State University which awarded him the M.A. and Ph.D. degrees in history in 1962 and 1966 respectively. His doctoral dissertation surveyed the development of professional revivalism in nineteenth century Ohio.

Mr. Pitzer embarked upon his academic career at Messiah College where he was an instructor from 1959 to 1961. He later spent three years as a teaching associate at The Ohio State University, and in 1966 he did research in the nature and content of the Warren G. Harding Papers as a manuscript librarian at the Ohio Historical Society in Columbus, Ohio. During the 1966–67 academic year he served as an assistant professor of history at Taylor University, and in 1967 he joined the faculty of Indiana State University.

Professor Pitzer's fundamental interest is the social and intellectual history of the United States during the nineteenth century. He has contributed an article to the special Harding edition of *Ohio History* and has presented a paper before the annual meeting of the Ohio Academy of Science. He was selected to become a member of the Phi Alpha Theta historical honorary society in 1961, and he also holds membership in the American Historical Association, Organization of American Historians, and Ohio Historical Society. His church affiliation is Brethren in Christ, and he belongs to the Democratic Party.

DONALD E. PITZER

Christianity in the Public Schools

Separation of church and state, perhaps the most delicate peren-
nial issue to face the Christian community in America, has been brought
into sharp, controversial focus in the 1960's. The current struggle re-
volves around the propriety of organized religious activities in the public
schools and centers in some recent Supreme Court decisions. The broad
interpretation which the court has given to the separation of church and
state and the rights of the individual under the "Establishment of Religion" and "Free Exercise" clauses of the First Amendment has caused
leaders in the church and the state to rethink their positions regarding
the role of the state as a propagator of religion in the public, tax-supported
schools. This problem is presently the theme of numerous books, articles,
and meetings, and some have even proposed Constitutional amendments to define the relationship more clearly. In order to resolve these
difficulties, it is first necessary to examine the role of religion in the establishment and development of American public education. Next, the
movement for separation of church and state and complete individual
religious liberty will be considered. This desire was expressed in the bills
of rights on the state and national levels during the Revolutionary period
and was reaffirmed by the courts with regard to the public schools as
American society became increasingly pluralistic. At the same time such
an investigation will provide the evangelical with an opportunity to form
an intelligent attitude toward state-sponsored religious activities in today's public schools.

Colonial Education—Protestant Controlled

From the earliest time in the English American colonies Christianity
underlay and permeated the educational as well as the religious and governmental institutions. In all of the colonies, nine of which had an established church, the various Christian denominations provided the primary

stimulus for educating the young. Under the prevailing philosophical atmosphere, the churches urged the necessity of at least an elementary education for each child in order that he might learn to read the Bible and the catechism and thus come to know the will of God for his salvation. The schools which were formed as a result of this motivation during the early colonial period quite naturally emphasized religious matters to the exclusion of history, geography, science, music, and secular literature.[1]

Where the Church of England was established (Maryland, North and South Carolina, Virginia, and Georgia), the English tradition of parents being responsible for seeing to their children's education by private tutors was the general practice. Those children whose parents could not afford tutors were taught, if at all, by local parish priests or teachers in scattered endowed schools. But, from planter's child to beggarman's orphan the education that was available placed high priority on instruction in Christian principles. In 1656 a Virginia law made moral and religious training compulsory for orphaned children, and subsequent legislation required the same for all offspring of the poor in order to relieve the threat of a possible vagabond and dangerous class in society.[2] In the Middle Colonies the situation was much more nationally and denominationally heterogeneous than in the South or New England. Therefore, the tutorial and parochial facilities which were established there served chiefly to indoctrinate the youth in the peculiar beliefs of the Anglicans, Dutch Reformed, German Lutherans, Mennonites, Quakers, Moravians, and Scotch-Irish Presbyterians. New England, however, was the location of the most important development with regard to the church-state relationship in education.

It was in Puritan New England that the first public tax-supported schools in America were created as the product of the intense desire of the established Congregational Church to insure a religiously literate younger generation. As early as 1635, the Bostonians evidenced their educational concerns by the establishment of an elementary school to be supported by private subscription and by the income of a parcel of land donated by the town. A few other towns soon followed the Boston example. The Massachusetts Legislature passed a law in 1642 requiring town officials to compel parents to provide elementary instruction for their children. The minimal ingredients of this education were the reading of English, a knowledge of the capital laws and the catechism, and apprenticeship in a trade. Finally, five years later the church leaders ordered the legislature to take the step which would make the fulfillment of the parental responsibilities under the 1642 law possible—free public elementary instruction. This famous law of 1647 stipulated that, by levying taxes if necessary, every town of fifty families was to hire an elementary school teacher and that every town of one hundred families was to establish a Latin grammar school. In this manner the precedent for civil-controlled, compulsory education was set, and by 1680 Connecticut, New Haven, Plymouth, and New Hampshire had followed suit.[3]

That the very fabric of the curriculum in the state-controlled public schools of New England should be as thoroughly religious as that in the private and parochial schools of the Middle and Southern colonies was insured from the outset. The Massachusetts law of 1647 based its demand for schools on the sole assumption that "one cheife proiect of ye ould deluder, Satan, [is] to keepe men from the knowledge of ye Scriptures." The Connecticut law of 1650 required that children be instructed "in the grounds and principles of religion" which required that they should at least "learn some short orthodox catechism." In 1684, schoolmasters in the New Haven Grammar School were required by statute to begin the class work of the day "with a short Prayer for a blessing on his Laboures & theire Learning."[4] Except for the instruction in Latin in the grammar schools, religious material composed the entire reading matter of classes in New England during most of the first century of their existence. The list of textbooks included the *Hornbook*, which was a sheet containing the alphabet and the Lord's Prayer attached to a board, the religious Primer, Psalter, Testament, and Bible. The *New England Primer*, which appeared in 1690 and became widely used in most schools throughout the colonies, is illustrative of the way in which all instruction was made to serve the desired religious purpose. In the *Primer* the alphabet was taught by assorted Bible verses which began:

A wise son makes a glad father, but a foolish son
is the heaviness of his mother.

Better is a little with the fear of the Lord, than great
treasure and trouble therewith.

Come unto Christ all ye that labor and are heavy laden,
and he will give you rest.

Do not the abominable thing which I hate, saith the Lord.

Except a man be born again he cannot see the Kingdom of God.

A typical section of student readings from the *Primer* was:

The praises of my tongue
I offer to the Lord,
That I was taught so young
To read his holy Word.

That I was brought to know
The danger I was in,
By nature and by practice too
A wretched slave to sin.

That I was led to see
I can do nothing well
And whither shall a sinner flee
To save himself from hell.[5]

The *Primer* also included the Lord's Prayer, Apostles' Creed, Ten Commandments, names of all the books of the Bible, and questions and answers of the Shorter Westminster Catechism which indoctrinated the pupils in Calvinistic theology.

In short, the New England public school system, while controlled by civil officials, was an adjunct of the church. Not only were the children expected to learn the catechism and to hear the Bible read and expounded, but also they were required to attend church. Grammar school pupils had the additional assignment of reporting each week on the Sunday sermon. And, there were civil sanctions against those who violated the religious atmosphere of the schoolroom as in the case of the girl who was hailed before the court in New Haven Colony and charged with "prophane swearing." She had used the expressions "by my soul" and "as I am a Christian."[6]

Throughout the colonial era and into the nineteenth century the overwhelming Protestant consensus which prevailed among the populace permitted the continuation of policies with regard to education and office holding which discriminated against Roman Catholics, Jews, Unitarians, and other dissenters. Both parochial and charity schools were religious in character. The free school system of New England continued to leave the certification of grammar school teachers in the hands of local Congregational clergymen.[7] Noah Webster recalled in 1840 that the textbooks used in the common schools of Connecticut in the decade just before the Revolution "were chiefly or wholly Dilworth's Spelling Books, the Psalter, Testament, and Bible."[8] Most of the colonies also maintained religious tests for the holding of public office. Maryland and Massachusetts required a belief "in the Christian religion." In 1776 Delaware adopted the stipulation that candidates for office had to profess "faith in God the Father, and in Jesus Christ, His only Son, and in the Holy Ghost, on God, blessed forever more." In Pennsylvania the officeholder in addition had to agree that God is "the rewarder of the good and punisher of the wicked."[9]

The Ideals of the American Revolution

While the homogeneous colonial setting provided an ideal environment for the perpetuation of Protestantism in the schools, two factors were at work during the eighteenth century to separate church from state, to lay the foundation for complete religious freedom for the individual, and ultimately to eliminate church influence in the public schools. The first of these sprang from the Protestant Christian community itself. It was an attempt to achieve equality of opportunity for every denomination, culminating in the disestablishment of the Congregational, Anglican, Episcopal, and Dutch Reformed Churches between 1776 and 1833. The second motivating force for reform grew out of the eighteenth century Enlightenment. Stressing the natural rights of man, it urged a thoroughgoing legal separation of church and state, and envisaged a complete implementation of the principle of voluntarism for the individual in matters of religion. Its success came not only with the adoption of bills of rights at the state and federal levels, but also with the progressive construction which the courts have tended to give to these guarantees since that time.

Thus, a period which began in the decade prior to the Revolution and lasted beyond the turn of the nineteenth century saw men of widely divergent religious viewpoints unite in a crusade to free all American churches and citizens from the hindrances of state religious sanctions. Calvinistic Baptists and Presbyterians on the one hand and Jeffersonian Deists and liberal statesmen on the other devoted their efforts to the achievement of this objective. The movement focused in Virginia where the establishment of the Anglican Church had long worked to the disadvantage of all dissenters. In 1772 the Baptists, who had long advocated that church functions should be entirely separate from the state, began placing their grievances before the House of Burgesses. Led by John Leland, they cited the fact that it was difficult for the Baptist poor to secure the money to pay the taxes for the state church and that Baptist clergymen were restricted from performing marriages and from preaching in meeting houses not specifically stated on their licenses. By 1774 the Presbyterians of Virginia added their own reasons for discontent to the Baptist list. They summarized these in a petition to the legislature as: disturbance of their meetings, lack of freedom to speak and write on religious topics of their choice, and the inability to own property for the support of their schools and churches. They pleaded that they might be permitted "to have and enjoy the full and free exercise of our religion, without molestation or danger of incurring any penalty whatsoever."[10]

While the clergymen aroused public sentiment for disestablishment, George Mason, Thomas Jefferson, and James Madison drew upon the philosophical concepts of John Milton, Algernon Sidney, and John Locke to give eloquent expression to the arguments for religious freedom and to formulate bills for its implementation. The first tangible results came in the passage of the Virginia Declaration of Rights on June 12, 1776. This statement combined the ideas of Mason and Madison and was a source for the first part of the Declaration of Independence and the Federal Bill of Rights. It read:

> That religion, or the duty which we owe to our Creator, and the manner of discharging it, can be directed only by reason and conviction, not by force or violence, and therefore all men are equally entitled to the free exercise of religion, according to the dictates of conscience; and that it is the mutual duty of all to practice Christian sidered as a subject of the governor of the universe.[13]

As the Presbyterians rejoiced in this act as "the rising Sun of religious Liberty, to relieve us from a long night of ecclesiastic Bondage," the movement for complete religious freedom gained speed.[12] In December 1776 the legislature relieved dissenters from paying taxes to the State Church and also from all penalties previously inflicted for not attending its services. By 1780 Virginia had discontinued the payment of salaries to Episcopal clergymen and granted the right of dissenting ministers to solemnize marriages. Complete freedom in religious matters seemed clearly in view, but this liberty was not realized until after a final battle with the entrenched conservatives over the General Assessment Bill which ended in the enactment of Jefferson's Bill for Establishing Religious Freedom.

The General Assessment Bill, which was proposed by Patrick Henry and which would have required every citizen of Virginia to contribute financially to some Christian church, occasioned Madison's well-known defense of religious freedom in his "Memorial and Remonstrance." Drawing upon the loftiest principles of the Enlightenment, Madison opposed the Assessment Bill on the grounds that "religion, or the duty which we owe to our creator, and the manner of discharging it, can be directed only by reason and conviction, not by force or violence. The religion, then, of every man, must be left to the conviction and conscience of every man; and it is the right of every man to exercise it as these may dictate." He forcefully asserted further that:

> That right is, in its nature, an unalienable right. It is unalienable, because the opinions of men, depending only on the evidence con-

templated in their own minds, cannot follow the dictates of other men; it is unalienable, also, because what is here a right towards men, is a duty towards the creator. It is the duty of every man to render the creator such homage, and *such only*, as he believes to be acceptable to him; this duty is precedent, both in order of time and degree of obligation, to the claims of civil society. Before any man can be considered as a member of civil society, he must be considered as a subject of the governor of the universe.[13]

Madison warned that in a democracy it *is* possible "that the majority may trespass on the rights of the minority" and "that the same authority which can establish Christianity, in exclusion of all other religions, may establish, with the same ease, any particular sect of Christians in exclusion of all other sects."[14] That his arguments against the legislative interference with complete religious liberty were effective was demonstrated when the assessment plan was defeated in October 1785.

Riding the crest of this victory, the religious reformers in Virginia brought their actions to a climax by calling for a vote in January 1786 on Jefferson's Bill for Establishing Religious Freedom which had been pending in the legislature since 1779. This act represented one of the most important documents in man's lengthy struggle for freedom of conscience. It acknowledged the corrupting effect which temporal establishment has upon the religious community itself, the way in which state-enforced religious restrictions violate the natural rights of man, and the irrationality of making civil rights dependent upon religious commitments. Therefore, it provided:

> That no man shall be compelled to frequent or support any religious worship, place of ministry whatsoever, nor shall be enforced, restrained, molested, or burthened in his body or goods, nor shall otherwise suffer on account of his religious opinions or belief; but that all men shall be free to profess, and by argument to maintain, their opinions in matters of religion, and that the same shall in nowise diminish, enlarge, or affect their civil capacities.[15]

If the quest for guarantees of religious freedom was spearheaded in Virginia, it also was carried forward effectively in other states and at the federal level. By 1780, all of the states except New Hampshire adopted the principles of religious liberty which were outlined in the Virginia Bill of Rights of 1776.[16] The disestablishment of state churches was completed in 1833 with the uprooting of the Congregational church in Massachusetts. Nationally, the Declaration of Independence itself proclaimed that man has derived certain basic rights from his Creator which no government can give or take away. In the bill of rights included in the Northwest Ordinance of 1787, the Congress under the Articles of Confederation initiated the process towards freedom in religious matters as a guarantee of the central government. The Ordinance explicitly stipulated that "No person, demeaning himself in a peaceable and orderly manner, shall ever be molested on account of his mode of worship or religious sentiments, in the said territory."[17] The Federal Constitution and the Bill of Rights contained in the first ten amendments further outlined the fundamental religious rights of the citizens and the nature of church-state separation. Article VI of the Constitution insured that "no religious test shall ever be required as a qualification to any office or public trust under the United States." The First Amendment, which was ratified in December 1791 and which was to become the cornerstone of religious liberty in the United States, provided that "Congress shall make no law respecting an establishment of religion, or prohibiting the free exercise thereof."

The Protestant Consensus

The writing of these great principles of religious freedom into constitutional law during the heat of the Revolutionary era did not immediately alter the fact that the Protestant Christian thought and practice saturated the nation's governmental, religious, social, and educational institutions. None of the moves taken by the state and national governments could, or was meant to, displace the Christian faith as the predominant one in the United States. The vast majority of the populace was at least nominally Protestant and evidenced no desire to lessen Protestantism's general influence upon American government, society, or education. A divine service held in St. Paul's (Episcopal) Chapel and presided over by the chaplain of the Congress was made a part of the first inauguration of George Washington in 1789. Only Jefferson and Madison of the early presidents declined to issue proclamations appointing days for national thanksgiving and prayer. Writing to a Presbyterian minister in 1808 Jefferson explained: "I consider the government of the United States as interdicted by the Constitution from intermeddling with religious institutions, their doctrines, discipline, or exercises. . . . No power to prescribe any religious exercise, or to assume authority in religious discipline, has been delegated to the General Government."[18]

Matters regarding public education originally were left almost totally in the hands of the states, but it was apparent from the first that, provisions for religious freedom notwithstanding, on both levels of government a religious purpose would be associated with education in the early republic. The Northwest Ordinance of 1787 provided that: "Religion, morality and knowledge, being necessary to good government and the happiness of mankind, schools and the means of education shall forever be encouraged."[19] A number of the seven states which had included a section regarding education in their constitutions indicated their desire to encourage schools as a means to promote morality within a Christian context. The Massachusetts Constitution of 1780 justified its continued support of Harvard College on the basis that "the encouragement of arts and sciences and all good literature, tends to the honor of God, the advantage of the Christian religion, and the great benefit of this and the other United States of America."[20] The Vermont Constitution of 1787 suggested that:

> Laws for the encouragement of virtue, and prevention of vice and immorality, ought to be constantly kept in force, and duly executed; and a competent number of schools ought to be maintained in each town for the convenient instruction of youth; and one or more grammar schools be incorporated, and properly supported in each country in this state. And all religious societies, or bodies of men, that may be hereafter united or incorporated, for the advancement of religion and learning, or for other pious and charitable purposes, shall be encouraged and protected.[21]

The Ohio Constitution of 1802 offered a peculiar combination of the guarantee of freedom of conscience and the religious purpose of the schools. It stated:

> That all men have a natural and indefeasible right to worship Almighty God according to the dictates of their conscience; that no human authority can, in any case whatever, control or interfere with the rights of conscience; that no man shall be compelled to attend, erect, or support any place of worship, or to maintain any ministry, against his consent; and that no preference shall ever be given by law to any religious society or mode of worship; and no religious test shall be required as a qualification to any office of trust or profit. But religion, morality, and knowledge being essentially necessary to the good government and the happiness of mankind, schools and the means of instruction shall forever by encouraged by legislative provision not inconsistent with the rights of conscience.[22]

As the establishment of free, tax-supported public education became a nationwide reality during the nineteenth century, the problem of deciding when religious practices in the schools were "inconsistent with the rights of conscience" was a matter that the states and ultimately the federal government had to face. Before the Civil War the solution was relatively simple. Since the overwhelming majority of citizens were committed in some degree to one of the Protestant sects, it was felt that nonsectarian religious activities in a Protestant vein could be carried on in the schools, while the rights and consciences of the Roman Catholic, Jewish, Unitarian, and other dissenting minorities could be overlooked.

According to Caleb Bingham, each child in the reading schools of Boston before 1815 was required to read a verse from the King James Version of the Bible or a paragraph from Webster's *Third Part* every schoolday. After 1815, when Bingham's own *American Preceptor* and *Columbian Orator* replaced the Bible as a reading book, the reading master himself was required to open and close the school day with a passage from the Scriptures as a religious exercise.[23] The rules of government for the public schools of Providence, Rhode Island in 1820 admonished teachers to "endeavor to impress on the minds of the scholars a sense of the Being & Providence of God & their obligations to love & reverence Him. . . , the happy tendency of self government and obedience to the dictates of reason & religion, [and] the observance of the Sabbath as a sacred institution."[24] The New Testament continued to be a part of the reading curriculum in the Providence primary schools at least until 1827.[25] In New York, the charity school established in 1805 which formed the basis for the development of the public schools there, set as "a primary object, without observing the peculiar forms of any religious Society, to inculcate the sublime truths of religion and morality contained in the Holy Scriptures."[26]

Horace Mann, secretary of the Massachusetts state board of education from 1837 to 1848 and in many ways the father of the American public school system, conceded that "the Bible is the acknowledged expositor of Christianity" and "is in our common schools by common consent,"[27] but nevertheless he championed a liberal position concerning the question of religion in the schools. He argued staunchly that any legally recognized sectarian instruction within the public schools could serve as a roadblock to the success of the growing movement for compulsory public education. In 1847 he summarized his views:

> It is easy to see that the experiment would not stop with having half a dozen conflicting creeds taught by authority of law in the different schools of the same town or vicinity. Majorities will change in the same place. One sect may have the ascendency to-day; another tomorrow. This year there will be three Persons in the Godhead; next year but one; and the third year the Trinity will be restored to hold its precarious sovereignty until it shall be again

dethroned by the worms of the dust it has made. This year, the everlasting fires of hell will burn to terrify the impenitent; next year, and without repentance its eternal flames will be extinguished, to be rekindled forever, or to be quenched forever as it may be decided at annual town meetings. . . . In controversies involving such momentous interests, the fiercest party spirit will rage, and all the contemplations of heaven be poisoned by the passions of earth.[28]

Therefore, Mann felt that a proper solution was the continued use of the Bible in the schools as a devotional reading, but *without comment*. In his final report as Massachusetts school board secretary, he asserted that "our system earnestly inculcates all Christian morals, it founds its morals on the basis of religion; it welcomes the religion of the Bible; and in receiving the Bible, it allows it to do what it is allowed to do in no other system—to speak for itself."[29] While the growing sector of non-Protestant dissenters in the United States could not have agreed with this aspect of Mann's "liberal" philosophy, they could have agreed with another Jeffersonian-like statement which he made in the same report. "If a man is taxed to support a school where religious doctrines are inculcated which he believes to be false, and which he believes that God condemns, then he is excluded from the school by the divine law, at the same time that he is compelled to support it by the human law. This is a double wrong."[30]

Challenges to the Protestant Consensus

The massive influx of Roman Catholics from Germany and Ireland after 1840 drew national attention to the "double wrong." During the 1830's as many as 65,000 Irish came to America annually, and by the end of the 1840's the yearly figure was over 200,000. Between 1845 and the beginning of the Civil War 1,250,000 Germans entered the country and they comprised 31 percent of the total foreign-born population.[31] With this increased numerical strength the Roman Catholic Church began to press its case against the exclusive reading of the Protestant Bible in the public schools. Much of the discontent centered about the use of the King James translation whose preface in some editions expressed its purpose of giving "such a blow unto that Man of Sin [the Pope] as will not be healed."[32]

Many Catholic communities had avoided any confrontation on the Bible-reading issue by educating their children in parochial schools in the manner of many of the Protestant groups, but by the 1840's the Catholic leadership began to draw attention to the need to change the religious practices in the public schools which an increasing number of Catholic youths were attending. Bishop Francis Kenrick of Philadelphia was one of the first to speak out. In 1843 he petitioned his city's school board to permit Catholic pupils to use the Douay Version of the Bible during the required daily Bible-reading exercises. Although the board granted the request, the nativist element in the city was not satisfied with this concession. Indiscretions by groups on both sides of the issue led to a series of riots in which two Catholic churches were burned, a convent was destroyed, many houses in the Irish section were set on fire, and several lives were lost.[33]

Throughout the nation there were instances of injustice and bloodshed. For instance, a Boston priest, Father Wiget by name, in 1859 advised the children of his parish not to participate in the required weekly recitation of the Ten Commandments in the public schools. When about sixty children in one school acted upon their priest's advice, the teacher made an example of one ringleader, an eleven-year-old boy named Tom Wall. He beat the boy's hands with a three-foot long rattan stick until Tom and his fellow rebels submitted to the customary repeating of the Ten Commandments. In Indiana a Catholic school girl who refused to memorize a chapter from the King James Bible and substituted a passage from "Maud Muller" was kept after school repeatedly in a futile attempt to break her resistance.[34]

In the latter half of the nineteenth century it became apparent that the exalted principles of religious liberty championed by Jefferson and Madison and established in the bills of rights could not continue to lie dormant in the American conscience. Although many native Americans resented the fact that a heterogeneous society was being produced by the continued immigration of Roman Catholics, Jews, and people of other faiths, they could not remain totally insensitive to their pleas for equal rights of conscience in the public classrooms. Therefore, by the 1870's the first signs of a stricter application of the principles of separation of church and state began to appear. The local school board of Cincinnati, Ohio pioneered by ending the traditionally required Bible reading in the city's public schools. After a period of heated litigation, the action of the board was upheld by the Ohio Supreme Court in 1872 in a decision that was a ringing victory for the separation principle. The state court asserted that:

> Legal Christianity is a solecism, a contradiction of terms. When Christianity asks the aid of government beyond mere impartial protection, it denies itself. Its laws are divine, and not human. Its essential interests lie beyond the reach and range of human governments. United with government, religion never rises above the merest des-

potism; and all history shows us that the more widely and completely they are separated, the better it is for both.[35]

President Ulysses S. Grant expressed a similar sentiment on the national level in 1876. In an address to the Convention of the Army of the Tennessee at Des Moines he urged,

> Let us all labor to add all needful guarantees for the security of free thought, free speech, a free press, pure morals, unfettered religious sentiments, and of equal rights and privileges to all men, irrespective of nationality, color, or religion. Encourage free schools and resolve that not one dollar appropriated for their support shall be appropriated for the support of any sectarian schools. Resolve that neither the state nor the nation, nor both combined, shall support institutions of learning other than those sufficient to afford every child growing up in the land the opportunity of a good common school education, unmixed with sectarian, pagan, or atheistical dogmas. Leave the matter of religion to the family altar, the church, and the private school, supported entirely by private contributions. Keep the church and state forever separated.[36]

The first of the states to effect reforms in the direction of freedom of conscience in its schools was Wisconsin. In 1890 its Supreme Court forbade devotional Bible reading and the saying of prayers in the state-supported schools. By 1915 three other states, Nebraska, Illinois, and Louisiana, had followed the Wisconsin example.[37]

The Supreme Court and the First Amendment

Beginning in the 1920's the United States Supreme Court began to assume a share in the responsibility of protecting individual citizens from the violation of their civil rights by state-controlled agencies, including public schools. The basis for federal action was the Fourteenth Amendment which had been ratified in 1868. Citizens in the twentieth century began arguing that it bound even the states to guarantee the civil rights provided by the first ten amendments to the Constitution. Since the Fourteenth Amendment forbids the states to deprive any person of "life, liberty, or property, without due process of law," the court took the position that not only physical but also intellectual, spiritual, and aesthetic freedom must be included in the term "liberty." Under this construction, neither the states nor Congress may violate any of the provisions of the national Bill of Rights which includes the Free Exercise and Establishment of Religion Clauses of the First Amendment.[38] Since public education has always been a state rather than a federal function and only a few of the states were taking effective measures to correct the violation of religious liberties which were occurring within their own borders, this development of federal protection can hardly be overestimated. It is also important in a broader sense because it is a reflection of the recent concerns for individual rights and separation of church and state which go beyond the initial protests of the immigrant groups to include the implications of urbanization and secularization upon American culture.[39]

Therefore, since the late 1940's the decisions of the Supreme Court have made that body the center of attention in a renaissance of the ideals of Jefferson and Madison regarding church-state separation. In the 1947 parochial school bus case, *Everson* v. *Board of Education*, the court made its initial attempt to define the meaning of the founding fathers in the First Amendment, and in so doing indicated its own broad interpretation of the Establishment Clause. It suggested that:

> The "establishment of religion" clause of the First Amendment means at least this: Neither a state nor the Federal Government can set up a church. Neither can pass laws which aid one religion, aid all religions, or prefer one religion over another. Neither can force nor influence a person to go to or remain away from church against his will or force him to profess a belief or disbelief in any religion. No person can be punished for entertaining or professing religious beliefs or disbeliefs, for church attendance or non-attendance. No tax in any amount, large or small, can be levied to support any religious activities, or institutions, whatever they may be called, or whatever form they may adopt to teach or practice religion. Neither a state nor the Federal Government can, openly or secretly, participate in the affairs of any religious organizations or groups and *vice versa*. In the words of Jefferson, the clause against establishment of religion by law was intended to erect "a wall of separation between church and State."[40]

The following year, in its decision in *McCollum* v. *Board of Education*, the highest court put into effect the conviction that "the First Amendment has erected a wall between Church and State which must be kept high and impregnable."[41] It held with the plaintiff that the voluntary classes in religious instruction held during school hours under the sponsorship of the interfaith Council on Religious Education in Champaign, Illinois were in violation of the constitutional guarantees of religious liberty on three accounts. First, this instruction gave certain Protestant groups an advantage over others in propagating their doctrines. Second, although the program was officially voluntary, it included religious censorship by both the Council on Religious Education, which selected the faiths to be represented and which teachers should present them, and the school superintendent, who could reject any teacher. Although the court declared that the states must remain neutral on matters of religious indoctrination, it added that "to hold that a state cannot consistently with the First and Fourteenth Amendments utilize its public school system to aid any or all religious faiths or sects in the dissemination of their doctrines and ideals does not manifest a governmental hostility to religion or religious teachings." On the contrary, it contended that:

> A manifestation of such hostility would be at war with our national tradition as embodied in the First Amendment's guaranty of the free exercise of religion. For the First Amendment rests upon the premise that both religion and government can best work to achieve their lofty aims if each is left free from the other within its respective sphere.[42]

Since that time the Supreme Court has not lost sight of this guiding principle in matters of religion in the public schools, that is, the protection of the rights of everyone by a strictly enforced religious neutrality in the tax-supported, compulsory-attendance state school system. The three most important cases in this regard and the ones whose decisions produced the greatest shock to the Protestant consensus which still prevails in many parts of the United States were argued before the court in the decade of the 1960's. These cases are *Engle* v. *Vitale* (1962), *School District of Abington Township, Pennsylvania* v. *Schempp* (1963), and *Murray* v. *Curlett* (1963).

The School Prayer Case

The decision in *Engle* v. *Vitale* involved the right of a state to require the students in its schools to recite a particular prayer as a daily exercise. The New York State Board of Regents had composed a short "nonsectarian" prayer—"Almighty God, we acknowledge our dependence upon Thee, and we beg Thy blessings upon us, our parents, our teachers, and our country"—and had recommended that it be repeated each morning in the public schools of the state. Soon after this was adopted by the school board of New Hyde Park on Long Island, the parents of ten pupils objected. As members of the Jewish faith, the Society for Ethical Culture, the Unitarian Church, and one as a professed atheist, these complainants maintained that the prayer was repugnant to their own beliefs and to the Establishment Clause of the First Amendment.

After three New York courts upheld the Regents' prayer on the basis that any child could be excused from reciting it at the request of his parents, the matter was appealed to the United States Supreme Court. By a six to one vote the Supreme Court reversed the decisions of the New York courts and declared that this prayer was in violation of the Establishment Clause. Speaking for the majority of the court, Justice Hugo L. Black observed that "the constitutional prohibition against laws respecting an establishment of religion must at least mean that in this country, it is no part of the business of government to compose official prayers for any group of the American people to recite as a part of a religious program carried on by government."[43] Then, using examples from English and American colonial history, he traced the path of coercion, persecution, and hostility which government-enforced prayer had traveled until the time of the American Revolution. He argued:

> The First Amendment was added to the Constitution to stand as a guarantee that neither the power nor the prestige of the Federal Government would be used to control, support or influence the kinds of prayer the American people can say—that the people's religions must not be subjected to the pressures of government. . . . Under that Amendment's prohibition against governmental establishment of religion, as reinforced by the provisions of the Fourteenth Amendment, government in this country, be it state or federal, is without power to prescribe by law any particular form of prayer which is to be used as an official prayer in carrying on any program of governmentally sponsored religious activity.[44]

Therefore, in the opinion of the court, neither the nondenominational nor the voluntary quality of the Regents' prayer could free it from being "inconsistent with both the purposes of the Establishment Clause and with the Establishment Clause itself."[45]

In handing down this decision the high court expressed two concerns. The first was that no one should suppose that the New York prayer was such a minor offense to religious freedom that the court should have overlooked it. The second was that the court should not be thought of as hostile to religion or prayer because of its ruling against a state prayer which some citizens found offensive. Justice Black expressed the first concern in the following way:

> It is true that New York's establishment of its Regents' prayer as an officially approved religious doctrine of that State does not amount to a total establishment of one particular religious sect to

the exclusion of all others—that, indeed, the governmental endorsement of that prayer seems relatively insignificant when compared to the governmental encroachments upon religion which were commonplace 200 years ago. To those who may subscribe to the view that because the Regents' official prayer is so brief and general there can be no danger to religious freedom in its governmental establishment, however, it may be appropriate to say in the words of James Madison, the author of the First Amendment: "[I]t is proper to take alarm at the first experiment on our liberties. . . . Who does not see that the same authority which can establish Christianity, in exclusion of all other Religions, may establish with the same ease any particular sect of Christians, in exclusion to all other Sects? That the same authority which can force a citizen to contribute three pence only of his property for the support of any one establishment, may force him to conform to any other establishment in all cases whatsoever?"[46]

The court's sensitivity to the preservation of religion in the nation's culture was summarized in this manner:

It has been argued that to apply the Constitution in such a way as to prohibit state laws respecting an establishment of religious services in public schools is to indicate a hostility toward religion or toward prayer. Nothing, of course, could be more wrong. The history of man is inseparable from the history of religion. And perhaps it is not too much to say that since the beginning of that history many people have devoutly believed that "More things are wrought by prayer than this world dreams of." It was doubtless largely due to men who believed this that there grew up a sentiment that caused men to leave the cross-currents of officially established state religions and religious persecutions in Europe and come to this country filled with the hope that they could find a place in which they could pray where they pleased to the God of their faith in the language they chose. And there were men of this same faith in the power of prayer who led the fight for adoption of our Constitution and also for our Bill of Rights with the very guarantees of religious freedom that forbid the sort of governmental activity which New York has attempted here. These men knew that the First Amendment, which tried to put an end to governmental control of religion and of prayer, was not written to destroy either. They knew rather that it was written to quiet well-justified fears which nearly all of them felt arising out of an awareness that governments of the past had shackled men's tongues to make them speak only the religious thoughts that the government wanted them to speak and to pray only to the God that the government wanted them to pray to.[47]

Thus, the highest tribunal concluded that: "It is neither sacrilegious nor antireligious to say that each separate government in this country should stay out of the business of writing or sanctioning official prayers and leave that purely religious function to the people themselves and to those the people choose to look to for religious guidance."[48]

Regardless of the care which the court took to suggest that its purpose in the *Engle* v. *Vitale* decision was to uphold individual rights and not to abolish religion from American life, few of its pronouncements were met with a more general and vociferous negative reaction. In the days following the decision, Congress served as an open forum for the critics of the Supreme Court's stand. Much of the adverse sentiment was expressed by Southern representatives who had resented the Warren Court ever since its school desegregation decision in May 1954. Senator Herman E. Talmadge of Georgia asserted that "the Supreme Court had set up atheism as a new religion" and "put God and the Devil on an equal plane."[49] Mississippi Representative John Bell Williams had read into the *Congressional Record* a statement concerning "the ungodly decisions of the apparently godless Supreme Court" which "offers an insult to Almighty God and invites His wrath upon the people of this Nation."[50] In the summer of 1962 forty-nine different amendments to the Constitution were proposed which would permit various forms of devotional Bible reading, prayer, and other religious exercises in the public schools. One of these even came from the Conference of American Governors which met in July. An initially hostile attitude to the decision also was taken by many major leaders of the Protestant and Roman Catholic faiths. Francis Cardinal Spellman combined his discontent with the prayer decision with his own crusade for federal funds for parochial schools. Therefore, he charged that the court was making "a two-pronged attack on the American way of life" which intended "to take God out of the public school and to force the child out of the private school."[51] Episcopal Bishop James A. Pike appeared before the Senate Judiciary Committee to voice his opinion that the court ruling was not consistent with the original intent of the framers of the First Amendment. Theologian Reinhold Niebuhr, Bishop Fred P. Corson, President of the World Methodist Council, and Evangelist Billy Graham agreed that the decision was a move to secularize American society completely.[52]

Although at first the opponents of the court's opinion received a great deal of attention, its supporters manifested the sober judgment that ultimately prevailed. Speaking at a news conference on June 27, only two days after the court ruling, President Kennedy defined the basic concerns of those who concurred with the decision:

> The Supreme Court has made its judgment. A good many people obviously will disagree with it; others will agree with it. But I think that it is important for us, if we're going to maintain our constitutional principle, that we support Supreme Court decisions even when we may not agree with them.
>
> In addition, we have in this case a very easy remedy, and that is to pray ourselves. And I would think that it would be a welcome reminder to every American family that we can pray a good deal more at home, we can attend our churches with a good deal more fidelity, and we can make the true meaning of prayer much more important in the lives of all of our children. That power is very much open to us. And I would hope that, as a result of this decision, that all American parents will intensify their efforts at home. And the rest of us will support the Constitution and the responsibility of the Supreme Court in interpreting it.[53]

In addition to the Jewish, Unitarian, and other traditionally liberal-oriented religious groups which one would expect to favor the decision, there was immediate support from some Baptists, a large section of the Methodists, and the editors of the ordinarily conservative evangelical journal, *Christianity Today.* Speaking for the Baptist Joint Committee on Public Affairs, Dr. C. Emmanuel Carlson argued that:

> When one thinks of prayer as sincere outreach of a human soul to the Creator, "required prayer" becomes an absurdity. The "recitation of a prayer" has been called morally uplifting without recognizing that hypocrisy is the worst of moral corrosion. Some have felt that our "national heritage" is in danger, without realizing that the distinctive of our heritage is not legislated prayer but a people praying in freedom under the guidance of their church and of the Spirit of God.[54]

The *Christian Century* found thirty-one Protestant leaders from twelve denominations, including a past president of the National Council of Churches, three Methodist bishops, the president of the Southern Baptist Convention, and a Presbyterian editor, who were willing to take the following stand for the prayer decision: "We believe the court's ruling against officially written and officially prescribed prayers protects the integrity of the religious conscience and the proper function of religious and governmental institutions."[55] *Christianity Today* advised that "a second look should lead all critics to second thoughts about the Supreme Court decision. It can be defended, and commended, as compatible both with a proper Christian attitude toward government stipulation of religious exercises, and with a sound philosophical view of freedom."[56] As more and more clergymen, religious publications, and secular newspapers came out in favor of the ruling, most of the politicians also swung into line as the fall elections of 1962 approached.

The Bible-Reading Cases

While the initial protest regarding the Regents' prayer decision was resolving itself into a few scattered waves of controversy, the Supreme Court heard two new cases which were to have a more sweeping impact on religion in the public schools than any previous attempt to apply the Free Exercise and Establishment Clauses. One of the cases, *School District of Abington Township, Pennsylvania* v. *Schempp*, grew out of a suit which was brought by the Unitarian parents of two children who attended high school in Abington. By Pennsylvania law ten verses of the Bible were read without comment by teachers and students at the opening of each school day. Edward Schempp objected to this practice as a violation of the First Amendment, but refused to ask that his children be excused from the room during the exercise because this might cause the other students to think of them as "odd balls" and even atheists or communists. The other case, *Murray* v. *Curlett*, was initiated by an avowed atheist, Mrs. Madalyn E. Murray, whose son attended the public schools of Baltimore. Her objection was to a 1905 Maryland school board ruling which required that classes be opened each day with the "reading, without comment, of a chapter in the Holy Bible and/or the use of the Lord's Prayer."[57] By agreeing to hear this and the Schempp case, the highest tribunal in the land accepted the responsibility of deciding the constitutionality of both the required reading of sectarian scriptures and the reciting of sectarian prayers in the public schools of the nation.

Months before the Supreme Court gave its single decision for both cases on June 17, 1963, it was obvious that many, if not most, Americans had come to recognize the detrimental implications of judicially-sanctioned devotional Bible reading and prayer in the schools and thus were anticipating the court's negative reaction. As early as October 1962, the editors of the *Christian Century* expressed the hope that the court would "strike down" the regulations in the states which had established the use of sectarian readings and prayer. They observed that "any other decision would not only breach the church-state wall but would also open the doors of the public schools to practices which abrogate the rights of minorities and which tend to embroil the churches in bitter, insoluble controversy."[58] They summarized the potential effects of such a situation in a very compelling fashion:

> If the court should decide that the reading of the Bible as a devotional exercise and the repetition of the Lord's Prayer are practices consistent with the intent of the First Amendment, tormenting and divisive questions will rise. What version of the Bible will be used—the Douay, the King James, the Revised Standard? Who will decide what ten verses should be read? The teacher? Can a public school teacher, an employee of the state, select a passage of Scripture for a public school class without violating the Constitution? Shall the children select the reading? Imaginative young people have been known to select passages of Scripture which appeal to their prurient rather than to their spiritual interests. Would not Jews demand readings from the Old Testament; Christian Scientists readings from *Science and Health*; Mormons, from the *Book of Mormon*? Which Lord's Prayer? When the Roman Catholic children complete their Pater Noster will they remain reverently quiet while the Protestant children add ". . . the kingdom and the power and the glory forever . . ."? Meanwhile, what about the Jews, the Unitarians, the atheists, the Moslems, the Hindus—have they no choice but to listen daily to Christian prayer or to suffer the embarrassment of withdrawing from the presence of their schoolmaster? Why should random passages of Scripture be read to children without comment? Is the Bible a talisman, a cabalistic charm? There will be no end to such questions and no end to the controversies they will raise.[59]

Church organizations also spoke out on this question. The General Assembly of the United Presbyterian Church in May 1963 adopted a resolution opposing religious practices such as Bible reading and prayer in the state school systems. As spokesman for the resolution, the Rev. Nevin Kendall said: "Public schools should not be part-time churches but full-time public schools. We dare not identify ourselves with people who insist on using a majority position to cram their religion down their neighbor's throat."[60] Ten days before the Schempp and Murray decision was handed down, the National Council of Churches, representing thirty Protestant and Orthodox groups with over forty million members, published the following policy statement dealing with religion in the public schools:

> Neither the church nor the state should use the public school to compel acceptance of any creed or conformity to any specific religious

practice. . . . We warn the churches against the all-too-human tendency to look to the state and its agencies for support in fulfilling
the churches' mission. Such a tendency endangers both true religion
and civil liberties.[61]

On June 17, 1963 the Supreme Court gave its own reasons why the
state must not promote mandatory religious observances, and, while
everyone was not in agreement, few were surprised by the decision. The
ruling followed the basic pattern of interpretation which the court has
followed since the Everson case of 1946 and declared the Pennsylvania
and Maryland statutes unconstitutional under the Establishment Clause
of the First Amendment as applied to the states through the Fourteenth
Amendment. After reviewing the facts in the cases, Justice Tom C. Clark
who wrote the majority opinion in the eight to one decision made the
point that the American national heritage is one which combines both
religious commitment and religious freedom:

> It is true that religion has been closely identified with our history
> and government. . . . The fact that the Founding Fathers believed
> devotedly that there was a God and that the unalienable rights of
> man were rooted in Him is clearly evidenced in their writings, from
> the Mayflower Compact to the Constitution itself. This background
> is evidenced today in our public life through the continuance in our
> oaths of office from the Presidency to the Alderman of the final sup-
> plication, "So help me God." Likewise each House of the Congress
> provides through its Chaplain an opening prayer, and the sessions of
> this Court are declared open by the crier in a short ceremony, the
> final phrase of which invokes the grace of God. Again, there are such
> manifestations in our military forces, where those of our citizens who
> are under the restrictions of military service wish to engage in vol-
> untary worship. Indeed, only last year an official survey of the coun-
> try indicated that 64% of our people have church membership . . . ,
> while less than 3% profess no religion whatever. It can be truly said,
> therefore, that today, as in the beginning, our national life reflects a
> religious people who, in the words of Madison, are "earnestly pray-
> ing . . . , that the Supreme Law-giver of the Universe . . . guide them
> into every measure which may be worthy of his [blessing. . . .]"
>
> This is not to say, however, that religion has been so identified
> with our history and government that religious freedom is not like-
> wise as strongly imbedded in our public and private life. Nothing
> but the most telling of personal experiences in religious persecution
> suffered by our forebears . . . , could have planted our belief in lib-

erty of religious opinion any more deeply in our heritage. It is true that this liberty frequently was not realized by the colonists, but this is readily accountable to their close ties to the Mother Country. However, the views of Madison and Jefferson, preceded by Roger Williams, came to be incorporated not only in the Federal Constitution but likewise in those of most of our States. This freedom to worship was indispensable in a country whose people came from the four quarters of the earth and brought with them a diversity of religious opinion. Today authorities list 83 separate religious bodies, each with membership exceeding 50,000, existing among our people, as well as innumerable smaller groups.[62]

Then he outlined the function of the First Amendment in the maintenance of the American system of religious freedom. Quoting Justice Wiley B. Rutledge in an earlier decision, Clark asserted that: "The [First] Amendment's purpose was not to strike merely at the official establishment of a single sect, creed or religion. . . . But the object was broader than separating church and state in this narrow sense. It was to create a complete and permanent separation of the spheres of religious activity and civil authority by comprehensively forbidding every form of public aid or support for religion."[63] Justice Clark argued further that, as the court had stated in the Everson case, this "requires the state to be a neutral in its relations with groups of religious believers and non-believers."[64] In the court's opinion this:

> Wholesome "neutrality" . . . stems from a recognition of the teachings of history that powerful sects or groups might bring about a fusion of governmental and religious functions or a concert or dependency of one upon the other to the end that official support of the State or Federal Government would be placed behind the tenets of one or of all orthodoxies. This the Establishment Clause prohibits. And a further reason for neutrality is found in the Free Exercise Clause, which recognizes the value of religious training, teaching and observance and, more particularly, the right of every person to freely choose his own course with reference thereto, free of any compulsion from the state.[65]

The high tribunal maintained that one simple test can determine the validity of statutes under the First Amendment: "what are the purpose and the primary effect of the enactment? If either is the advancement or inhibition of religion then the enactment exceeds the scope of legislative power as circumscribed by the Constitution."[66] Applying this test, the court found that the Pennsylvania and Maryland laws prescribing daily

Bible reading and recitation of the Lord's Prayer "as part of the curricular activities of students who are required by law to attend school" is an establishment of religion and therefore unconstitutional.[67]

As in *Engle* v. *Vitale*, the Supreme Court on this occasion emphasized that it was acting to protect religious liberty and freedom of conscience, not to favor secularism over religious belief. Justice Clark observed:

> It is insisted that unless these religious exercises are permitted a "religion of secularism" is established in the schools. We agree of course that the State may not establish a "religion of secularism" in the sense of affirmatively opposing or showing hostility to religion, thus "preferring those who believe in no religion over those who do believe." We do not agree, however, that this decision in any sense has that effect.[68]

In fact, he declared that "one's education is not complete without a study of comparative religion or the history of religion and its relationship to the advancement of civilization." He added that "the Bible is worthy of study for its literary and historic qualities. Nothing we have said here indicates that such study of the Bible or of religion, when presented objectively as part of a secular program of education, may not be effected consistently with the First Amendment."[69]

Justice William J. Brennan, Jr., in his concurring opinion which masterfully traced the historical and legal facets of the issues in question, reinforced Justice Clark's estimation of the non-devotional use of the Bible in the public schools. "The holding of the court today," he affirmed, "plainly does not foreclose teaching *about* the Holy Scriptures or about the differences between religious sects in classes in literature or history. Indeed, whether or not the Bible is involved, it would be impossible to teach meaningfully many subjects in the social sciences or the humanities without some mention of religion."[70] The concurring opinion of Justice Arthur J. Goldberg emphasized the same idea by quoting from the *Engle* v. *Vitale* ruling which states that:

> There is of course nothing in the decision reached here that is inconsistent with the fact that school children and others are officially encouraged to express love for our country by reciting historical documents such as the Declaration of Independence which contain references to the Deity or by singing officially espoused anthems which include the composer's professions of faith in a Supreme Being, or with the fact that there are many manifestations in our public life of belief in God. Such patriotic or ceremonial occasions bear no true

resemblance to the unquestioned religious exercise that the State . . . has sponsored in this instance.[71]

Finally, the Schempp and Murray decision defined the limitation which the lofty principles of the Free Exercise Clause has placed upon the majority itself in the American democracy. The Supreme Court stated that it could not "accept that the concept of neutrality, which does not permit a State to require a religious exercise even with the consent of the majority of those affected, collides with the majority's right to free exercise of religion." In the tribunal's opinion, "While the Free Exercise Clause clearly prohibits the use of state action to deny the rights of free exercise to *anyone*, it has never meant that a majority could use the machinery of the State to practice its beliefs."[72] Quoting from a previous decision by Justice Robert H. Jackson, the court reemphasized that: "The very purpose of a Bill of Rights was to withdraw certain subjects from the vicissitudes of political controversy, to place them beyond the reach of majorities and officials and to establish them as legal principles to be applied by the courts. One's right to . . . freedom of worship . . . and other fundamental rights may not be submitted to vote; they depend on the outcome of no elections."[73] Thus, the Supreme Court, by its continued enforcement of the First Amendment, was taking cognizance of the fact that both religion and the individual hold places of highest esteem in the American way of life. In conclusion the spokesman for the court stated:

> The place of religion in our society is an exalted one, achieved through a long tradition of reliance on the theme, the church and the inviolable citadel of the individual heart and mind. We have come to recognize through bitter experience that it is not within the power of government to invade that citadel, whether its purpose or effect be to aid or oppose, to advance or retard. In the relationship between man and religion, the State is firmly committed to a position of neutrality. Though the application of that rule requires interpretation of a delicate sort, the rule itself is clearly and concisely stated in the words of the First Amendment.[74]

An Evangelical Response to Religion in the Schools

Both court decisions have implications for the current evangelical attitude, and that of other religious groups as well, concerning state-sponsored religious activities in the public schools. The homogeneous Protestant environment in which the first public and charity schools were begun in colonial America stands in sharp contrast to the heterogeneous religious environment in which today's public schools exist. Not only have the minority religious groups multiplied in size and number, but also the American conscience has become increasingly more sensitive to the rights of the individual. Therefore, it is no longer consistent with the nature of this society or its concept of justice to permit any religious body to use the public schools as a device to indoctrinate children in the tenets of its own particular faith. The concern for religious freedom has not grown out of a desire by the state to tyrannize over religion or to eradicate it from national life, but rather it has come mainly from the desire of the religious community to preserve for its exclusive use the spiritual arena. As contemporary society has become increasingly pluralistic, one is forced to the position that Christianity itself must be considered a "sect" which cannot expect, and should not desire, state support any more than any other faith. In his concurring decision in the Schempp and Murray cases, Justice Brennan noted that in an earlier case the Illinois Supreme Court had recognized that "the Bible, in its entirety, is a sectarian book as to the Jew and every believer in any religion other than the Christian religion, and as to those who are heretical or who hold beliefs that are not regarded as orthodox . . . its use in the schools necessarily results in sectarian instruction."[75]

Voluntarism for the individual in all religious matters is a cherished principle which originated in America during the time of the Revolution and which puts every faith on an equal footing in seeking adherents and support. Violation of this ideal in any way by either the church or the state injures the unique place which religion and the individual hold in American society. By its very nature, the public school has been a focal point for coercion of the dissenting individual by majority religious groups. Where else can be found a captive audience of impressionable children drawn from the whole community? But the church has gradually come to realize that this is neither a legitimate nor an effective method of disseminating the gospel or securing members. The Great Commission of Christ to go and teach all nations his commandments certainly did not imply the solicitation of state aid or the coercion of people to hear the message against their will. The formal and compulsory recitation of a sectarian prayer by a group of pupils and the reading of verses from the Bible by a teacher or student without comment are not commensurate with the spirit of the divine command. Episcopal Bishop Brooke Mosley admitted that until the 1963 Supreme Court decision he "had assumed that since prayer is good, prayer in schools must be good too," but since then he had come to feel that:

> Even the simplest prayer, when supervised by the teacher in a public school—the authority symbol—is a subtle form of coercion. Prayer

is the expression of a personal relationship between a human being and the God he worships. . . . It is as wrong to force a person to pray as to force him to marry someone he doesn't love. Even for the majority group, classroom prayer—sometimes piped in by a public-address system from the principal's office—may well become no more than a magical incantation. Prayer is entering into a conversation with God—it's listening as well as speaking. That can't be achieved by a rote prayer in a public-school classroom. And Bible reading without comment can be just as valueless.[76]

Recent research has brought to light the fact that the short devotional exercises in the public schools have a very minimal effect upon the students. Three studies of religiously-oriented Catholic and Lutheran parochial schools have shown that even in such protected and enriched atmospheres the students show no greater advancement toward ethical behavior than do similar students who attend the public schools.[77]

In the light of these findings, *Eternity* magazine was absolutely correct in concluding that in the Schempp and Murray decision the Supreme Court did the church a favor by taking away "the rubber crutch" of ineffective religious activities in the schools.[78] Because of this, the church has rediscovered the vast array of opportunities which it possesses in a free society to propagate the faith effectively without having to give up part of its responsibility or its rights to the state which is in no way equipped to carry out the spiritual role of the church. The Rev. Dean Lewis, Secretary for Social Education of the United Presbyterian Church, emphasized that parents must realize "you can't pay your debt to God by having your children mumble a two-minute prayer in school."[79] The obligation must be met by exploiting every resource and activating every function of the family and the church to inculcate religious values and to seek converts on a personal basis. A family unit in which the love of Christ prevails is an invaluable foundation for Christian outreach. This is the place where prayer, Bible reading, and counseling can take on their most poignant meanings—without any interference or aid from the state. On a larger scale, the avenues of outreach for the church under the guarantees of the First Amendment are innumerable. The church is free to assemble, preach, win converts, publish and distribute literature, educate its adherents in its own schools and colleges, possess and use property, raise and spend funds, and create associations for the study and propagation of its beliefs. No extension of activity into an area under state control is necessary or desirable to further the cause of the Christian faith. As far as the public schools are concerned, it is highly significant that the Supreme Court in the Schempp and Murray decision declared the study of comparative religion, the history of religion and its relationship to the advancement of civilization, and the Bible for its literary and historic qualities is completely legitimate. Religious instruction, however, is to be conducted in the homes and churches where no one's rights will be violated and where personal faith can take on its true meaning.

Those sincere individuals who are still advocating the amendment of the Constitution in order to permit the practice of state-sponsored devotional Bible reading and prayer in the public school systems are unwittingly calling for the establishment of a meaningless "cultural" or "patriotic" religion. By their very nature any religious exercises devised by the state to satisfy virtually everyone cannot be considered true religion. Nevertheless, the participants may be deceived into thinking of themselves as religious or Christian because they have gone through forms which appear to be religious or Christian. Such insipid ritualism cannot be tolerated as a substitute for the vital conversion experience and committed Christian life which the evangelical community envisages as the standard for true religion. In this connection, Dr. Ben Sissil, Secretary for National Affairs of the United Presbyterian Church, has warned against "patriotism faith" which he feels is more harmful to Biblical faith than idol worship. Forcefully but effectively he asserts:

> When men bowed down to idols of stone and wood at least this was obvious idolatry. Much more subtle is the modern idolatry, where we make profession of faith an object of worship. We surround ourselves with symbols, with the outward signs of piety—sanctimonious slogans on coins, prayers for every public occasion—and feel that is enough. We have faith, we say virtuously. But it is a poor substitute for the real thing.[80]

So long as the First Amendment remains unaltered to insure separation of church and state and protection of individual freedom of conscience, the future of Christianity in the United States will be secure. If vital religion promoted by vigorous churches under the direction of the Spirit of God cannot flourish in an atmosphere of religious liberty, it could not do so under conditions of state support. During the difficult struggle for religious liberty in Virginia, Thomas Jefferson declared profoundly that: "It is error alone which needs the support of government. Truth can stand by itself."[81]

NOTES

1. Ellwood P. Cubberley, *Public Education in the United States* (Boston: Houghton Mifflin, 1934), p. 41.

2. R. Freeman Butts, *A Cultural History of Education* (Boston: Houghton Mifflin, 1947), pp. 296–97.

3. *Ibid.*, pp. 294–95.

4. Ellwood P. Cubberley, *Readings in Public Education in the United States* (Boston: Houghton Mifflin, 1934), pp. 18–19, 64.

5. *Ibid.*, pp. 45–51.

6. Cubberley, *Public Education in the United States*, p. 41.

7. Anson P. Stokes and Leo Pfeffer, *Church and State in the United States* (New York: Harper & Row, 1964), pp. 264–65.

8. Ellwood P. Cubberley, *Readings in the History of Education* (Boston: Houghton Mifflin, 1920), p. 369.

9. Anson P. Stokes, *Church and State in the United States* (New York: Harper, 1950), I, p. 274.

10. *Ibid.*, I, pp. 368–76.

11. *Ibid.*, I, p. 303.

12. *Ibid.*, I, p. 376.

13. Stokes and Pfeffer, *Church and State*, p. 56.

14. *Ibid.*, pp. 56–57.

15. *Ibid.*, p. 70.

16. Robert R. Rutland, *The Birth of the Bill of Rights* (Chapel Hill: University of North Carolina Press, 1955), pp. 41–42. The colonial charters of Connecticut and Rhode Island already contained such guarantees. The other states enacted them either as a part of their new constitutions or as separate bills of rights.

17. Henry Steele Commager, ed., *Documents of American History* (7th ed., New York: Appleton-Century-Crofts, 1963), I, p. 130.

18. Stokes and Pfeffer, *Church and State*, pp. 87–89. President Adams proclaimed May 9, 1798 a day of prayer to save America from the influx of the liberal ideas of the French Revolution which Jefferson generally embraced.

19. Commager, *Documents of American History*, I, p. 131.

20. Massachusetts, *Constitution* (1780), Chap. 5, Art. 1.

21. Vermont, *Constitution* (1787), Chap. 2, sec. 38.

22. Ohio, *Constitution*, Art. 8, sec. 3.

23. Cubberley, *Readings in the History of Education*, pp. 545–46.

24. *Ibid.*, p. 549.

25. *Ibid.*, p. 636.

26. *Ibid.*, p. 553.

27. *The Life and Works of Horace Mann* (Boston: Lee and Shepard, 1891), IV, p. 316.

28. Cubberley, *Readings in the History of Education*, p. 575.

29. *Life and Works of Horace Mann*, IV, pp. 311–12.

30. *Ibid.*, IV, p. 313.

31. Carl Wittke, *We Who Built America* (New York: Prentice-Hall, 1939), pp. 130–31, 187–88.

32. Arthur Frommer, ed., *The Bible and the Public Schools* (New York: Pocket Books, 1963), p. 26.

33. Stokes, *Church and State in the United States*, I, p. 830.

34. Frommer, *Bible and Public Schools*, pp. 27–28.

35. *Ibid.*, pp. 28–29.

36. Donald E. Boles, *The Bible, Religion, and the Public Schools* (Ames: Iowa State University Press, 1965), pp. 30–31.

37. Chester J. Antieau, *et. al.*, *Religion under the State Constitutions* (Brooklyn, N.Y.: Central Book Co., 1965), p. 53.

38. Stokes and Pfeffer, *Church and State*, pp. 100–101.

39. See Harvey Cox, *The Secular City* (New York: Macmillan, 1965).

40. 330 U.S. pp. 15, 16 (1947). Nevertheless, the court ruled in this case that tax monies could be used to transport children to parochial schools.

41. 333 U.S. p. 212 (1948).

42. *Ibid.*, pp. 211–12.

43. 370 U.S. p. 425 (1962).

44. *Ibid.*, pp. 429–30.

45. *Ibid.*, p. 433.

46. *Ibid.*, p. 436.

47. *Ibid.*, pp. 433–35.

48. *Ibid.*, p. 435.

49. *Congressional Record*, 87th Cong., 2d Sess., 1962, CVIII, Part 13, p. 17590.

50. *Ibid.*, p. A5957.

51. *New York Times*, Aug. 3, 1962, p. 21.

52. Paul Blanshard, *Religion and the Schools: The Great Controversy* (Boston: Beacon Press, 1963), pp. 57–58, 64–65.

53. *New York Times*, June 28, 1962, p. 12.

54. U.S., Congress, Senate, Committee on the Judiciary, *Hearings, Prayer in Public Schools and Other Matters*, 87th Cong., 2d Sess., 1962, p. 107.

55. "Churchmen Support Supreme Court," *Christian Century*, LXXIX (July 18, 1962), p. 882.

56. "Supreme Court Prayer Ban: Where Will It Lead?" *Christianity Today*, VI (July 20, 1962), pp. 25–26.

57. 374 U.S. pp. 205–09, 211–12 (1963).

58. "Prayers, Bibles, and Schools," *Christian Century*, LXXIX (Oct. 24, 1962), p. 1279.

59. *Ibid.*, pp. 1279–80.

60. "School Prayers? The Presbyterians Say 'No,'" *U.S. News and World Report*, LIV (June 3, 1963), p. 10.

61. "Supreme Court Decision on Bible Reading and Prayer Recitation—Comments by Lay and Religious Leaders," *National Education Association Journal*, LII, (Sep. 1963), 56. Within a year after the court decision, leaders from the following churches had taken official stands in favor of the ruling: Protestant Episcopal, American Baptist, Southern Baptist, American Lutheran, Methodist, Lutheran Church in America, Missouri Synod Lutheran, United Church of Christ, United Presbyterian, and Disciples of Christ. See Arlene and Howard Eisenberg, "Why Clergymen Are Against School Prayer," *Redbook*, CXXIV (Jan. 1965), p. 38.

62. 374 U.S. pp. 212–14 (1963).

63. *Ibid.*, p. 217.

64. *Ibid.*, p. 218.

65. *Ibid.*, p. 222.

66. *Loc. cit.*

67. *Ibid.*, p. 223.

68. *Ibid.*, p. 225.

69. *Loc. cit.*

70. *Ibid.*, p. 300.

71. *Ibid.*, pp. 307–08.

72. *Ibid.*, pp. 225–26.

73. *Ibid.*, p. 226. This is an effective answer to the question raised by Evangelist Billy Graham: "Eighty percent of the American people want Bible reading and prayer in the schools. . . . Why should the majority be so severely penalized by the protests of a handful?" Quoted in *National Educational Association Journal*, LII, p. 56.

74. 374 U.S. p. 226 (1963).

75. *Ibid.*, p. 282n.

76. Eisenberg, *Redbook*, CXXIV, p. 97.

77. Andrew M. Greeley and Peter H. Rossi, *The Education of Catholic Americans* (Chicago: Aldine, 1966); *Catholic Schools in Action: The Notre Dame Study of Catholic Elementary and Secondary Schools in the United States* (South Bend:

University of Notre Dame Press, 1966); and Ronald L. Johnstone, *The Effectiveness of Lutheran Elementary and Secondary Schools as Agencies of Christian Education* (St. Louis: Concordia Seminary, 1966).

78. Cited in Eisenberg, *Redbook*, CXXIV, p. 104.

79. *Ibid.*, pp. 96–97.

80. *Ibid.*, p. 96.

81. *Notes on the State of Virginia* quoted in Stokes, *Church and State in the United States*, I, p. 384.

Earl J. Reeves is Associate Professor of Political Science at the University of Missouri at St. Louis. He was born on March 16, 1933 at Muskogee, Oklahoma and obtained his undergraduate training at the University of Wichita where he was awarded the B.A. degree in 1954. He earned an M.A. in 1959 at the University of Wichita and a Ph.D. in political science at the University of Kansas in 1962. Mr. Reeves taught at the University of Kansas for three years and then served as an assistant professor at the University of Omaha, 1962–64. He was appointed to an associate professorship at the University of Missouri at St. Louis in 1964 and was named Acting Director of the Center of Community and Metropolitan Studies at this institution in 1965.

He is author of the *1960 Kansas Voters Guide* and the *1962 Kansas Voters Guide*, published by the Governmental Research Center, University of Kansas. He has also contributed articles to Richard L. Stauber, ed., *Approaches to the Study of Urbanization* and the *Midwest Review of Public Administration*, and he edited the *Report on the Inter-University Seminar on Urban Extension* (1966). He is a member of a number of professional organizations, including the American Political Science Association, Midwest Conference of Political Scientists, Missouri Political Science Association, American Society for Public Administration, and American Association of University Professors. He is currently Vice-President of the St. Louis Metropolitan Chapter of the American Society for Public Administration.

Professor Reeves is quite active in civic life in Berkeley, Missouri. He was chairman of a bond issue committee in his city, and he is currently Vice-President of the Berkeley City Council and engaged in developing research and training programs for local officials. He has also served on the Committee to Extend the Merit System to employees of St. Louis County and has worked for county and regional parks as a member of the Open Space Council. Mr. Reeves is a member of his local United Presbyterian Church, and he is active in a variety of interdenominational religious activities, including teaching a graduate seminar in urban problems at the Eden Theological Seminary in St. Louis.

EARL J. REEVES

The Population Explosion
and Christian Concern

On October 26, 1966 evangelical Christians from around the
world met in the Berlin Congress Hall for a World Congress on Evangelism. One of the dominant features in the Hall for this conference was
a population clock. This giant thirty foot display flashed pictures of
eleven babies every second to dramatize the rapidity of the growth of the
world's population. So great is the rate of increase that it was estimated
that the population of the world increased by two million persons during the ten days the Congress was in session.[1]

The main purpose of this great population clock was to remind the
delegates that the population of the world is rapidly outstripping the
churches' efforts to fulfill the great commission. And the explosive nature
of the population increase of recent decades does present the evangelical
Christian with a great challenge to carry the gospel more effectively and
more quickly than ever before.

But the rapid increase in the world's population presents other problems as well and these too represent a great challenge to all men, including the evangelical Christian. For example, the rate of population
increase is so great that we are haunted by the spectre of a world so
crowded with people that life becomes impossible or at least unbearable.
There is some disagreement about the extent of the threat and some
question about the precise timetable but the possibility of a world filled
with starving, overcrowded masses of people as a result of the awesome
prolificacy of human reproduction is far too real to be ignored.

The Dangers of Present Population Trends

In this century the population of the world has risen from about a
billion and a half to over three billion. If the present population trends

183

continue without significant change, it is estimated that the world population will double again by the end of this century, giving us a population of between 6 and 8 billion persons.

There is no agreement on precisely how many people the world can contain. Some optimists contend that the "world of 100 years hence with its population of perhaps some 20 billion people will be able to feed itself, provided that most people live in cities and offer enough money for the production of their food."[2] Others, taking a more pessimistic view, contend that the question is not merely whether man can survive in a world of 20 billion people but whether it would be worthwhile to survive in such a world. Furthermore, they note that this population explosion is not taking place at a uniform rate throughout the world. The more advanced industrial nations have a much lower rate of increase than do the non-industrial developing nations. These nations are much less able to cope with the problem. In fact, for much of the world the question is not whether the population will exceed the food supply by 2068 or even by 2000 but, according to one recent study, possibly by as soon as 1975.[3] In some parts of India, famine is perilously close to reality even today.

Nearly two centuries ago Thomas Malthus, an English clergyman, took note of two basic principles: first, "that food is necessary to the existence of man;" and second, "that the passion between the sexes is necessary and will remain nearly in its present state." On the basis of these two principles he concluded that "the power of population is indefinitely greater than the power in the earth to produce subsistence for man."[4] The only thing that had prevented the total population of the world from outracing the food supply was vice, disease and famine.

> The power of population is so superior to the power in the earth to produce subsistence for man that premature death must in some shape or other visit the human race. The vices of mankind are active and able ministers of depopulation. They are the precursors in the great army of destruction and often finish the dreadful work themselves. But should they fail in this war of extermination, sickly seasons, epidemics, pestilence, plague advance in terrific array and sweep off their thousands and ten thousands. Should success be still incomplete, gigantic inevitable famine stalks in the rear and with one mighty blow levels the population with the food of the world.[5]

Malthus apparently felt that only the "natural" processes of misery, vice, and famine could restrain the pressure of population growth. Therefore he contended that all attempts to ameliorate the living conditions of those at the bottom of the economic system were not only foolish and self-defeating but even dangerous as they could only encourage an increasing population which would leave man's later condition worse than the present. Therefore he rejected the possibility of any effective political intervention in the natural order. About the only possible way to deal with the problem, he felt, was to lower the birth rate through late marriage and by sexual abstinence within marriage. Even here he believed that the pressure of the passions would overcome the dictates of reason.

Methods of Limiting Population Growth

Abstention and late marriage are not likely to prove very helpful in family planning as they tend to run counter to nature, and if the hope of population control was limited to these two devices the hope would indeed be slim. But the possibility of preventing overpopulation by controlling the birthrate is, nonetheless, regarded today as one of the best hopes of mankind. And in fact, the modern advances in methods of contraception do make family planning a real possibility, at least in the developed nations.

Even in earlier times techniques of birth control were known and used. Withdrawal or *coitus interruptus* is one of the oldest and most widely accepted devices for avoiding pregnancy. It was extensively used in western and northern Europe and in fact was apparently the principal method by which pregnancy was avoided in premarital love affairs. The practice was carried into married life, on a scale sufficient to depress the birthrate, in France and other European countries during the eighteenth and nineteenth centuries.[6] Another older technique was the use of douching or flushing out the vagina with water in order to remove the semen. Both withdrawal and douching had the advantage of being inexpensive and available. But both were risky, with a high potential for failure and both raised serious questions about interference with the complete psychological satisfaction of sexual intercourse. Therefore, even in earlier times a third technique, one which is much more closely related to some modern methods, was developed. This method involved plugging the upper vagina with leaves, sponges, or other barriers. This form of contraception again is inexpensive and easily secured. But it may be psychologically offensive and it is only moderately effective in preventing conception.

In recent years the desire for smaller families in the economically more advanced nations has spurred a renewed interest in contraception. One technique which has been endorsed by some religious groups, especially the Roman Catholic Church, is the rhythm method. This is based on the fact that a woman normally releases only one fertilizable egg during each menstrual cycle. This egg has an active life of around twelve hours and a man's sperm generally lives about forty-eight hours. Therefore, a woman can only become pregnant during a period of approximately sixty hours each month, and if intercourse is avoided during this time, normal relations can be enjoyed during the rest of the month without serious risk of pregnancy.

Unfortunately, there is as yet no certain way of knowing exactly when this safe period occurs. Because most women are somewhat irregular in their menstrual cycle, the sixty hour period must be expanded considerably to provide a margin of safety. It is necessary, therefore, for those who use this method to rely on formulae based on the average length of the menstrual cycle in order to determine the safe period. Dr. Alan Guttmacher, President of the Planned Parenthood Association, argues in his excellent book on birth control that the rhythm method is far better than no method at all but less effective than other techniques which are now available.

Substantial progress has been made in recent years in developing "mechanical" devices which prevent conception either by preventing the semen from entering the vagina through the use of a condom or from entering the womb through the use of a diaphragm. Both of these devices are highly reliable but they require some advance preparation which may, in the case of the condom, interfere with the normal process of the sex act. These devices have also been supplemented by jellies, foams, and tablets which combine a certain blocking function with a spermicidal agent.

A variation on the process of mechanically blocking the entry of the sperm into the womb is the intrauterine device (IUD). This device is a ring, which may be made of silver wire, silkworm gut, or plastic, and is inserted semi-permanently into the cavity of the womb. The ring is far superior to the diaphragm in that it can be left in place for a year or more. The IUD is quite effective in preventing pregnancy but it may be somewhat painful to have it inserted and it does require the assistance of a physician. There have also been instances of the IUD working loose and either being expelled from the body or in some rare instances eroding through the uterus into adjacent tissues where it can cause painful complications. In spite of its drawbacks the IUD is generally convenient and it has been widely used in Taiwan, Ceylon, India, and Mexico because once it is inserted, the woman does not need to take additional precautions.

By far the most dramatic and significant development in the contraceptive process is the development of the oral contraceptive, now simply known as the "pill." A cover story in *Time* hailed this new development with the statement that "in a mere six years it has changed and liberated the sex and family life of a large and still growing segment of the U.S. population: eventually, it promises to do the same for much of the world."[7] There are about a dozen variations of "the pill" but their basic effect is two-fold: first, they regularize a woman's monthly cycle and secondly, they prevent ovulation, making pregnancy impossible by preventing the release of a fertilizable egg from the woman's ovaries.

The pill has only been available for about six years and in its early stages popular acceptance was hampered by the fear of possible dangerous side effects. But after several years of use and continuing intensive research programs, the evidence is overwhelming that the only significant side effects are possible increase in weight for some women and occasional nausea (similar to "morning sickness") for others. There has been absolutely no evidence identifying the pill as a cause of cancer or blood clots as was originally feared. And in addition to preventing pregnancy they may even help a woman in making the menopause adjustment.

Because of its convenience and almost 100 percent guarantee against pregnancy the pill has been widely accepted in the United States and some of the other industrial nations, and major efforts are being undertaken to introduce it in the underdeveloped areas where population growth is greatest. While the current pill represents a highly successful device, further research is being conducted which may result in the development of injections or implants which could give longer lasting protection and eliminate the counting of days. Some researchers are working on a one-shot "morning after" pill for the woman who rarely has intercourse or who is the victim of rape.

Unfortunately, many parts of the world, including some of the advanced industrial societies, are still relying on abortion (the destruction of the embryo or fetus after conception has occurred) as a means of eliminating unwanted children. In its survey of birth control *Time* noted that in West Germany the number of abortions each year equals the number of live births. In France and Italy, where birth control materials are prohibited, abortion is also very widespread. Today, in some of the industrial nations, such as the Soviet Union, abortions are performed quickly and safely. But among the masses of the underdeveloped nations, modern sterile techniques are not available and folk methods of abortion such as crouching on the ground and aborting oneself with a sharp stick are prevalent. The result, as might be expected, is that the victims of bungled abortions crowd the hospital wards of many of the underdeveloped areas, and many women die leaving large numbers of orphaned children behind.[8]

Moral and Religious Questions Regarding Birth Control

Most of the practical problems associated with birth control—uncertainty, messiness, interruption of the normal pattern of intercourse—have, therefore, been either eliminated or drastically reduced by the advent of the pill. Even the remaining problems of counting days and remembering to take the daily dosage may soon be eliminated by new techniques. But, while the practical problems have been largely eliminated there still remain certain moral and religious questions about the use of birth control devices.

The first question is whether the various mechanical and chemical methods of preventing conception are contrary to nature and represent a distortion or perversion of the basic purpose of the sexual relationship. This question has been of special concern to the Catholic Church and their basic doctrinal position was set forth by Pope Pius XI in his encyclical "*Casti Connubii*", issued in 1930, and is summarized by William Graham Cole in his *Sex in Christianity and Psychoanalysis*. In the second part of the encyclical the Pope rejected all of the familiar arguments in favor of birth control because "the conjugal act is destined primarily by nature for the begetting of children." Any who frustrate the intention of nature are guilty of a shameful and vicious sin. Even concern for the health of mothers is no excuse for breaking the laws of God. The "rhythm method" of birth control is legitimate in certain circumstances because abstention from sexual relations in marriage at certain times in order to avoid periods of fertility is in accordance with nature. The sexual relationship in marriage has secondary ends, such as mutual love and the quieting of lust and may therefore, be pursued with impunity as long as they are subordinated to the primary end of marriage.[9]

Cole further illustrates the restrictive nature of the Catholic position on birth control by citing a three volume summary of Roman teaching on sex and marriage by E. C. Messenger entitled *Two in One Flesh*. In this work three principles of moral theology governing the sexual act are set forth. First, anything which contributes to the generation of children is lawful. Second, whatever is not directly related to generation but is not against it is in danger of being a venial sin but can be without sin if it is performed for a good end, such as the expression of love. Third, action designed to prevent conception is a mortal sin. Therefore, the use of contraceptives, *coitus interruptus*, and the achievement of orgasm by "unnatural" connections are prohibited. In fact, Father Messenger insists that those who marry have a duty to be fruitful and multiply—even suggesting that they should have more than two children and hopefully more than four.[10] An important part of the Roman Catholic attitude toward contraceptives is based on their interpretation of the sin of Onan in Genesis 38. This interpretation holds that Onan through *coitus interruptus* spilled his seed upon the ground and thereby incurred the wrath of God.

Therefore, any action which prevents the seed from being deposited in the proper place (the vagina) is both unnatural and contrary to the law of God. Even the "natural" rhythm method of birth control is not above suspicion and should perhaps only be used when there is a strong reason for it. Thus the official teaching of the Church is in keeping with the Augustinian doctrine that procreation is the purpose of the sexual relationship and that any interference with this basic purpose is a sin or at best a questionable practice to be used only under extenuating circumstances.

In spite of this strong traditional opposition there has been a considerable acceptance of birth control by Catholic laymen. According to the Ryder-Westoff survey, 53% of American Catholic couples now use some form of birth control other than rhythm. And many Catholic doctors will now prescribe the pill for their patients. *Time* quotes gynecologist Francis C. Mason as stating that "the pill is the most acceptable method of birth regulation. Use of the pill by a large Catholic population acts to make them psychologically sound and to create a sound family relationship. I don't practice medicine as a Catholic. If a woman asks me for medical advice, I give her medical advice."[11]

Perhaps the most striking symbol of the rebellion within Roman Catholicism over birth control is the case of the "Singing Nun." Sister Luc-Gabrielle, who gained world fame with her beautiful and reverent hymn to "Dominque," has now left the convent to pursue a recording career. And one of her first recordings is a hymn celebrating the liberation offered to women by the "Golden Pill."

Thus strong pressures for change have developed within the Catholic Church on the question of birth control. And the strongly negative reaction to Pope Paul's most recent encyclical, rejecting artificial birth control, raises serious questions about the church's ability to enforce its position.

It is impossible to describe any one position on birth control as representing *the* official Protestant view. But it can be noted that a basic difference of interpretation of the role of the sexual relationship was an important part of the conflict of the Reformation. Luther specifically rejected the traditional Roman emphasis on the virtue of celibacy. While Luther accepted the idea of Augustine and Aquinas that the "highest good of married life is offspring to be reared in the faith," his whole attitude toward sex reflected a greater freedom of conscience for the individual than that which prevailed within Catholicism.[12] Both Luther and John Calvin emphasized that marriage was ordained by God not only for procreation but also to provide an acceptable release of sexual passion in order to prevent fornication.

The overwhelming majority of Protestant groups today accept most forms of birth control and many Protestant groups are active promoters of the Planned Parenthood movement. Cole summarizes the prevailing Protestant attitude as one which gladly accepts the advantages provided by contraceptive devices among which are:

> The protection of maternal health from the ravages of continual childbirth, the enabling of persons with disease or undesirable heredity traits to have intercourse without passing on their affliction to another generation, and the advancement of a happy family life, in which couples can express their love as often as they desire without fear of producing children who cannot be properly cared for. This represents one of the chief differences in the interpretations of sex held by contemporary Protestants and Catholics.[13]

A special report in a recent issue of *Christianity Today*, a leading "conservative" Protestant publication, noted that all Christian groups today accept some form of family planning. And while Roman Catholics permit only the "rhythm" method of periodic abstinence from sexual relations, most Protestants accept mechanical or chemical techniques as well. It is interesting to note, however, that this widespread Protestant acceptance of contraception is a relatively new phenomenon. "Rome merely believes what the Protestants did until several decades ago. The U.S. state laws against birth control recently overthrown were Protestant hangovers."[14]

But while the use of contraceptives by married couples is now generally accepted by most Protestants (and unofficially by a substantial number of Catholics), the question of their use by the unmarried does raise serious moral questions for many. The basic fear, of course, is that contraceptives, by removing the fear of pregnancy, will encourage promiscuity. It seems unlikely, however, that convenient contraception alone will undermine the basic moral structure of society. For the most part it can be assumed that a girl who is promiscuous because of the pill would have been promiscuous without it. And in any case its benefits for those who want to use it legitimately far outweigh the possibility of its misuse.

A more difficult moral problem may be raised by the question of deliberately providing contraceptives to college and high school students or to unmarried mothers. Even here, however, any potential increase in temptation must be weighed against the benefits of avoiding the psychological damage of an unwanted pregnancy for those who already find the temptation overwhelming. Furthermore, it is apparent that once a teenager has become pregnant, been expelled from school, and has had either a baby or an abortion, the chances are great that she will soon be pregnant again. It may be possible through the judicious use of contraceptives to break this cycle and give these girls a second chance. This type of approach may not improve a girl's morals but it may help her to avoid becoming a burden on society and from bringing additional children into a life in which they are unwanted and inadequately provided for.

Another basic moral problem related to birth control is the question of abortion. Most religious groups join in condemning abortion (except in certain very special circumstances) because it involves the destruction of life rather than its prevention. But the problem of distinguishing between birth control and abortion may be rather complicated in the case of the IUD and perhaps even the pill.

A small ethical controversy has arisen in which it is contended that the IUD stops the reproductive process after the female egg is fertilized and may, therefore, be a "mechanism for microscopic murder." This point of view has been presented by William F. Campbell, a missionary doctor in Morocco. Dr. Campbell accepts the use within marriage of "condoms, diaphragms, spermicidal drugs, medicine to suppress ovulation, and drugs to suppress formation of sperm in the male."[15] But because of the possibility that the IUD may destroy the fertilized egg rather than prevent fertilization, he opposes its use. On the same grounds he would reject the experimental "morning after" pill as well.

Other missionary doctors have responded to Campbell's view by pointing out that there is no proof that the IUDs destroy a fertilized egg. It may work, for example, by causing the ovary to release the egg before it is ripe enough to be fertilized. Furthermore, they charge that Campbell's "legalistic nit-picking" might prohibit not only the IUDs and the "morning after" pill but also quite possibly the general pill now widely used. Most discussion of the pill emphasizes its "anti-ovulant" effect—

preventing the release of the egg by simulating conditions of pregnancy. But the progesterone estrogen combinations also make the cervical mucus impenetrable to the sperm and render the womb unsuitable for implantation of a fertilized egg. This reaction is similar to the interference charged against the IUD and has been cited by some Catholics as a reason for rejecting the pill.[16]

An Evangelical Position on Birth Control

In seeking to formulate an evangelical position on birth control it may be helpful to group the various methods into three basic categories —abstention, prevention, and abortion. Abstention, which includes late marriage, periodic abstention (or rhythm), and celibacy, has traditionally been regarded as an acceptable method for Roman Catholics. But in general, abstention is a highly unreliable method for restraining the population explosion. Late marriage may limit the number of child-bearing opportunities if it is accompanied by pre-marital abstinence. But given the strength of the sex drive, it may simply increase the temptation for pre-marital intercourse and result in an increase in illegitimate children. Likewise, celibacy if accompanied by sexual abstinence removes some units from the population production line. But the number of such persons is far too small to make any significant change in the rate of population increase.

Within the marriage relationship complete abstention from intercourse is not only unnatural but contrary to Paul's warning in I Corinthians 7:5 that husbands and wives should be careful not to deny one another the sexual rights of marriage lest they be tempted into unfaithfulness. And even the practice of periodic abstention, while perhaps better than no family planning at all, is both unreliable and for many people unpleasant. The precise counting of days and keeping of charts that is required to give any hope of success would seem to most observers, including many Roman Catholics, to be so cumbersome and mechanical as to destroy much of the normal enjoyment of the sexual act.

Therefore, the evangelical Christian would probably not regard abstinence as a very realistic or even particularly desirable method of birth control. This is especially true in view of the improvements which have been made in mechanical and chemical contraception. If one accepts the general Protestant viewpoint that the creation of one flesh through the sexual relationship is both natural and desirable even when procreation is not the basic purpose, then there would appear to be no particular moral or religious basis to prevent the evangelical Christian from using any of the generally accepted means of preventing conception. Even *coitus interruptus*, though it may be rejected on aesthetic grounds or regarded as an unpleasant interruption of a natural process, would not seem to be morally objectionable. In contrast to Roman Catholic teaching, for example, the sin of Onan is best understood as resulting not from the use of *coitus interruptus* but from his disobedience to God's direct commandment to raise up seed in his brother's name. And the sin would have been just as great if he had abstained from the sex relationship completely.

In general there would appear to be no Scriptural reason to deny a married couple the right to use any of the standard mechanical or chemical methods of preventing pregnancy. Even the question of the possibility of destroying life by destroying a fertilized egg through an IUD or a pill seems likely to be dismissed by most evangelicals as a highly theoretical and legalistic controversy.

Even the development of a "morning after" pill would seem to be a real boon for mankind and therefore, should be welcomed rather than condemned. The fact that it could be taken after intercourse would permit a tailoring of the use of the pill to the requirements of specific individual patterns, especially for those who have intercourse rarely or irregularly. It would eliminate the necessity for taking a regular cycle of pills and might provide a method that could be exported most easily to the underdeveloped areas where population control is most desperately needed. It would also be a far more acceptable solution to the problem of pregnancies resulting from rape than that provided by abortion.

It is in fact this last category of population control through abortion (defined as destruction of the embryo or fetus after conception has occurred) that represents the most difficult moral challenge. There is a strong movement both internationally and in the United States toward legalized abortion for certain cases, particularly where the mother's life is endangered by the pregnancy or for victims of rape. The American Medical Women's Association, for example, in their convention in November 1966 joined with the American College of Obstetricians and Gynecologists and the American Law Institute in urging limited legalized abortion. They note that there are an estimated one million abortions performed in the United States each year and few of them are performed under sanitary medical conditions. Therefore, they recommend that licensed hospitals be permitted to provide abortions in cases where there is substantial danger to the mother's mental or physical health, where there is strong probability that the child will be born with severe mental or physical abnormality, or where the pregnancy is the result of rape or incest.[17] The State of Colorado has adopted a law which permits abortion, and serious consideration is currently being given to similar moves in several other state legislatures. Where they are designed to provide careful medical and legal controls, such laws may be desirable if they are used only in extreme emergencies. In general, however, abortion should not be considered as a significant device for limiting population and its widespread use for that purpose represents a very callous disregard for human life.

Birth Control Is Not Enough

Even the most optimistic projections for the impact of these new birth control techniques would seem to indicate that the world population will continue to increase rapidly, especially in the underdeveloped, non-industrial nations. In part, this is because the population growth of the last three decades has not been so much a result of an increase in the birthrate as a decrease in the death rate. But the decline in the mortality rate itself tends to raise the birthrate because women have fewer miscarriages and their husbands live longer, thus increasing their child-bearing potential. And with continued medical advances the death rate will probably continue to decline.

Another complicating factor which slows the impact of birth control is the hold of traditional attitudes which regard prolific childbearing as desirable (see Psalms 127:3–5 for a reflection of this attitude). Robert Heilbroner notes, for example, that in many parts of the underdeveloped world, children represent a symbol of manliness and prestige. They are also an important source of domestic and field labor for families who cannot afford machinery. And in general a large family provides the only form of "social security" which can provide for the parents in their old age.

For these reasons, combined with the fear that a small family might be wiped out by sudden disaster and the apprehension that birth control might be expensive and bothersome, the resistance to widespread use of birth control is likely to be very great. In fact, where birth control has been successful, as in Japan, it has followed rather than preceded economic development. Perhaps, as Professor Heilbroner suggests, the best hope for population control lies in industrialization itself because of the forces which it brings to bear on the birthrate. He points out that:

> The altered status of women, the economic disadvantages of children in an industrialized environment, the delayed age of marriage,

and, not least, the expanded horizon of expectations, all exert pressures which seem to depress the natural birth rate. . . . The trouble is, however, that this takes time—a very long time. Meanwhile, the terrible rates of increase, especially in the years during which the death rate falls dramatically, themselves provide perhaps the most discouraging barrier to the achievement of rapid industrialization.[18]

And in fact some of the areas of the most rapid population growth have not yet even begun to make their numbers felt. The impact of modern medicine is just beginning to be felt in tropical Africa, for example. As the infant mortality rate, which now averages 300 to 500 per thousand, drops toward the American rate of 26 per thousand, the potential population increase will be staggering.[19]

Any attempt by evangelical Christians to face up to the implications of the population explosion must therefore, involve not only a concern with the methods of limiting population but also an awareness of the need to control the impact of the population increase. The area where the impact of increasing population is most often feared and discussed is food supply. As noted earlier, it was the fear that the geometric increase in population would rapidly outpace the arithmetic supply of food which haunted Malthus and the spectre of famine in India reminds us of the staggering problem we face in feeding the world's population. Even so, the great advances in modern agricultural techniques provide a very real hope that we may be able to produce enough food to meet basic human needs if we can solve some of the subsidiary problems. One of these problems, for example, involves the religious attitudes of the Hindus which not only eliminate certain items from the food supply but also create additional competition for the available food supply by permitting vast numbers of animals to consume food which otherwise could be used for human consumption.

Another of these problems is the limited productivity of agricultural labor in the underdeveloped world. A major cause of this limited productivity is the prevalence of too many farmers trying to subsist on tiny plots of land. This pattern of fragmented farming severely limits the applicability of modern technology.

> For peasants working their tiny strips [of land] cannot efficiently utilize—nor could they possibly afford—the physical, mechanical, and chemical means by which agriculture in the West attains its rich returns. On the minuscule farms of the backward lands reapers and binders and sowers are totally uneconomic. Worse yet, because

the peasant earns no investable surplus he cannot even exchange his wooden plow for a steel one, or substitute chemical fertilizer for animal or human dung. Indeed, even animal fertilizer is seldom applied; it is used instead as the slow-burning fuel over which the peasant cooks his bowl of rice.[20]

Thus, the problem of providing an adequate food supply is inextricably intertwined with the general problem of the economic development of the underdeveloped areas, and any efforts by the industrial nations to stave off famine must involve not just gifts of food but assistance toward general economic development. In particular, assistance must be given which will enable the developing nations to move peasants off the farms and into the cities. Evidence from experimental programs in the underdeveloped nations indicates that some 15 to 30 percent of the farmers in underdeveloped areas produce "zero net output." If the number of peasants on the farms could be reduced by one third or perhaps even one half, the remainder could probably produce at least as much food as the present total and perhaps even more. The surplus labor, which would no longer be required on the farms, could provide the labor supply which is required for industrialization.

Unfortunately, labor alone is not enough to promote economic progress. Labor must be combined with capital. One way to achieve the accretion of capital may be the siphoning off of some of the increased agricultural production. If the peasants who remain on the soil can increase their food production, some of this gain must be used to feed those laborers who are transferred to the cities where they can work on capital-producing projects.[21]

Again, however, the process of taking excess labor and food off the farms and transferring it to capital-producing projects is a complex and difficult one. There must be governments which are capable of directing and enforcing this redistribution. There must be adequate natural resources and there must be a diversity of production which will permit the new economy to survive periodic cycles of oversupply of certain goods. Diversified production in turn requires a skilled labor force and a skilled labor force requires increased educational facilities. Even in the developed nations like the United States the post war "baby boom" created an educational crisis because of the shortage of teachers and classrooms. The problem is even greater where whole new educational systems must be developed.

In addition to food, jobs, and education the increasing urbanization of the world's population will create an ever increasing demand for safe, adequate, and sanitary housing. At present we are still unable to provide adequate housing for even a population of 3.3 billion persons. The achievement of even a minimum level of decency in housing for the vast population of the future will require the full inventiveness of modern technology to develop housing units which can be mass-produced in sufficient number, at low enough prices, and in some form that will still provide some degree of privacy and individuality.

One example of the type of imaginative thinking that will be required in the attempt to solve some of these basic problems is Moshe Safdie's "Habitat 67" at the Montreal Expo 67 exhibition. This exhibit consists of 354 prefabricated concrete boxes placed into a pattern of terraces in which every living unit is open to the sun and can use the roof of a neighboring unit as a private yard and garden.[22] The need for adequate shelter around the world is so great that we must think in terms of a million human beings at a time. We cannot continue to depend on spacious single family suburban developments. We must instead build great cities which incorporate the functions of living, commerce, industry, entertainment, and art into one vital whole.

By producing a basic unit which can be mass produced and yet still be flexible enough to be adjusted to individual desires, we may be able to solve the problem of retaining individualism in a thickly populated world. Safdie contends, for example, that in "Habitat 67" there can be almost infinite variety of design for the interior of his units. And the development of such compact cities would increase the range of experience within reaching distance of a home because of the higher population density and a reasonable system of public transportation.

Conclusion

It is not possible to detail all of the problems which must be overcome in order to meet the housing, health, transportation, education, employment, and other needs of the world's rapidly growing population. But the development of methods to cope with these problems will require an unprecedented degree of collective cooperation within and between the nations of the world. There must be some general consensus developed about the significance of human life and the basic requirements which must be met to make life truly human. Mere existence on the thin edge of starvation, living in hovels surrounded by poverty and disease, denied the opportunity for work and education—such a standard can no longer be accepted as permissible or tolerable. Furthermore, it is obvious that massive programs of assistance from the industrial nations will be required. Only rarely, if at all, can these undeveloped nations pull themselves up by their own bootstraps. Whatever specific programs or channels may be developed, all of the industrial nations must accept the fact that they cannot isolate themselves from the problems of their neighbors.

There are still men who, like Thomas Malthus, proclaim that the prolificacy of human reproduction can only be controlled by the natural processes of poverty, war, disease, and famine. And they warn that any attempt by men or their governments to relieve the agony of the poor and the starving can only be self-defeating. Unfortunately, many evangelical Christians in their desire to reject the "social gospel" have adopted this or similar positions. It seems impossible, however, to reconcile such a viewpoint with the Biblical concept that we are our brother's keeper. Anyone who reads through the Scriptures will be struck again and again by the emphasis on the obligation to remember the poor and to protect widows and orphans. James warns that "If a brother or sister is ill-clad and in lack of daily food, and one of you says to them, 'Go in peace, be warmed and filled,' without giving them the things needed for the body, what does it profit?" (James 2:15, 16). And John echoes this concern when he writes that "if anyone has the world's goods, and sees his brother in need, yet closes his heart against him, how does God's love abide in him?" (I John 3:17).

In fact, evangelical Christians have accepted this challenge and through their missionary programs they have carried not only the gospel of personal salvation but also medicine, education, and even new techniques of agricultural production. Unfortunately, the combination of rising nationalism, which has severely restricted the work of Christian missions, and the very magnitude of the population explosion, which has dwarfed all of the work that has been done thus far, make it necessary to go beyond our previous efforts. We must be willing to use the greater resources and decision-making power of government to deal with the challenge that confronts us. Too often, evangelical Christians have not only supported the idea of separation of church and state but they have regarded the state with considerable suspicion and even hostility. And when this is combined with the rejection of the "social gospel," it has often resulted in a negativisitic withdrawal from reality. In the present world situation, government is inevitably going to be a major vehicle through which basic decisions are made. Only government with its power to tax can obtain and allocate the resources which will be necessary in order to make possible the economic development which must be achieved if we are even to keep up with, much less get ahead of, the population increase.

The processes of economic development will not come easily. They will require social and political changes along with modifications in the means of production. In many cases these changes may be revolutionary and violent and in others progress may be so slow that it will breed discontent and perhaps political authoritarianism. Even in the industrial nations the growth of population will produce strain and conflict. And if these more fortunate nations shoulder the burden of economic assistance which will be required to give the underdeveloped nations any hope for success, it will demand sacrifice and vision on the part of their people. Fortunately, the United States and some of the other industrial nations have shown some willingness to share the burden of the underdeveloped nations. Through financial, educational, and technical assistance programs they have tapped their human and technical resources and shared them with others.

Some evangelicals may view these programs with concern because they are political and not strictly Christian. But since they permit us as Christians to express, through the state, our concern for the needs of others and since they result in part from our Christian heritage, we should rejoice in this opportunity to open the "bowels of compassion" and share with those in need. This does not mean that we must automatically and uncritically approve of every program that goes under the label of international assistance. But it does mean that we must seek to encourage those programs which are in keeping with the commandment that we love our neighbor as ourselves. H. F. R. Catherwood in his excellent little book *The Christian in Industrial Society* expresses rather clearly the social obligation of the evangelical Christian in a secular society.

> Society in any of its sectors can be made more or less righteous and the Christian must be concerned that, as far as he is able to accomplish it, righteousness shall prevail in those spheres in which he is involved, whether it is a school, a faculty, a local community or a business. To leave them to secularism or humanism would be a complete abdication of our responsibility as Christian citizens.[23]

In a world in which more and more of the basic decisions of life must be made collectively through the governmental process, it is especially important that the Christian citizen be prepared to support that which is good and to oppose that which is wrong and oppressive. We must be prepared to accept and utilize new ideas and new techniques but we must also be on guard against those forces which would reduce man to a machine or a unit of production. This obligation is especially heavy on those of us who live in the comfort and luxury of the modern industrial nations. Unless we find a way to stem the tide of population and poverty, we may well find our little islands of prosperity swept under by a flood of judgment as devastating as that in the days of Noah.

NOTES

1. "The World Congress on Evangelism," *Christianity Today*, XI (Dec. 9, 1966), p. 43.
2. Christopher Tunnard and Boris Pushkarev, *Man-Made America: Chaos or Control?* (New Haven: Yale University Press, 1963), p. 7.
3. William and Paul Paddock, *Famine 1975* (Boston: Little, Brown and Company, 1967).
4. Thomas Malthus, "Essay on Population," in Robert M. Hutchins and Mortimer J. Adler, eds., *The Great Ideas Today* (Chicago: Encyclopedia Britannica, 1963), p. 475.
5. *Ibid.*, pp. 500–501.
6. Alan F. Guttmacher, *Planning Your Family* (New York: Macmillan, 1964), pp. 86–87.
7. "Contraception: Freedom from Fear," *Time*, LXXXIX (Apr. 7, 1967), p. 78.
8. *Ibid.*, p. 82.
9. William Graham Cole, *Sex in Christianity and Psychoanalysis* (New York: Oxford University Press, 1955), p. 139.
10. *Ibid.*, pp. 152–53.
11. *Time*, LXXXIX, p. 80.
12. Cole, *Sex in Christianity and Psychoanalysis*, p. 113.
13. *Ibid.*, p. 169.
14. "Birth Control: Which Methods Are Moral?" *Christianity Today*, XI (Feb. 17, 1967), p. 43.
15. *Ibid.*, p. 44.
16. *Loc. cit.*
17. *St. Louis Post-Dispatch*, Nov. 6, 1966.
18. Robert Heilbroner, *The Great Ascent* (New York: Harper & Row, 1963), p. 93.
19. *Ibid.*, p. 57.
20. *Ibid.*, p. 42.
21. *Ibid.*, p. 79.
22. "Prototype of New City Design," *St. Louis Post-Dispatch*, Mar. 5, 1967.
23. H. F. R. Catherwood, *The Christian in Industrial Society* (London: Tyndale Press, 1964), p. xi.

William W. Adams, Jr. is a political scientist whose specialty is Soviet government and law. Born in Tuscaloosa, Alabama on July 8, 1929, he earned the B.A. and M.A. degrees in political science at the University of Kansas in 1951 and 1954. He did advanced graduate work in the field of Soviet Studies at Columbia University where in 1960 he was awarded the Certificate of the Russian Institute and the M.A. and Ph.D. degrees in 1960 and 1967 respectively. Mr. Adams has also studied abroad in Monterrey, Mexico and Munich, Germany and has traveled extensively in the Soviet Union. He has taught at several institutions including Park College, the University of Missouri at Kansas City, Tulane University, and William Jewell College where he is currently Professor and Chairman of the Department of Political Science.

Included among Professor Adams' honors and awards are membership in Pi Sigma Alpha (Political Science honorary), a Ford Foundation Foreign Area Training Fellowship in 1959–60, a travel grant from the Kansas City Regional Council on Higher Education in 1964, and a Danforth Teacher Grant in 1966–67. He is a member of the American Political Science Association, American Association for the Advancement of Slavic Studies, Mid-West Slavic Conference, Kansas-Missouri Bi-State Slavic Conference, and Missouri Political Science Association. He was one of the founders and served as secretary of the Kansas-Missouri Bi-State Slavic Conference in 1962–64, and he held the offices of vice-president in 1962–63 and president in 1963–64 of the Missouri Political Science Association. In addition, he has contributed articles to the *Dictionary of Political Science* (New York: Philosophical Library, 1964) and *The Baptist Student*.

Mr. Adams served as chairman of the Municipal Charter Study Committee in Liberty, Missouri in 1963–65, and he has taken a keen interest in various local political and civic activities in this community. From 1948 to 1956 he was an enlisted man in the Kansas National Guard. He is also an active member of a Southern Baptist church in Liberty.

WILLIAM W. ADAMS, JR.

Communism, Realism, and Christianity

"[H]ealthy public opinion can arise only . . . in an atmosphere of questing. . . . An indispensable condition . . . is a clash of different opinions, an exchange of controversial ideas, discussion, debate." These Jeffersonian notions are the words of Peter Kapitsa, a leading Soviet physicist, which were expressed in a January 1967 interview with a Soviet youth magazine. He continued: "It is easier to ignore an adversary than to argue with him, but to turn away from an adversary, to refuse to know him, to 'shut him up,' is to damage science, the truth and society." Asked whether his remarks were valid only for science, he replied: "I think not. The laws of development are the same everywhere."

In some ways Kapitsa sounded more like John Stuart Mill or Oliver Wendell Holmes, Jr. than Karl Marx or Lenin. "[E]rrors always give way under the onslaught of truths despite all obstacles; at the very worst, it is a matter of time and the number of victims, as the history of mankind shows, beginning with the bonfires of the Inquisition and even earlier."[1] Compare Justice Holmes: "The best test of truth is the power of the thought to get itself accepted in the competition of the market;" and Mill: "The peculiar evil of silencing the expression of opinion is that it is robbing the human race. . . . If the opinion is right, they are deprived of the opportunity of exchanging error for truth; if wrong, they lose . . . the clearer perception and livelier impression of truth, produced by its collision with error."[2]

The remarkable thing is not that some Soviet citizen, even a prominent one, holds such views, but that they were published by an official Soviet press organ. Was this an isolated incident? In the March 1967 issue of the leading Soviet journal on party history, F. F. Petrenko suggested that his country's present collective leadership may not be infallible. "Collective leadership and the scientific approach . . . guarantee to a considerable extent against serious mistakes. But even they cannot fully exclude them. . . ."[3] Previously Khrushchev had blamed Stalin's errors on the "arbitrariness" of the "personality cult," and his successors blamed Khrushchev's errors on his "subjectivism," while collective leadership, it was said, "excludes the adoption of erroneous decisions."[4] But now Petrenko advocated creation of "an appropriate, effectively operating mechanism for correcting [errors] so that ultimately freedom of discussion and criticism might become the unquestionable norm of party life—from its lowest units to its central organs."[5] In essence, this would mean freedom to criticize top Soviet leaders. Recently a leading Soviet literary magazine hailed the publication of a Russian translation of "Biblical Tales," a Polish edition of the Old Testament. Breaking with the "conspiracy of silence" which had surrounded Biblical literature, the review stated that the "majestic literary monument"—the Old Testament—was available to the Soviet reader.[6] In May 1967 Alexander Solzhenitsyn caused a sensation with a letter to the Writers' Union which called for an end to censorship. "Literature which cannot on occasion put people on guard against moral and social dangers does not deserve the name of literature. . . . I propose that this congress demand and obtain the suppression of all censorship—open and hidden—on artistic production and that it free the publishing houses from the necessity to obtain authorization before publishing anything."[7] Although his advice was not followed, Solzhenitsyn was not imprisoned for his opinion.

Has the Soviet Union suddenly become a democracy with elemental freedoms and has it abandoned atheism? No, but neither is it the same as in Stalin's day. Soviet society is still not free as Americans understand freedom since the press is censored and the one party system remains. Pasternak's *Dr. Zhivago* was banned in 1958, and the writers Siniavskii and Daniel were jailed in 1966 for publishing anti-Soviet literature abroad under pseudonyms.[8] But these reprehensible elements of continuity should not be allowed to obscure the dramatic changes—changes which affect not only the Soviet people but also the lives of many others. It is essential to take these changes into account while at the same time regarding communist regimes and movements as enemies of democracy and religion. How to deal with such enemies and the difficulty of evaluating such changes are the twin problems to be dealt with here.

Treatment of One's Enemies

Jesus instructed his followers to:

> Love your enemies, do good to those who hate you, bless those who curse you, pray for those who abuse you. To him who strikes you on the cheek, offer the other also; and from him who takes away

your cloak do not withhold your coat as well. (Luke 6:27–29.)
Do not resist one who is evil. . . . and if any one forces you to go
one mile, go with him two miles. (Matt. 5:39, 41)

In the mid-twentieth century, this advice almost sounds like "Better red
than dead!"

Nevertheless, there are those who justify violent resistance to communism in Christian terms. "Suppose you see an insane hoodlum kicking a little girl to death a hundred yards down the street. Before you can
get there, the little girl will be dead. In your hand you have a gun. How
do you show love in a situation like that?"[9] If all communists were insane
hoodlums interested in kicking in little girls' heads, the chilling implication that it is our duty to shoot communists might be defensible, though
still difficult to reconcile with Jesus' words.

More often, Christian precepts are simply ignored. Some regard it as
"unrealistic" to love enemies and return good for evil especially when
one's enemies are communists. Determining whether Jesus' teachings are
actually unrealistic necessitates an evaluation of the system and movement known as communism.

All descriptions of communism resemble the three blind men and the
elephant. One grasped the tail and concluded an elephant was like a
rope; another took the trunk and likened the elephant to a snake; the
third, holding a leg, compared it to a tree. All had an element of truth,
but none described an elephant. The Cold War image of communism
pictures an "international communist conspiracy," which is directed
from Moscow by iron discipline and is irretrievably committed to revolution everywhere and ultimate world domination. Thus violent resistance
and "victory" over communism offer the only security for democracy.

Such a view has an element of truth, yet the brief glimpses of Soviet
life at the beginning of this article do not jibe with it. This is due to an
inadequate understanding of communism which is rooted in two types
of flaws in thought. Growing out of these two general categories are ten
common errors. The first grouping is that of *analytical errors*, that is,
distortions, deliberate or otherwise, by writers and commentators on
communism which are manifested in one way credibility, selective quotation, the numbers game, and comparisons with the west. The second
category, *errors of perception*, arising from the tendency to seek simple
explanations and to screen out data in conflict with fixed notions, produce such erroneous views as the devil theory, the iron law of immutability, the myth of monolith, the messianic myth, the motivational fallacy,
and the responsibility of the communists for everything that has apparently gone wrong.

Analytical Errors

Communists quote their voluminous scriptures to support their views. Ironically, so do anti-communist propagandists. If Lenin said that communists must continually advance the cause of world revolution, should those who love freedom not heed the warning? But this "Doubtful Art of Quotation"[10] faces the twin difficulties of credibility and selectivity.

One Way Credibility. "You can trust the communists to be communists," reads the title of Dr. Fred Schwarz's best-selling book. This influential work argues that communists mean what they say and quotes extensively from communist sources. Yet, the reader is asked to believe only those statements which promise increasing tensions, greater violence, and unbending determination to conquer the world. Quotations at variance with this picture are either ignored or explained away as mere deception or maneuver.[11] For example, Schwarz correctly notes (without sources)[12] that Marx accepted the possibility of peaceful transition to socialism in some countries. He then quotes Lenin correctly (with source) rejecting this possibility.[13] Yet he ignores Khrushchev's 1956 statement that the transition "need not be associated with civil war under all circumstances" and that in some instances a parliamentary struggle might supplant a revolutionary one.[14]

On what grounds can a person "trust" one statement but not another?[15] Each quotation must be considered in the light of its historical context, and none may be assumed valid for all time. In the example just cited, if Khrushchev's statements were mere deception, he certainly fooled the Chinese, for they have been denouncing the idea ever since!

Selective Quotation. Schwarz chooses quotations to show communist dedication to violence in principle. Communists do not "use violence only because the exploiting class resists their assumption of power," he states, and quotes Engels and Lenin on the virtues of violence.[16] However, differing views can be found in the theoretical literature of communism. For example, in June 1917 Lenin discussed possible tactics for a Soviet seizure of power. He compared the French and Russian Revolutions and portrayed the workers and peasants as contemporary Jacobins, similar to those French radicals who had fostered the reign of terror. But, he argued that there was a difference. "The twentieth century 'Jacobins' would not guillotine the capitalists; imitation of a good model is not duplication. It would be enough to arrest 50–100 magnates and bigwigs of banking capital . . . for a few weeks to expose their intrigues. . . . [Then] they could be released."[17] Even after the Bolshevik seizure of power, Lenin did not at once advocate mass repression. Ten days after the October Revolution he declared: "We are reproached with using terror. But such terror as was used by the French revolutionaries who guillotined unarmed people we do not use and, I hope, shall not use."[18] It is beside the point that Lenin's expectations were not fulfilled. The point is that one cannot prove by the technique of selective quotation an affirmative commitment to violence for the sake of violence, as Schwarz tries to do.

Perhaps an analogy would place the tricky problem of quotation in better perspective. What would one think of a revolutionary who adopts as his motto the slogan, "The outcome justifies the deed"? What about a revolutionary who defends terror as follows?

> In the struggle which was necessary many guilty persons fell without the forms of trial, and, with them, some innocent. . . . It was necessary to use the arm of the people, a machine not quite so blind as balls and bombs, but blind to a certain degree. . . . [R]ather than [the revolution] should have failed, I would have seen half the earth desolated.

Are these the utterances of a Bolshevik? No, the slogan is an English translation of George Washington's motto, *Exitus acta probat*, while the quotation is Thomas Jefferson's defense of Jacobin terrorism in the French Revolution.[19] The implication is not, of course, that there is no difference between George Washington and Lenin, but that one can prove what one wishes by selective quotation. The problem of relative credibility of conflicting quotations demands careful analysis rather than arbitrary or doctrinaire affirmation of some and rejection of others.

Quotations may also be misrepresented, often because of their very simplicity. Khrushchev's "We will bury you" is frequently cited as proof of Soviet aggressiveness. The question is seldom asked: who is "we" and who is "you" (if the reader will pardon the grammar)? It is commonly understood as a threat that Russia will bury America. "We [the United States] must be buried if the Communists are to achieve Communism."[20] Actually, the statement is an expression of faith in Marx's dialectical interpretation of history. According to Marx, historical development is determined by impersonal forces, quite apart from human will. Change comes through a series of climactic clashes between opposing forces, a class struggle. Each new ruling class reorganizes human institutions to suit itself. Capitalism will inevitably be overthrown by the proletariat who will establish socialism and end class exploitation for all time. Then communism, a classless, stateless, perfectly free society, can come into existence.

In the statement, "We will bury you," "we" can be seen as the forces of socialism and "you" as the forces of the decaying capitalist order.

There is no substitute for the revolutionary struggle of the "oppressed" of each country. Khrushchev emphasized this point in a speech in Bucharest on June 19, 1962: "Of course the time will come . . . when the red banner of socialism will wave over the United States of America too! . . . It is not we who shall raise this banner but the American working class itself, the American people will do it."[21] Thus "We will bury you" becomes less of a threat and more a prediction. *If* Marxism is valid, the prediction will come true—but that is a very big "if" indeed! In any case, placing the quotations side by side well illustrates the twin problems of selectivity and credibility of quotes.

The Numbers Game. According to Schwarz, "Lenin established Bolshevism with seventeen supporters in 1903. He conquered Russia with forty thousand in 1917. Today, the party of Lenin has conquered one billion. The population of the world is two and three quarter billion. By what year will that figure be reached?"[22]

There are at least two difficulties with this frightening numbers game, namely, the myth of monolith and the game of "blame it on the communists." "Today, the party of Lenin has conquered one billion." The truth is that today the Soviet Communist Party controls far fewer people than at the time of Stalin's death. Disintegration of the Soviet empire is well advanced. Many parties and regimes call themselves communist, but for a great many of them Moscow no longer pulls the strings. This does not mean that Moscow has no influence, but influence can result as well from corresponding national interests as from any capacity of Moscow to give orders. The United States influences British policy, and the two countries usually vote together in the United Nations, but Britain is not an American satellite.

In the second place, the mere existence of a revolutionary, disciplined communist party never "caused" a revolution. Communists are able to come to power only when a revolutionary situation is present. Soviet apologists have often sought to prove that Bolsheviks played a key role even in the February Revolution of 1917 which toppled the Tsarist regime. Ironically, they have often found support for this contention from reactionaries who blame it on them. Actually, the Bolsheviks took advantage of a spontaneous revolution and the same has been true in other cases. When the old order has already decayed and no peaceful transition to a new order is possible, it may be too late to prevent a communist takeover.

The tendency of rightists to render unwitting aid to communism by giving it undue credit is not new. In the spring of 1871 following the French collapse in the Franco-Prussian War, moderates and leftists who were anti-clerical and anti-militarist seized control of Paris and declared a commune, but the newly-formed government of the Third Republic crushed it within a short time. In the following year the International Workingmen's Association (First International) met at The Hague, Holland. It had had no hand in planning the Paris Commune, but the delegates found to their surpise that they were popular with the common people. French rightists had blamed the Commune on the International and the masses had believed them![23] Frequently, radicals have gained mass support when the enemies of social change inaccurately blamed them for actions on behalf of change.

Let's Play Comparison. Teaching that merely compares and contrasts certain features of capitalist and communist economics is dangerous indeed. According to anti-communist spokesman Fred Schwarz: "The issue is clear cut—freedom versus slavery."[24] Although he argues that "there is no substitute for knowledge,"[25] he is in reality advocating a form of indoctrination. Naturally this is not likely to produce sound knowledge. But there is a sense in which the warning against comparisons is valid. In the first place, what the Soviet (or other) people have under communism may be more meaningfully compared with what they had before than with what Americans have now. In the second place, when comparisons are made between the communist and "free" worlds, one should be sure he is comparing things which are comparable.

A prime example of comparing incomparables is the practice of formulating lists of "how things are" there and here. One of the most extensive is "Basic contrasts: Communism versus Freedom," drawn up by J. Edgar Hoover.[26] Consider just one of these contrasts. Under communism, "There is a total disregard for the inherent dignity of the individual." Under freedom, "There is a deep and abiding respect for the inherent dignity and the worth of the individual."[27] The difficulty here is that the "is" and the "ought" are not distinguished. Our assessment of Soviet reality is contrasted with our understanding of the American ideal. Accuracy would demand contrasting either the ideal or the reality of each system. A Soviet contrast of their "ought" with our "is" might read: "Under communism the material basis of racial and national hatred is eliminated, while under capitalism discrimination and even lynch law is the lot of oppressed minorities." In fact, both systems fall short of their expressed ideals.

Errors of Perception

Fed by the foregoing analytical errors, a set of six myths has grown up. These must be carefully scrutinized if one's perception of the problem of communism is to be clarified.

The first of these is *the devil theory* of politics which sees every move of the adversary as part of a gigantic monolithic conspiracy, fraught with ulterior motives. It is a closed system of thought that utilizes circular logic and the device of the self-proving hypothesis to demonstrate its own validity no matter what the adversary may do. The enemy himself is seen not as a human being sharing common traits with other men but as an inhuman super-devil.

Official communist analysis of Western behavior often exhibits this outlook. For example, in 1956 Britain and France invaded the Suez region to thwart Egyptian President Nasser's nationalization of the Suez Canal. Had the United States supported them, the Soviets would have interpreted these actions as proof that Western capitalist and imperialist powers were conspiring to reestablish colonialism in the Middle East. But the United States supported Egypt and, along with the Soviet Union, pressed for the withdrawal of the invading armies. Did Soviet spokesmen take this as an indication that the United States, in this case at least, was interested in protecting the territorial integrity of small nations and in preserving peace? On the contrary, the Russians contended that American policy "proved" she was seeking to displace Britain and France as the leading colonial power in the Middle East. Thus, whatever policy the United States followed, it "proved" that American capitalist "ruling circles" were fomenting imperialist aggression.

This same attitude is seen in conservative interpretations of communism. Customarily, conservatives claim to see in human nature a built-in power drive, a basic self-interest, and this dark, Hobbesian view lies at the root of their mistrust of centralized political power.[28] But at least this view implies the existence of a common humanity. When they look at a communist, however, many of these same observers suddenly see not a human being sharing a common nature and similar instincts with other humans, but a de-humanized superman, capable both of limitless evil and superhuman feats. The warning is sounded against assuming "that the Soviet people are—'ordinary people' just like ourselves; that Communism is just another political system."[29]

Consider the recurring theme that the Sino-Soviet dispute just cannot be real but must be a hoax to trick the West into making concessions. Since this cleavage has produced splits and defections within many communist parties throughout the world and obstruction to Soviet interests by Albanian, Rumanian, and other communist regimes, the hoax theory requires acceptance of a truly superhuman capacity for conspiracy. To hold the movement together and still put across the hoax, most of the forty million practicing communists in the world would have to be privy to it. At the very least, tens of thousands of party cadres would have to be aware of the secret unity behind the facade of division. What are the odds that a conspiracy could be shared by so many without a leak? When Khrushchev denounced Stalin at the 20th Party Congress, there were only a few thousand people present at the closed session. The full speech was never published by the Soviet regime, yet the State Department released it a few months later. If a few thousand Soviet communists could not keep such a secret, how could many millions of diverse nationalities do so?

It has been said that war dehumanizes the enemy and the Cold War is no exception. The devil theory sees even the most innocuous activity by the "other side" as part of the inhuman "plot." For example, Schwarz describes his discovery in an American communist bookstore of some English language children's books which had been published in Russia and China. The stories contained no propaganda and were well written, but what is his evaluation? "The trouble with these books is that there is nothing wrong with them." They are like candy a kidnapper offers a child![30] Is there, then, no one in the Soviet Union who loves children and wishes to make them happy with beautiful stories? Is there no state censor who would pass such stories from such motives? Might we not welcome any sign of common humanity in communist behavior? Should "Peter and the Wolf" be banned because it was written by Sergei Prokofiev, a Soviet composer?

From the devil theory of communism springs *the Iron Law of Immutability*, a notion that the communist movement cannot change. But predictions based upon this iron law have often failed. To take a case in point, Schwarz had an easy answer in 1960 for those who pointed out that Stalin executed his opponents while Khrushchev did not.

> Such people have no knowledge of history. Lenin died in 1924 Stalin came to total power in 1929. The expellees from the Politburo were not executed until 1936. In the meantime, they were frequently given jobs appropriate to their abilities in distant areas. The same thing has happened since Stalin died. Immediately after [his] death . . . there was a period of collective leadership followed by the emergence of Bulganin and Khrushchev. Bulganin was eventually overthrown and appointed to some minor position.[31]

The implication was that soon Khrushchev could be expected to begin executing his enemies, but this never came to pass. Elsewhere, Schwarz adds: "The dictatorship becomes ever more intense. The powers in the hands of the top few become greater and greater until finally there emerges the man of all power, the Joseph Stalin, who sits in the seat of the mighty while millions of slaves rush to and fro to do his bidding."[32]

Again, the prophecy was not fulfilled. Instead, Khrushchev himself was dismissed in 1964 and his successors have continued his avoidance of domestic political bloodshed.

Similarly, the present writer in 1964 heard Dr. Nicholas Nyardi of Bradley University, a main exponent of the devil theory, portray the Sino-Soviet dispute as merely a personality clash between Khrushchev and Mao. (At least he did not claim it was a hoax!) He compared it with the Stalin-Tito rift in 1948. As soon as Stalin died, he said, the breach disappeared; as soon as either Khrushchev or Mao disappears, China and the Soviet Union will again be allies. But this is grossly inaccurate! In the first place, Stalin's death did not bring Tito back under Soviet discipline, and his relations with Moscow fluctuated throughout the Khrushchev era.[33] Moreover, Khrushchev's removal has not been followed by any Russian-Chinese rapprochement.

Another faulty conclusion based on the "iron law" is Schwarz's interpretation of the Lysenko controversy in Soviet genetics. He correctly recounts the debate of the late 1940's over Lysenko's theory of inherited acquired characteristics—a position at variance with universally accepted Mendelian genetics. After vigorous debate among Soviet biologists, the Central Committee of the Soviet Communist Party endorsed Lysenko, and the dissenters were silenced. Schwarz then notes that Lysenko has since been dethroned, adding:

> The question at issue is not the rightness or wrongness of the Lysenko theories, but the right of the Communist Party to determine scientific truth by edict. That situation has not changed. Russian scientists may have changed their views, but only because they have been permitted to do so by the Party. "Truth" remains the exclusive province of the Party.[34]

No one devoted to free inquiry will disagree with this condemnation. The error lies in the implied immutability of the situation. In 1962 a controversy broke out between Soviet medical scientists over what was known as the "Kachugin method" of cancer treatment. In traditional fashion, one of the factions appealed to the Party's Central Committee for support. Then a remarkable thing happened. The Central Committee refused to decide the issue, declaring:

> The Party Central Committee does not consider it possible to assume the role of arbiter in the approval of methods of treatment. Only medical men can determine whether the use of one or another method of treating illness is correct. Attempts to administer science by injunction can come to no good, and it is common knowledge that in the not too distant past such attempts led to undeserved

accusations against and the discrediting of certain prominent scientists and doctors in our country. . . .[35]

Thus the very change which Schwarz ruled out has come to pass. Yet, if he had only carefully studied the history of other monoliths, he might have avoided this error. For example, at one time the Roman Catholic hierarchy insisted that the theories of Copernicus and even the observations of Galileo could not be true. Galileo was forced to recant what he had seen through a telescope, while his inquisitors refused even to look. In time, however, the Catholic hierarchy adjusted to the new scientific truths and abandoned the role of arbiter. Why should the Soviet communist hierarchy be any less capable of learning and changing?

The Myth of Monolith. In 1967 a State Department official told the present writer: "I believe that in a showdown all communist countries would fight on the same side." Is this statement really valid? Has the communist ideology accomplished what no other ideology has ever been able to do—effectively bridge diverse national interests? In the Crusades and the religious wars of the sixteenth century, Christians and Moslems, Protestants and Catholics often fought with their opposites against their religious compatriots. Are communists less likely to respond to power interests than adherents of other ideologies? The fact of the matter is that not monolithism but rather factionalism characterizes the communist movement. If the American goal is "victory over communism," then it would be foolish to treat all communists as identical toy soldiers marching to Moscow's drum beat. Divide and conquer would be a much sounder strategy.

When Tito successfully defied Stalin in 1948, many observers regarded it as a fluke. Yet today, Moscow can "give orders" to ever fewer communist parties and even fewer communist regimes. At the Moscow Conference of November 1960, Chinese delegate Teng Hsaio-ping asserted the right of the Chinese Party not to be bound by Soviet Party positions, adding: "We shall not yield!"[36] The reason for the dispute lies deeper than just differences over strategy to deal with capitalism. The Chinese, motivated by nationalism, repeatedly denounce "imperialist treaties" which had brought originally Chinese territories under Tsarist Russian control and which Soviet Russia retains. And each side has hurt the other's power position. In 1961 pro-Chinese Albania closed down Soviet submarine bases, depriving her of her only naval outlet in the Mediterranean at the time. Moscow withdrew Soviet technicians, failed to continue aid to the Chinese nuclear program, supported India against China in 1962, and finally ousted all Chinese students from the Soviet Union in 1966.

International communism has not merely undergone a mitosis into two monoliths, Soviet and Chinese, but also is facing almost total disintegration. Initial challenges came from parties in power—Yugoslavia, Poland, Hungary, and China. But other Communist Parties soon followed. Palmiro Togliatti's Italian Communist advocated "poly-centrism" in 1957. At the 1960 Moscow Conference the usually docile Maurice Thorez, French communist leader, called for discarding phrases like "dictatorship of the proletariat." Swedish party leader Hagberg agreed, saying: "It is incorrect to try to analyse the events of the day by recourse to the theories of yesterday. . . . There is no sense in going on repeating what Lenin said once without taking note of the changes since his day."[37] In late 1964 many Communist Parties demanded an explanation from Moscow regarding Khrushchev's ouster. Togliatti's memorandum, published after his death a short time later and adopted as official policy by the Italian Communist Party, declared: "Every party must know how to act in an autonomous manner."[38]

One of the more remarkable delayed reactions involves Rumania. In the early 1960's, COMECON (East European equivalent to the Common Market) attempted an area-wide economic plan. When Rumania received an essentially agrarian role, its communist government flatly refused integration into the plan. This independence in domestic policy was augmented in the summer of 1967 by self-assertion in foreign policy when Rumania was the only communist government which refused to support the Arabs in the new Middle East war and she was the first Soviet bloc state (except Russia) to establish diplomatic relations with West Germany.

Nothing has happened in the last three years to alter the 1965 evaluation by an authoritative Western source that "Moscow's influence in the world Communist movement has sunk even lower under the post-Khrushchev leadership than it had under Khrushchev."[39] Recent Moscow efforts to organize a joint conference to denounce the Chinese have met decreasing success: 67 parties took part in the Budapest Consultative Conference in February 1968, but only 54 showed up for the Preparatory Commission in April.[40]

> Between the Soviet Union and China there is a straightforward conflict of power and prestige as between two great powers bordering each other and growing mightily. . . . [E]ven if Moscow and Pekin could reach apparent ideological compromise, the movement would still be split. The sophisticated Parties of Western Europe are moving ever farther not only from the Chinese position but also from the position set out in the Moscow Declaration of 1957. . . .
>
> If one thing is certain, it is that the world Communist movement, as a monolithic phenomenon controlled from a single centre,

whether Moscow or Pekin, is finished. This is not to say that Communist Parties in all lands . . . will cease to exist as highly disruptive forces, operating either in the interests of the Soviet Union (or China) as a power, or in order . . . to seize power for themselves. It is simply to say that there can no longer be any question of the existence of a single master plan. In future, each Communist Party, each Communist-controlled country must be studied individually and treated individually.[41]

The Messianic Myth. An author recently indicated that his purpose for writing was "to demonstrate the ideological basis of Soviet foreign policy." He contended: "The Soviets, then, are motivated by ideology, not by natural causes. . . . Marxism-Leninism . . . is the motivation of Soviet foreign policy and of the international Communist movement."[42]

Purveyors of the devil theory almost invariably see ideology as the significant force behind communism. According to Barry Goldwater: "Our wars in the past have all sprung from clashes of interests between nations. They have involved international power rivalries." But this is "a new kind of war," and "our enemy is not a nation but a political movement made up of ideologically possessed people. . . . Communism . . . is not a 'system' to be dealt with in the conventional, time-tested manner of the past. It is a disease."[43] This view denies the influence of traditional power motives, the geographical setting, and national interest. The opposite extreme insists, however, that every move of a communist regime is determined by power considerations, and thus whether a particular country has a communist or non-communist regime makes little difference in its policy.

Scholars are divided on the question of whether power or ideology determines Soviet actions.[44] There is, however, no doubt that an attempt to explain every communist move by ideology ignores other possible explanations. For example, the Chinese attack on India in the fall of 1962 is generally regarded as just one more instance of "communist aggression." Yet Chiang Kai-shek's Nationalist regime had also laid claim to the Indian territories which were seized. If Chiang were still in power on the mainland, might he not also have sought the "liberation" of Chinese territories from India? Did communism or frustrated nationalism lie behind the clash? Moreover, how did Soviet support of India and Pakistani support of China square with the view of the world as divided into "communist" and "free" camps?

The Motivational Fallacy. Even if ideology is the motive behind communist behavior, it does not necessarily follow that policy is derived from ideology. Criminal law distinguishes between motivation and intent, a useful distinction in analyzing this problem. One may be acceptable, the other not. For example, one may commit murder under the apprehension that the victim is an evil sorcerer about to enslave the world. If the killing was intentional, not accidental, the charge is murder, although a mitigation of punishment might be granted because of the noble motive. Communists moved by visions of a future society free from class division and oppression, and rightists motivated by the hope of a future free from the threat of communism may both be credited with admirable motives. However, the worthiness of the intent in a given instance, say the suppression of the "reactionary" Hungarian uprising or support of apartheid in South Africa because it is "anti-communist," may reasonably be questioned. Conversely, one may render service to persons in need in order to gain their confidence preparatory to defrauding them. In such an instance the motive—fraud—is unlawful even though no overt crime has been committed.

By the same token, even if communist regimes are motivated by ideology, it does not follow that they cannot be dealt with. Eschatology— ultimate expectation—does not determine tactics. Ideology did not prevent the Soviets from withdrawing troops from Northern Iran in 1947, lifting the Berlin blockade in 1949, withdrawing from the occupied zone of Austria in 1955, nor mediating in the India-Pakistan conflict in 1965.

Blame It on the Communists. Adherents to the devil theory and the messianic myth often see communism at the root of all troubles. The allies of communism are "chaos and confusion, no matter who generates it." Social and economic conditions are irrelevant. "Communism is spawned by Communists, and Communists alone."[45] From this it follows that whoever stirs up trouble of any kind aids communism.

One difficulty with this approach is that it maximizes the ranks of the enemy. "We are at war with . . . communism—all kinds and varieties." It must be fought "regardless of whether it happens to be in the Kremlin's good graces."[46] This policy of absolute opposition to all forms of communism must be pursued in spite of the fact that Yugoslavia threatens Moscow's control over its empire by providing an example of independence, that testy little Albania might weaken the Soviet position in the Mediterranean by ousting Soviet submarine bases, that the Soviet Union might hinder China's power position by withdrawing technical advisers, no matter whether Rumania refuses to join other communist regimes in supporting Israel in the Mid-East war of June 1967, and no matter whether Dubcek and other liberal Communists in Czechoslovakia seek to expand freedom of speech and press!

Maximization of enemies does not stop there. "Every time we insist on a coalition government with a Communist and a neutral we automatically set up a two-to-one situation against freedom."[47] Thus, Goldwater adds neutralists to the ranks of "enemies." He was speaking of the Laotian coalition government—an unfortunate example, because subsequently the neutralists and communists split and Souvanna Phouma's neutralist regime accepted American aid in the fight against the Pathet Lao. Had the United States thrown all support to the rightist Boun Oum, as Goldwater suggested, either American forces would soon have been fighting in Laos or Boun Oum would have been overwhelmed by combined neutralist and communist forces. The coalition produced instead a two-to-one situation against communism capable of holding the line without large-scale commitment of American troops.

The basic fallacy of blaming the world's ills on communism can be demonstrated by an exercise in imagination. Suppose that overnight all communists somehow abandoned their ideology. How many existing problems would be solved, for example, the Arab-Israeli tensions, the Greek-Turkish dispute over Cyprus, nationalist uprisings in Africa, the India-Pakistan dispute over Kashmir, the Chinese-Indian, Chinese-Russian, Russian-Rumanian, and Polish-German border disputes, the population explosion, and the crisis of economic development in the emerging nations?

Some argue that the existence of communist powers helps to stir up some of these troubles—Soviet arms shipments to the Middle East, for instance. But, to say that communists fish in troubled waters is not the same thing as saying communists cause the trouble. Moreover, it can be questioned whether even such "fishing" as Soviet arms shipments are due to the communist ideology. A non-communist regime in Russia would also be a great power with interests in the Middle East and elsewhere. Goldwater himself observes that "[t]here have always been men and states that would not hesitate to use arms to advance their national policies and defend their special interests."[48] If so, then the question becomes, "Why victory?" What would be accomplished? Virtually all of the troubles which the nation and the world now face would remain.

The attitude which maximizes enemies is based upon the proposition, "He who is not for me is against me." A much more rational approach to foreign policy would be to assume that "My enemy's enemy is my friend" —at least potentially. Such a stance holds the possibility of maximizing one's friends (as in Laos).

A Human View of Communism

If the three blind men had concluded that an elephant was a snake tied in a tree, they would have distorted reality more than the observation of any one of them. Similarly, the composite distortion of communism produced by these aforementioned errors is greater than any one of them. An alternative might be called the human view. It begins with a recognition that communists are, after all, human beings.[49] This follows from the conservatives' own insistence on a basic human nature which includes a power drive—original sin, if one prefers this term. But it is no compliment, for this means that humans are capable of fanaticism, hatred, and brutality as well as reason, love, and kindness. If there is such an innate power drive, one should not be surprised to discover that communists have one.

The human view recognizes that communism is *not* a more effective ideological cement than Christianity, Islam, or some other faith. Communists may be motivated by power and interests as well as by ideology and they quarrel among themselves. Moreover, communism may change as readily as any other system. "There was a day when it was considered the normal thing for Christians to die for their faith."[50] Yet, "victory over Christianity" was not necessary for the non-Christian world to stop the spread of Christianity by military means.

Thus, dealing with communism is not all or nothing; defeat is not "the only alternative to victory."[51] The Soviets distinguish between peaceful coexistence of states with differing social systems, and *ideological* coexistence, ruling out the latter. It is a useful distinction. For the Christian ideological compromise with communism is impossible. But this need not rule out dealing with communist states and parties when they act as power units and not as ideological missionaries with a messianic complex.

> [T]he task of the non-Communist world is not to worry itself sick over the ultimate goals of the Soviet leadership. . . , but to concentrate on multiplying situations in which the Soviet Union either will be forced or will choose to play the game of international politics in an essentially traditional setting. How the Kremlin leaders will square this with their Marxist conscience is not really our problem.[52]

Since the various communist regimes and parties respond to power and ideological interests in different proportions, they require differential treatment. This means distinguishing between: (1) communist revolts controlled by a major power (China or Russia); (2) communist revolts free of external control; and (3) non-communist revolts. The first should generally be resisted unless physically impractical (Tibet), including the use of armed force. Whether the second or third is opposed at all should depend upon the type of government facing overthrow. If the regime is a democratic one, American military and economic aid and advisers might be in order; if it is a reactionary one, aid should be denied. In either case, if the regime is so unpopular as to be incapable of defeating insurgency without large scale outside assistance, America's own national interest would dictate that she not tie her fortunes to its fate. Otherwise this country would be fighting not Chinese or Soviet expansion but rather nationalism. And *anyone's* nationalism, even in independent communist form, can potentially bar such expansion.

Differential treatment is hamstrung not only by the myth of monolith but also by frequent use of pronouns with no antecedent. We (the United States) are fighting "them" in Vietnam because if we do not stop "them" there, "they" will capture Cambodia, Laos, Thailand, Burma, India, Malaysia, Indonesia, the Philippines, and soon we will be fighting "them" on the beaches of Waikiki. *Who* will do all this? Ho Chi Minh? To say, "the communists," is no answer. *Which* communists? There is no "Asian communism" in the form of a Chinese monolith. China is isolated from other communist countries as well as from the West. American spokesmen occasionally admit that Hanoi is independent and potentially hostile to China.[53] The Vietnamese have fought the Chinese for a thousand years. If the American aim is to contain China, it can be argued that the most effective way would be to unite Vietnam under Hanoi and extend military aid. The present writer would not advocate this policy, but it is as sensible—and as likely to contain China—as a policy of undifferentiated holy war against all things communist in Asia. This only renders Hanoi ever more dependent on China.

Differential treatment should extend even to individual communists within the same regime or party. Moscow, Hanoi, and other centers have their "hawks" and "doves," their conservatives and liberals, just as do non-communist centers. Communism may attract both humanitarians and sadists, fanatics and practical politicians. So much the better for the peoples of communist countries—and the West—if the humanitarians, practical politicians, "doves," and liberals win out. Some of those working hardest to humanize the system are party members, and they sometimes do obtain substantial modifications.[54]

One should not dismiss out of hand the idea that Western behavior can influence trends in communist countries. Goldwater condemns cultural exchanges with arguments which boil down to "We send students, they send spies."[55] This has a rather hollow ring in view of recent disclosures of C.I.A. activity among American student groups. In reality, the breakdown of the iron curtain is a major factor weakening Soviet ideology, as Daniel Bell showed in 1965:

There are four broad factors . . . that put Marxism-Leninism
increasingly on the defensive these days: (1) the inherent contra-
dictions that appear in the logic of the doctrine (particularly the
"dialectic" and its conflict with science); (2) the incompatibility of
the doctrinal structure with the complex differentiation of Communist society . . . ; (3) the influence of Western thought, partly
through the emergence of a world community of science, partly
through the interchange of literature and ideas; and (4) the crum-
bling of the "walls of faith," as a result of Khrushchev's 1956 speech
and the bewildering reversal of his own fortunes. The sense of be-
trayal about the past and the uncertainty about how far present
leaders can be trusted undermine the certitudes of the faith.
Marxism-Leninism is no longer an all-embracing, aggressive doctrine. As in the breakup of Islam, perhaps, different elements of the
doctrine may now become of differential importance for different
groups in various Communist countries.[56]

The Main Battleground

The main battleground in this revolutionary age is the developing areas
of the world. British economist Barbara Ward sees four revolutions in
progress: the idea of equality, the idea of progress (or "revolution of
rising expectations"), the population explosion, and the scientific revolution. They "all started in the North Atlantic arena," and "spring essentially from our triple inheritance: Greek thought, Judaism, and Christianity."[57] The revolutions are of *our* making, yet they are often turned
against us. The North Atlantic peoples "are the privileged aristocracy
of world society." With "some sixteen percent of the world's population. . . , [we] enjoy steadily about seventy percent of its annual income."[57] To others, we often appear as the main barrier to their realization of our ideals of freedom, equality, and progress.

Our failure to understand this is compounded when we assume that
emerging nations need only establish democracy and free enterprise, and
they will prosper as we have. This view is wrong for several reasons. The
initial impact of technical development is to lower death rates, leaving
birth rates high, and this results in rapid population growth. Europe and
the United States began with sparse populations, but many developing
countries are overpopulated to start with (China, 800,000,000; India,
500,000,000). India must increase her gross national product nearly
ten percent annually just to maintain her present wretched living standards. (The American growth rate is about four percent.) There is insuffi-
cient private capital to do that. Moreover, democracy and capitalism grew

in the West as the middle classes grew. But in Asia, Western industrialism "tore up the local structure of small-scale handicraft industry
and with it that substratum of artisan skill upon which in Europe the
Industrial Revolution was built."[59] In addition, the peoples of developing nations often view capitalism differently than we in the West.
"[F]oreign entrepreneurs under colonial occupation invested a great deal
of capital . . . but the local population . . . felt . . . that their country
was simply an area for foreign exploitation."[60] The American colonists
in 1776 regarded British mercantilism, with its Corn Laws, Stamp Acts,
and shipping restrictions, as exploitation while Englishmen perceived it
as essential to British prosperity. Americans might remember this when
they wonder why others do not cherish their institutions as they do.

Peoples of the emerging nations may seek economic advance with
much or little emphasis on private investment, but it is inevitable that
their governments will have to play an extensive and positive role. And
communists of various sorts—both independent and agents of great
powers—will undoubtedly fish in these troubled waters. Does Christendom, home of mankind's white aristocracy, have any obligation toward
a world where 10,000 die daily of starvation?

> This ultimately is the ethical problem which our society has to
> solve. But our religious traditions do not leave us without guidance.
> We have, after all, given lip service for two thousand years . . . to
> the idea that all men are brothers. Of course, if the Christian idea
> is wrong, if mankind is not a brotherhood, then all obligations may
> be held to stop at the national frontier. We can keep our seventy
> percent of the world's income until somebody else comes and takes
> it away from us. But if by any chance what we Christians have al-
> ways been saying is true—that all men are brothers, and that the
> man who falls in the ditch can be of whatever color but we still
> have to behave like good Samaritans when we pass by—if that is
> the case, then we face a profound moral decision in our relations
> to Asia. For they are our brothers and, while we are the "haves,"
> they, most decidedly, are the "have-nots." They are the men in the
> ditch.[61]

Christian Realism

A realistic analysis of communism, the "de-devilization" of communists, differential treatment of communist regimes and parties, and the
maximization of potential allies rather than enemies—these practical
considerations suggest that we treat communists as human beings while

at the same time we seek to limit Soviet or Chinese imperialism. And, the main place of contest is in the underdeveloped world. Indeed, the question of whether India's democratic approach or China's communist approach to the problems of building national unity and economic strength proves more successful may well determine the fate of the uncommitted third of humanity.

Early in this essay it was noted that there is an apparent divergence between Jesus' advice to "love your enemies" and the practical demands of Cold War politics. Actually, the dichotomy is not so sharp. Realism demands fostering the material advancement of millions in want. Does Christianity demand anything less? "If a brother or sister is ill-clad and in lack of daily food, and one of you says to them, 'Go in peace, be warmed and filled,' without giving them the things needed for the body, what does it profit? So faith by itself, if it has no works, is dead." (James 2:15–17)

Jesus often won converts only after a miracle which met a physical need. Our age demands miracles on a grand scale; our civilization has the knowledge to work such miracles. Shall we do so? Or shall we one day see an increasing number of peoples concluding that communism offers the only hope, while we hear a whisper saying, "As you did it not to one of the least of these . . ."? (Matt. 25:45)

NOTES

1. "Invitation to Debate" (Victor Bukhanov, interview with Pyotr Kapitsa), *Yunost* [Youth], No. 1 (Jan. 1967), 79–81, translated in *Current Digest of the Soviet Press* (hereafter cited as *CD*), XIX, No. 16 (May 10, 1967), p. 15.

2. John Stuart Mill, "Essay on Liberty" in Edwin A. Burtt, ed., *The English Philosophers from Bacon to Mill* (New York: Modern Library, 1939), p. 961.

3. F. F. Petrenko, "Kritika i samokritika v deiatel'nosti KPSS" (Criticism and self-criticism in the work of the CPSU [Communist Party of the Soviet Union]), *Voprosy istorii KPSS* [Problems of the history of the CPSU], No. 3 (March 1967), 21. Some excerpts here quoted are translated with commentary in Christian Duevel, "Is Collective Leadership Infallible?" *Radio Liberty Dispatch*, May 26, 1967, p. 1.

4. A. A. Kolesnikov, "Sobliudenie leninskikh printsipov rukovodstva—osnova uspekhov v bor'be za general'nuiu liniiu partii" (Observance of Leninist principles of leadership—the foundation of successes in the struggle for the general party line), *Voprosy istorii KPSS*, No. 4 (April 1967), 106. The article was an orthodox answer to Petrenko.

5. Petrenko, *Voprosy istorii KPSS*, p. 31.

6. A. Kazhdan, "Bilbiia—eto znachit 'knigi' " (The Bible—that means 'books'), review of Zenon Kosidovskii, *Biblical Tales* in *Novyi mir* [New World], XLIII, No. 6 (June 1967), 274–77; commentary in Olivia Gilliam, "The Bible Rehabilitated," *Radio Liberty Dispatch*, Oct. 13, 1967, p. 1.

7. "A Man of Courage," *Newsweek*, LXIX (June 12, 1967), p. 44.

8. Tragic as the Siniavskii-Daniel affair is, there is something hypocritical in the

tendency of some Western observers who formerly hailed their writings as anti-Soviet to condemn the Soviet court for finding that their literary productions were indeed anti-Soviet!

9. Fred Schwarz, *You Can Trust the Communist (to be Communists)* (Englewood Cliffs, N. J.: Prentice-Hall, 1960), p. 178. Soviet military intervention in Czechoslovakia as this book goes to press has provoked the indignation not only of the West and most neutralist nations, but also of many communist parties and some communist regimes. Far from proving any monolithic communist dedication to brutality, these responses clearly illustrate the diversity of attitudes within to-day's communist movements.

10. The phrase is taken from Samuel L. Sharp, "National Interest: Key to Soviet Politics" in Alexander Dallin, ed., *Soviet Conduct in World Affairs* (New York: Columbia University Press, 1960), p. 48.

11. See, for example, Schwarz, *You Can Trust the Communists*, chap. 10, where the dialectic is misrepresented as a tactic rather than a theory of change. Cf. Anthony T. Bouscaren, *Soivet Foreign Policy: A Pattern of Persistence* (New York: Fordham University Press, 1962), where a statement on the bookjacket affirms that shifts in Soviet policy "are simply adjustments considered by the Communists tactically necessary and temporary."

12. Marx developed the idea in a speech in Amsterdam on his journey back to England after the First International's Hague Congress of 1872. See Carl Landauer, *European Socialism: A History of Ideas and Movements* (Berkeley: University of California Press, 1959), I, 132ff; and Hans Gerth, ed., *The First International* (Madison: University of Wisconsin Press, 1958), pp. 236–37.

13. Schwarz, *You Can Trust the Communists*, pp. 68–69.

14. N. S. Khrushchev, "Report of the Central Committee of the Communist Party of the Soviet Union to the 20th Party Congress," *Pravda*, Feb. 15, 1956, pp. 1–11, tr. in *CD*, VIII, No. 4 (Mar. 7, 1956), pp. 11–12. It was here that Khrushchev also developed new departures from Lenin on peaceful coexistence and the non-inevitability of war.

15. A parallel problem is Fidel Castro's 1961 declaration that he had been a Marxist-Leninist all along while earlier he had said that he was not. Which time did he lie?

16. Schwarz, *You Can Trust the Communists*, pp. 70–71.

17. V. I. Lenin, "O vragakh naroda" (On enemies of the people) in *Sochineniia* [Collected Works] (Moscow, 1932), XX, 505, as quoted in N. V. Krylenko, *Lenin o sude i ugolovnoi politike; k desiatilutiiu do dnia smerti, 1924–1934* [Lenin on the court and criminal policy; on the tenth anniversary of his death] (Moscow, 1934), p. 164.

18. Lenin, *Sochineniia*, XXII, p. 50, quoted in E. H. Carr, *The Bolshevik Revolution* (Baltimore: Penguin Books, 1966), I, p. 161.

19. Paul Leicester Ford, ed., *The Writings of Thomas Jefferson* (New York: G. P. Putnam's Sons, 1904), VII, p. 203. Letter to William Short, Philadelphia, Jan. 3, 1793.

20. Bouscaren, *Soviet Foreign Policy*, p. 1. This work holds that ideology is the overriding motive of Soviet foreign policy throughout the history of the USSR, a position which is highly debatable.

21. *Pravda*, June 20, 1962, p. 2, tr. in *CD*, XIV, No. 25 (July 18, 1962), 5.

22. Schwarz, *You Can Trust the Communists*, p. 105.

23. Gerth, *First International*, xii–xiii.

24. Schwarz, *You Can Trust the Communists*, pp. 177–78.

25. *Ibid.*, p. 126.

26. J. Edgar Hoover, *A Study of Communism* (New York: Holt, Rinehart and Winston, 1962), pp. 194–203.

27. *Ibid.*, p. 199.

28. Barry Goldwater, *Conscience of a Conservative* (New York: Macfadden Books, 1960), p. 17.

29. *Ibid.*, p. 108.

30. Schwarz, *You Can Trust the Communists*, p. 112.

31. *Ibid.*, p. 48. He adds: "Today at the top is the all-powerful Khrushchev, projected by the Communist Party to leadership of the Communist movement throughout the world." Criticism of Khrushchev by China, Albania, and others belied such a role for him.

32. *Ibid.*, pp. 100–101.

33. See, for example, Khrushchev's condemnation of "Yugoslav revisionists" at the 21st Party Congress, *Pravda*, Jan. 28, 1959, tr. in *CD*, XI, No. 5 (Mar. 11, 1959), p. 16. Tito's vigorous denunciation of Soviet intervention in Czechoslovakia is but the latest fluctuation in Yugoslav-Soviet relations.

34. Schwarz, *You Can Trust the Communists*, p. 12.

35. "In the Party Central Committee," *Pravda*, Aug. 1, 1962, p. 2, tr. in *CD*, XIV, No. 31 (Aug. 29, 1962), p. 6.

36. Edward Crankshaw, *The New Cold War: Moscow v. Pekin* (Baltimore: Penguin Books, 1963), p. 129. Some of the ideas treated here and below are developed in more detail in W. W. Adams, "Communism in Transition," *The Baptist Student*, Dec. 1965, pp. 24–28.

37. Crankshaw, *The New Cold War*, p. 150.

38. "Nineteen Parties Finally Meet in Moscow," *Communist Affairs*, III, No. 1 (Jan.–Feb. 1965), p. 15.

39. *Loc. cit.*

40. Christian Deuvel, "34 Communist Parties Absent at Session of Preparatory Commission in Budapest," *Radio Liberty Dispatch*, May 2, 1968. Far from disproving the assertion that the monolith is no more, reaction of communists to the recent Czech crisis illustrates it conclusively. East Germany, Poland, and Bulgaria urged intervention, Hungary went along reluctantly; Rumania and Yugoslavia condemned it, along with China (how odd to find Mao and LBJ on the same side for once!); the French, Italian, and Indian Communist Parties denounced it; the American party supported the move. Even if a puppet regime is established in Czechoslovakia (and events a few days after intervention indicate the Dubcek regime may survive), the disintegration of the Soviet empire is revealed for all to see.

41. Crankshaw, *The New Cold War*, pp. 163–64.

42. Bouscaren, *Soviet Foreign Policy*, Preface and pp. 7, 11.

43. Barry Goldwater, *Why Not Victory?* (New York: McGraw-Hill, 1962), pp. 165–66, 169, 170–71.

44. See "Ideology and Power Politics: A Symposium" in Dallin, *Soviet Conduct in World Affairs*, pp. 37–74; and "Discussion," *Slavic Review*, XXIV (Dec. 1965), pp. 591–621.

45. Goldwater, *Why Not Victory?* pp. 167, 171.

46. *Ibid.*, p. 172. There is irony, if not cynicism, in the tendency of some to condemn all communists until Moscow moves against a communist regime, then to do an about-face and hail Imre Nagy of Hungary or Alexander Dubcek of Czechoslovakia as freedom fighters. The time to aid such regimes through quiet diplomacy, increased trade, cultural exchange, and similar "bridge-building" exercises is while they are in power and enjoying increasing popular support, not after the Kremlin has acted to depose them.

47. *Ibid.*, p. 169.

48. *Ibid.*, p. 157.

49. Goldwater, *Why Not Victory?* pp. 185–86, pleads with citizens to regard

political leaders as humans: "They put on their pants one leg at a time just like you do." Would he concede as much for communists?

50. Schwarz, *You Can Trust the Communists*, p. 171.

51. Goldwater, *Why Not Victory?* p. 152.

52. Sharp, "National Interest" in Dallin, *Soviet Conduct in World Affairs*, pp. 57–58.

53. Comments of Walt Rostow as quoted by Emmet John Hughes, "On the Time of Jabberwock," *Newsweek*, LXX (Dec. 11, 1967), p. 23. The fact that Hanoi approved Soviet intervention in Czechoslovakia while Communist China condemned it is but the latest evidence that North Vietnam is no Chinese puppet.

54. For an interesting account of the success of Soviet jurists in broadening the chances for a Soviet citizen to recover damages from the government for torts committed by its agents, see Donald D. Barry, "The Specialist in Soviet Policy Making: The Adoption of a Law," *Soviet Studies*, XVI (1964), pp. 106–109.

55. Goldwater, *Conscience of a Conservative*, pp. 106–109.

56. Daniel Bell, "Ideology and Soviet Politics," *Slavic Review*, XXIV, (Dec. 1965), pp. 599–600.

57. Barbara Ward, *The Rich Nations and the Poor Nations* (New York: W. W. Norton, 1962), pp. 16, 21.

58. Barbara Ward, *The Interplay of East and West* (New York: W. W. Norton, 1957), pp. 91–92.

59. *Ibid.*, pp. 61–62.

60. *Ibid.*, pp. 63–64.

61. *Ibid.*, pp. 92–93.

George Giacumakis, Jr. is Assistant Professor of Middle East History at California State College at Fullerton. He was born in New Castle, Pennsylvania on July 6, 1937 and attended Shelton College where he majored in Hebrew and Hellenistics and in 1959 received the B.A. degree *summa cum laude*. He did graduate work in Mediterranean and Near Eastern Studies at Brandeis University and earned an M.A. in 1961 and a Ph.D. in 1963. During this period Mr. Giacumakis was also the recipient of a National Defense Foreign Language Fellowship in Arabic and Islamic Studies. In 1963 he joined the faculty of California State College at Fullerton.

He is the author of *The Akkadian of Alalah* (The Hague: Mouton, 1967) and the contributor of articles which are included in *The Biblical World: A Dictionary of Biblical Archaeology* (Grand Rapids: Baker, 1966), the *International Standard Bible Encyclopedia* (rev. ed., Grand Rapids: Eerdmans, 1967), and *Zondervan's Pictorial Encyclopedia* (to appear in 1968). He has also traveled extensively throughout the Middle East.

Professor Giacumakis belongs to a number of professional organizations, among which are the American Historical Association, American Oriental Society, Middle East Studies Association, Institute for Mediterranean Studies, Evangelical Theological Society, and American Scientific Affiliation. He is an associate member of the California Republican State Central Committee and also is a member of the Evangelical Free Church of America.

GEORGE GIACUMAKIS, JR.

The Israeli-Arab Conflict
in the Middle East

The state of Israel occupies a very small piece of land in comparison to the conflict surrounding its existence. Before the June 1967 Irsaeli-Arab War it was approximately the size of New Jersey, slightly over 7,800 square miles. The Negev Desert in the south comprised sixty percent of the nation before the Sinai desert was occupied. Israel's population has increased rapidly during the last two decades because of the immigration of about one million Jews. The population just prior to June 1967 was 2,500,000 and this included 250,000 non-Jews, most of whom were either Muslim or Christian Arabs. Israel gained about one million refugees and another 19,000 square miles of territory from her recent victory.

The whole issue of Israeli-Arab relations is a highly emotional one. Discussions about the question, which may begin in a subdued and rational tone, usually conclude with raised voices and tempers. The most dramatic display of the emotional fervor produced by this was the assassination of Senator Robert F. Kennedy in Los Angeles on the first anniversary of the June War by a young Jordanian, Sirhan Bishara Sirhan, who deeply resented the senator's public espousal of the Israeli cause. Twenty years of wrangling accomplished little in resolving the differences between these Middle Eastern peoples. The tensions between the Jews and the Arabs have climaxed on several occasions, resulting in armed confrontations. The pressures of the Great Powers as well as the presence of the United Nations Emergency Force generally have discouraged the conflicts from developing into open wars.

Recently, however, a situation evolved which led to war between the state of Israel and the neighboring Arab states. Various Arab pressure groups such as the Palestine Liberation Organization and the leaders of Syria, Algeria, Iraq, Jordan, and Egypt expressed a desire to "push Israel into the sea." Fortunately for Israel, these groups or countries had been disunited in their endeavors because of internal problems, but with the United States distracted by Vietnam, Nasser and the other Arab leaders saw a golden opportunity to eliminate this "cancer" from the East Mediterranean. In spite of their united effort in the June 1967 encounter, it was nevertheless evident that they were no military match for the Israeli forces.

It is only natural that the evangelical Christian is immensely interested in the outcome of this problem. During the last two centuries there has been an increasing amount of discussion concerning the restoration of the state of Israel. Many a minister has donned the prophet's robe and preached sermons in which he predicted either the restoration or the impossibility of the restoration of Israel by Diaspora Jewry. Thanks to the effective public relations program of the World Zionist Organization and wide press coverage, evangelical Christians have been aware of the efforts to bring the state of Israel into a reality. To some evangelicals, 1948 marked the beginning of the end of the age, for after two thousand years the Jews had once again established a national home in Palestine. This, they felt, was what the Scriptures had prophesied would precede the return of Jesus Christ to set up his earthly kingdom.

The Arabs, on the other hand, did not have a world-wide organization to proclaim their side of the issue. Their inability to unite, their lack of a large educated group that could communicate with the West, and the general separation between the Eastern and Western cultures hampered the presentation of a complete picture to the Western world. Moreover, spokesmen defending the Arab point of view often presented an ineffective case in such countries as the United States because of their difficulty in understanding the Western thinking process.

In this day of instant communications it is important for the informed Christian to investigate both sides of the complex Jewish-Arab problem. Only after this has been done should he attempt to reconcile this contemporary question with the Scriptures. The following essay will endeavor to view the various facets of the problem before offering any definite proposals concerning the Christian's attitude. The first part will deal with Zionism and the development of the modern state of Israel. The rise of Arab nationalism and its relationship to the Israeli-Arab problem will follow. Since the United States is very much committed to the continuance of the State of Israel, the third part will attempt to show how its official position has changed over the years. Next, the attitude of the Western evangelical Christian concerning the Jewish restoration during the last two centuries will be dealt with. The last part will discuss the dilemma which the Christian faces as he seeks to correlate this international affair with his understanding of the Bible.

Zionism and the Development of Israel

History is filled with examples of peoples who over a period of time have become integrated into other societies or nations, especially groups which do not have a common homeland with which to identify. Yet, most of the history of the Jewish people has been spent in lands outside of the Palestinian area which they considered their home, but still they have been able to maintain their religious and cultural identity. After the nation of Israel came into existence in the thirteenth century B. C., it took approximately 250 years to consolidate Hebrew power under the monarchy of David and Solomon. It was not long until the unified monarchy broke up into two political entities. The northern state—Israel—passed out of existence in the eighth century B. C., while the southern state—Judah—lasted until the first part of the sixth century B. C. Only a relatively small number of Jews returned to Palestine and reestablished their nation at the end of the sixth century B. C. The majority had scattered throughout the Middle East, the Mediterranean basin, and even into East Asia. Palestine experienced a further exodus of its Jewish population during the first century A. D. because of the Roman conquest. From then until the twentieth century, some 1900 years, the Jews as a group of people have lacked a geographical area with which to associate nationally. This normally would have caused a historical ethnic group to lose its identity and integrate with other societies.

The Jewish people did not experience this loss of identity for two reasons. One was the intense persecution which they often experienced in the lands where they lived. This naturally resulted in ghetto-types of living conditions and forced them to band together for security. Another factor was the role of Judaism within each of these communities. The rabbi was not only in charge of religious activities and responsible for the education of the youth, but he also acted as the chief spokesman of the Jewish community. The Jews usually lived in separation from those around them. The continuation of Jewish identity led to a movement for a national homeland.

In order to understand the twentieth century creation of Israel, it will be necessary to examine the role of the international movement of Zionism and to see how it maneuvered the idea of the state into realization. Simply stated, Zionism advocated a Jewish return to the homeland. The inspiration for this movement was drawn from the Old Testament which several times portrayed the people attempting to acquire possession of the land of Palestine. Zionism was directly fostered by the economic, political, and social conditions of nineteenth century European Jews. In many places the Jews found it extremely difficult to hold any type of public office or to possess property because of the bigotry directed against them. Not only were they isolated from the sphere of public life, but also they were forced to leave some countries including Spain, France, and Poland.

Although a more tolerant attitude toward the Jew had emerged in Western Europe (a feeling also carried over into the United States), this tolerance was not found in Eastern Europe. For that reason the Zionist movement, centered upon the dream of a nation in Palestine, began there. The anti-Semitic feeling so prevalent in Czarist Russia caused Jews to feel they had no real future in that land. When the political pressures increased against the Russian Jews during the 1880's, a movement called *Hoveré Zion* (Lovers of Zion) came into existence which advocated a return to Palestine in order to establish a national home and thus provide a measure of relief from the political pressures.[1] Anti-Semitic feeling was not limited to Russia but was also found in Poland and throughout much of Eastern Europe. Many immigrants who left Russia at that time came to the United States, but some were attracted to Palestine because of their orthodox theology. Although population estimates are difficult to make, the best figures indicate that around 25,000 Jews were in Palestine in the 1880's, a number which increased to about 60,000 by 1918.

Even though the earliest Zionist activity took place in Eastern Europe, the form of organized Zionism which brought about the development of the state of Israel was essentially a Western European movement founded by a Viennese journalist, Theodor Herzl. Originally he had little interest in the Jewish nationalist feeling which looked toward the formation of a Palestinian state, but his views changed after he had reported the celebrated Dreyfus Case in Paris. This case involved a Jewish captain in the French army who was accused of giving secrets to Germany, and it seemed evident to Herzl that Captain Dreyfus had been convicted and sentenced to prison because of the strong hatred for Jews. Herzl was emotionally stirred by the anti-Semitic overtones of the affair and in 1895 published a book, *Der Judenstaat*, which advocated the creation of a Jewish state.[2] He called for the acquisition of a piece of land which should be set aside for a Jewish state, and the establishment of a world-wide organization to provide funds both for the purchasing of land and for aiding the immigration of Jews to this state. Two years later Jewish leaders from a number of countries gathered at Basel, Switzerland and drafted a four point Zionist program. First, there would be the promotion of the colonization of Palestine by both agricultural and industrial workers. Second, those immigrants who came to Palestine would attempt to establish certain appropriate institutions which would bind the whole of Jewry together. Third, Jewish national sentiment would be strengthened, and fourth, government consent where necessary would be sought in order to carry out the aims of Zionism.[3]

The Zionist organization had become a potent pressure group by the time of World War I. It had accumulated a large amount of money, and its voice was heard in a number of the Western governments. An example of its influence is seen in the famous Balfour Declaration. The Zionist leaders in England, particularly Dr. Chaim Weizmann and Lord Lionel Rothschild, sought to obtain British aid for a Jewish state in Palestine. The British government on November 2, 1917 released a declaration from Arthur James Balfour to Lord Rothschild which guaranteed his government's backing for the establishment of a Jewish national home in Palestine. It was quite apparent that the regime did not have any idea how this would be carried out. Specifically, the promise was not for a Jewish state but simply a "national home," a concept later reaffirmed in the White Paper of 1922 which defined the Jewish national home as a center in which the Jews of the world could take interest and pride.[4] In none of these British statements was there any indication that Palestine should lose its Arab character. Obviously, the British really desired the immediate backing of world-wide Jewry for the Western war effort in Europe. The government evidently felt that it would deal with its promise to the Zionists after the heat of the conflict subsided.

The British had assumed control over Palestine in 1922 by virtue of a League of Nations mandate, and rapidly they became deeply embroiled in the Jewish-Arab problem. As Jewish immigration increased, Arab nationalism also increased. The Arabs became thoroughly disgusted with the indecision expressed by the British. Hitler's rise to power heightened the tempo of immigration into the Holy Land, which reached a climax in 1936 when a civil war broke out that lasted to the beginning of World War II. The Jews, with the Zionist organization behind them, were able to attract millions of dollars in investments to Palestine from all over the world. Land was purchased on a piecemeal basis and at inordinately high prices from absentee Arab landlords who generally lived in Beirut, Damascus, or Turkey and oppressed the indigenous Palestinian population. It is estimated that between 1919–1939 Zionist groups spent approximately $79,000,000 on agricultural and other interests in Palestine.[5]

The British vacillated by sending one investigating committee after another. One of these was the Peel commission of 1936–37 which suggested that the Palestinian mandate was based on a weak assumption and should be terminated. It also proposed a partition of the area into a Jewish state and an Arab state. At the time this suggestion was regarded as unsatisfactory, although a decade later it was adopted by the United Nations as a solution. To the Arabs it appeared the British were yielding to the Zionists, but the Jews felt that the British were giving in to Arab demands.

Both the Jews and the Arabs attempted to set up unofficial governments under the British mandate. The Arabs were not very successful, but the Jews were. The Jewish quasi-government (the *Yishuv*) was a remarkable political achievement. During the years of the mandate the *Yishuv* developed a political system, a civil administration, police and security forces, an educational system, and other aspects of a normal government. The Jewish settlers even developed a well-organized defense system. This illegal army was called the *Haganah*, and it had trained soldiers by 1936. When World War II came, the Zionists were presented the opportunity to sharpen the military expertise of these troops and to obtain weapons from the British which they hoped to use at the time when the mandate would be terminated.

Under the shadow of World War II and weary of the continuing frustration of Palestine, the British issued the White Paper of 1939.[6] This document declared that within ten years an independent Palestinian state would come into being. The Arabs and Jews would share in the government in such a way as to insure the interests of each group. Moreover, Jewish immigration during the next five years was to be limited so the Jewish population would not exceed one-third that of the entire country. The paper set annual immigration quotas of approximately 10,000 for the next five years after which no further Jewish immigration would be permitted without the approval of the Palestinian Arabs. Although Arab moderates considered it a victory, the extremists feared that it would establish a strong Jewish minority within the future government. The Jews, on the other hand, strongly objected to the immigration restrictions and launched a number of violent demonstrations against the British in which government offices were stoned and shops throughout Palestine were looted. The World Zionist Organization felt the British had reneged on the Balfour Declaration of 1917.

World War II lessened the enthusiasm for nationalist interests on both sides. The Jews, including both the Palestinian Jewish government (the *Yishuv*) and the Zionists, had no choice but to support the Allies against the Nazis. The Arabs adopted a more neutral stance and some of them were even sympathetic with the German ambitions. During the war the Jewish agency illicitly smuggled immigrants into Palestine, but unfortunately some of the weather-beaten vessels used to bring Jews to Palestine were refused port by British sea patrols and a few were even sunk. This did not help reduce the growing anti-British feeling among world Jewry.

After the war the world was shocked to learn that six million Jews, almost one third of the total Jewish population, had been exterminated by the Nazis. These atrocities evoked tremendous expressions of sympathy for the Jews and rallied public support for the establishment of a Jewish homeland. International concern and sympathy developed for the illegal immigration into Palestine, and the Jewish question became a major concern of both British and American policy. A United Nations Special Committee on Palestine (UNSCOP) was created in 1947 and dispatched to the Holy Land to find a solution. The majority report of the committee was that Palestine should be partitioned into two separate states.

As soon as the United Nations accepted the UNSCOP partition plan, civil war broke out in Palestine. The Arabs were greatly dissatisfied because of the unbalanced population percentages of each group living under the other government. In the sector set aside for the Arab state, the Jewish minority would have been only 1.5% of the total population. While in the Jewish state the plan would have left an Arab minority of approximately 45% of the population.[7] Although the resolution was adopted on November 29, 1947, neither the U.N. or the British did anything to implement the partition. The Jews celebrated because of the U.N. decision while the Arabs took up arms against it. The British had refused to accept the U.N. vote, but they had decided to terminate the mandate on May 15, 1948. The chaotic events which transpired in the months prior to the end of the mandate would seem to indicate that the British probably could not have done anything to bring about the two states because the situation was beyond their control.

As the civil war spread, atrocities increased on both sides and the loss of life was heavy. The most outstanding barbarity was the massacre by the Irgun (National Military Organization—a Jewish terrorist group) of the entire population of Deir Yassin, a village near Jerusalem, which contained about 250 Arab men, women, and children. The government of Israel condemned this action, but the news spread and a general exodus of panic stricken Arabs resulted. The wealthier Arabs had left earlier, but after the massacre the lower classes, especially the peasants, poured into the neighboring countries. The total number of Arab refugees numbered somewhere between 700,000 and 900,000. Finally, during the first half of 1949 Dr. Ralph Bunche of the U.N. was able to establish an armistice agreement between Israel and her neighbors. Israel felt she had reached maturity when in May of the same year she was admitted to the United Nations.

The Israelis have constantly argued that the Arab refugees left Israeli-held Palestine because of the strong orders issued over Arab radio stations to do so. Further, Israel claims that the solution to the resettlement problem of these peoples lies in the hands of the various Arab governments. The Arabs, on the other hand, place the blame entirely upon the Israelis for forcing them out of their homes.

The Rise of Arab Nationalism

Many people are not familiar with the glorious past of the Arab world, a history which overshadowed that of contemporary medieval Europe.

This past, often called the Golden Age of the Arab or Islamic world, had its beginnings with the appearance of Muhammad in the seventh century A. D. Muhammad proclaimed his monotheistic message about Allah and united the peoples of the Arabian peninsula under the banner of the new faith of Islam, a political accomplishment without precedent in Arabian history.[8]

The original Arabs soon went out from their homeland and conquered the land from Spain across North Africa to Central Asia. Under the leadership of the Umayyad dynasty, they briefly united this whole area under a single government. By the ninth century the political unity of the region had disintegrated but in spite of this there was highly significant scientific and intellectual advancement. The Islamic world drew upon the reservoir of Greek and Oriental knowledge to build a cultural edifice to which the Western world is deeply indebted. Arab accomplishments were particularly remarkable in the field of mathematics, science, and literature, and the Arabs today longingly look back to that period. They dream of a future when this area again will be looked up to by the other world powers as a source of economic, political, and cultural power.

The Abbasid dynasty, which had gained power in the Middle East, recruited a large number of mercenary soldiers from a central Asian people known as the Turks. Abassid Al-Mutasin (833–842) began using Turkish slaves and mercenaries to counterbalance the mounting influence of the Persians. Eventually the Turks were able to penetrate the higher branches of the military, and finally they took political control over many parts of the Middle East. In the Crusades of the twelfth century, European Christians fought against Muslims who were subjects of various Turkish rulers. The Crusades assisted in establishing the Turks in the Middle East and eventually one of their tribes, the Ottomans, took full control of this region. For the first time Western Europe became aware of the rich Muslim culture through the contact afforded by the Crusades.

The Arabs were dominated by the Ottoman Turks between the fifteenth and twentieth centuries, and during this time Arab interests or considerations were seldom taken into account. Since the Turks did not continue the cultural advancements of the Arabs, the Golden Age came to an end. However, two potential unifying factors existed among the Arabs during the Turkish domination: their religion and common origin. The Arabs continued to maintain their loyalty to Islam, while hating their Islamic Turkish masters. Beneath the surface of the Turkish bureaucracy Arab culture and language continued to exist. Since the Bible of Islam, the Koran, was written in Arabic, this language had to be taught along with Turkish.

It was not until the latter part of the nineteenth century that Arab nationalism started to blossom. The printed page was an important factor in spreading nationalistic ideas. With the founding of the famous Bulag Press in Cairo in 1822, Egypt provided the nationalists an important tool for disseminating their ideas throughout the Middle East. It also gave Cairo the distinction of being an important literary center, and thus drew many Arab intellectuals to Egypt. There they exchanged and debated their notions about the uniqueness of the Arab people and their desire to be independent from Turkish rule. Education also helped to implant nationalistic ideas in the minds of the Arabs. In 1875 the University of St. Joseph was founded in Beirut by French Jesuits. In 1866 the American Presbyterian Mission opened the Syrian Protestant College which later was called the American University of Beirut. In these academic halls many of the outstanding leaders of Arab national and cultural life have been educated.

Arab nationalism was directed not only against the Ottomans because of their Turkification practices, but also against the French and the British who were penetrating the Middle East under the guise of the Ottoman Empire. In the early twentieth century Arab nationalists began to formulate the concept of an independent Arab nation-state or states. Most of them threw their support behind the ruler of Western Arabia, Sherif Hussein, and his two sons. They had, along with the colorful Colonel Thomas E. Lawrence, organized an effective resistance which led to the defeat of the Ottomans in World War I.

By the end of the War, however, the nationalist movement began to splinter in several directions. The Egyptians, for example, were concerned with their struggle against Great Britain and did not really identify with problems in other parts of the Middle East. When the Western powers repeatedly disregarded Arab interests in the Paris Peace Conference of 1919 and in other meetings during the next few years, it became apparent to the Arabs that they would have to unite if they wished to achieve their desired goal of full national independence.

The catalyst for Arab unity was found in Palestine. In 1936 the Arabs of Palestine rose up against the British over Jewish immigration. As the mandatory power in Palestine, Great Britain was resented by the Arabs for its seeming indecision in the immigration question. The Palestinian Arabs were, however, highly disorganized and unable to carry out any effective actions against the British. Their leaders, the Husayni family which owned large tracts of land in southern Palestine, frequently were more concerned with their own interests than with the larger cause of nationalism. Moreover, the nationalist movement was weakened by the rivalry between the Muslims and the Christians.

World War II itself did not offer them much hope as far as unity and independence were concerned. Each Arab state was wrapped up in its own selfish concerns and they were not very interested in the fortunes or misfortunes of their brothers in neighboring states, except in Palestine. The Arabs were neutral, with certain exceptions, toward the conflict between the Allies and the Axis powers. Their leaders anxiously awaited the end of the struggle in order to resume the drive for self-determination. These nationalists then began using radio, motor vehicles, and airplanes to carry their message to the Arab population which lived in rural areas. Soon after the close of the war self-determination was gained by most of the Arab world. In the late 1940's and during the 1950's Arab nationalists took over the reins of government from Morocco eastward to Iraq. Many of the monarchical regimes were supplanted by more democratic governments sponsored by the nationalists. Thus, Tunisia established a presidency, Egypt deposed its monarch and paved the way for Gamal Abdel Nasser to assume power with his socialist regime, and Iraq revolutionaries ousted their monarch.

For the Arabs, Palestine was the one point of failure to obtain self-rule. This was a defeat which was never accepted, and it provided the fuel for the fire of Arab nationalism after 1949. The Arab was convinced in his own mind that he had been beaten not by a Jewish state in occupied Palestine but by a world-wide conspiracy known as Zionism headquartered in the West. This is illustrated by a statement frequently made by Arab spokesmen that they have nothing against Jews but they hate Zionism. Arabs often compare Zionism with communism in order to show its foreign ideological origins. It should be stressed that foreign ideologies are resented in the Middle East, whether they be from the West or the Communist world. For example, Egypt today accepts a great amount of aid from the Soviet Union, such as military armaments and assistance in the construction of the Aswan Dam, and yet continues to outlaw the Egyptian Communist Party. Even after the June 1967 defeat many of the Egyptian communists still remained in jail.

The United States and Palestine

American foreign policy has been inconsistent during the last century and most commentators adhere to either one or the other of the following interpretations. One group feels the United States was simply not interested in the rest of the world before the Spanish-American War and then manifested a slight concern until it became a world power as the result of World War II. The other assumes that the United States has always been against colonialism in any form and therefore has continuously attempted to assist other nations.[9] Neither of these views really explains American foreign policy. The official attitude towards Palestine is a good example of policy fluctuation. Part of the reason for the lack of a definite Palestine policy prior to the establishment of Israel was that the United States' interests were limited and divergent. Before World War I American functions in this area of the world were primarily academic, missionary, or philanthropic, but by 1920 the United States government had helped American oil companies to acquire shares in Middle Eastern oil endeavors. American Zionist leaders who later became justices of the Supreme Court, Felix Frankfurter and Louis Brandeis, served as indirect links between European Zionism and the United States government. President Wilson sided with them by giving his support to the Balfour Declaration. Brandeis' influence can be seen in Wilson's statement: "I welcome an opportunity to express the satisfaction I have felt in the progress of the Zionist movement in the United States and in the Allied countries since the declaration by Mr. Balfour, on behalf of the British Government."[10] Wilson had put the American government on record as backing the Zionists in their attempts to establish a Jewish state.

In 1924 the United States and Great Britain negotiated a treaty which established guidelines regarding their relationship to the Palestine mandate and for the protection of American interests in Palestine. At the beginning of World War II this treaty was mentioned when a majority of the members of the House Foreign Affairs Committee and twenty-eight senators strongly protested the limiting of immigration into Palestine which the British had announced in the White Paper of 1939. They claimed that the desires of the Jews in Palestine were "a moral obligation of the United States" and that the White Paper was a violation of the 1924 Treaty.[11] It seems, however, that the executive branch of the government was not convinced of this during the 1930's.

The Roosevelt Administration followed the same fence-straddling policy which the British had followed during the first half of their mandate of Palestine. Neither the State Department nor President Roosevelt paid much attention to the pressures brought by the American Zionists and the Palestine Economic Corporation, an American development company in Palestine, for an official endorsement of the principle of a Jewish homeland, and in fact the State Department displayed an almost hostile attitude toward Zionist intervention. The chief executive did not really want to get involved. Acting Secretary of State Joseph Grew indicated this to President Truman in 1945 in a memorandum which stated that Roosevelt had given assurances to the Arabs that he would respect their rights and that these assurances were regarded by the State Department as "definite commitments on our part." Roosevelt further declared: "In the view of this Government there should be no discussion altering the basic situation in Palestine without full consultation with both Arabs and Jews."[12]

The official position of the United States was somewhat confused by a congressional resolution adopted in January 1944. The Congress went on record as favoring the establishment of a national home for the Jews in Palestine, and it urged the United States government to "take appropriate measures to the end that the doors of Palestine shall be opened for free entry of Jews into that country, and that there shall be full opportunity for colonization, so that the Jewish people may ultimately reconstitute Palestine as a free and democratic Jewish commonwealth."[13] Part of the responsibility for obtaining this strong expression could be laid at the door of the American Zionists' public relations program, but the majority of Christians also favored the establishment of a Jewish Palestinian home. This has often been regarded by historians as simply an outgrowth of the rising wave of international sympathy evoked by the revelation of Jewish sufferings in Europe. The fact is that Biblical prophetic writings proclaiming a golden age of Israel under the leadership of the Messiah have had a profound influence on American Christians, including those occupying decision-making positions. This matter will be dealt with in detail later.

The immediate post-war years saw the direct involvement of the American government in Middle Eastern affairs. When Britain announced in the spring of 1947 that it would no longer take responsibility for upholding the Greek and Turkish governments, President Truman declared that the United States would guarantee the security of these countries. As a result of the Truman Doctrine, large amounts of financial and military aid flowed into Greece and Turkey to assist their regimes in warding off communist threats.

The Truman administration's policy toward the Palestine question was notoriously inconsistent. Mr. Truman at first went along with the neutral to pro-Arab State Department's recommendation not to get involved in the war between the Jews and the Arabs which was bound to occur as soon as the mandate expired. He was, however, subjected to pressures to commit American troops to executing the United Nations partition plan which the British had declined to do. In spite of this he instructed the American ambassador to the United Nations to propose a United Nations Trusteeship over Palestine and to state that the partition plan proposed by the world body was unworkable.[14]

A substantial segment of the American public, including the Zionists, protested vigorously about this reversal of policy. Truman's experience with the Zionists was not always a pleasant one. In his *Memoirs* he complained about their lobbying efforts:

> I do not think I ever had as much pressure and propaganda aimed at the White House as I had in this instance. The persistence of a

few of the extreme Zionist leaders—actuated by political motives and engaging in political threats—disturbed and annoyed me. Some were even suggesting that we pressure sovereign nations into favorable votes in the General Assembly . . . As the pressure mounted, I found it necessary to give instructions that I did not want to be approached by any more spokemen for the extreme Zionist cause.[15]

While debate proceeded in the United Nations over the Trusteeship proposal, the Palestinian Jews took matters into their own hands. They seized large portions of land which had not been allotted to them by the provisions of the partition, and the provisional Jewish government declared Israel a state. President Truman then acted on his own initiative and quickly announced *de facto* recognition of Israel without informing the State Department of his intentions. In fact, the American ambassador at the United Nations was still supporting the Trusteeship idea when he was informed of the President's announcement.

Some feel the President merely yielded to the pressures of public opinion and was not really committed to the establishment of a Jewish state, in other words he was a Zionist dupe. Probably a more accurate explanation is that Truman, disgusted with his own State Department, simply exerted his own strong will in the matter, and "let the chips fall where they may."

The relationship between the United States and the Middle East once again was fraught with tensions in 1956. Many questions still surround the action of John Foster Dulles and the State Department in rejecting Egypt's application for a loan to finance the construction of the greatly desired Aswan High Dam in Upper Egypt. This step started a chain reaction leading to President Nasser's decision to nationalize the Suez Canal on July 26, 1956. In October of that same year French Premier Guy Mollet, British Foreign Secretary Selwyn Lloyd, and Israeli Premier David Ben Gurion met at Sevres, France and planned an attack upon Egypt to restore Western control over the Suez Canal. The United States was not informed of these secret plans and was quite shocked when on October 29, 1956 Israeli Army paratroopers descended on Egyptian fortifications in the Sinai region about forty miles from the Suez Canal. It took Israel only one hundred hours to reach the Suez Canal, and many still ask why they or the British and French decided to stop. The United States played the principal role in halting the war by pressuring Israel to return to her Negev borders (she did however, gain a southern port on the Gulf of Aqaba) and probably was responsible for the failure of Britain and France to regain control of the Canal. While Dulles condemned the action of the three American allies, President Gamal Nasser emerged as the paramount leader in the Middle East. In all probability the State Department did not wish to establish Nasser so securely but ironically this is what resulted from the inconsistent American actions.

In the most recent conflict between Israel and the Arab States, the United States acted more consistently than it had in the past. Israel vanquished the Arab opposition in half the time it took to get to Suez in 1956 and increased its territory from slightly under 8,000 square miles to over 27,000 square miles. Just prior to the outbreak of hostilities President Lyndon B. Johnson stated that the United States was committed to maintaining the borders which existed in the Middle East. What he apparently meant were the borders of Israel as constituted in 1948 even though they were not recognized by the Arab states. After the Israeli victory Mr. Johnson modified his position: "There are some who have urged, as a single, simple solution, an immediate return to the situation as it was on June 4th. As our distinguished Ambassador Goldberg has already said, this is not a prescription for peace, but renewed hostilities."[16] This clearly indicated support for some of Israel's territorial gains, including the old city of Jerusalem formerly held by Jordan.

Many Israelis did not agree with the moderate attitude expressed by the United States in the recent conflict. They felt that this country should have broken the blockade which Nasser imposed at the southern end of the Gulf of Aqaba (Strait of Tiran) on May 22, 1967. While the United States was trying to end the blockade through diplomatic negotiations, the impatient Israelis resorted to direct action against the Arab states. They probably gained far more this way than they would have from diplomatic endeavors. It is quite possible that Israeli dissatisfaction with American moderation was the reason for the unprovoked attack on a United States Navy communications ship, the *Liberty*, about 15 miles off the north coast of the Sinai Peninsula. The official reports were construed to make it appear as an accident, but this is impossible to accept. Israeli planes first made six strafing runs over the ship, and then twenty minutes later three torpedo boats attacked the vessel, producing a rather high casualty toll. During this time the American flag was clearly flying above the ship.

An overall view of the United States attitude toward Palestine during the past four decades reveals that it has been favorable to the Jewish position in spite of the inconsistencies. If Israel did not have this support together with the financial backing of American and European Jewry, it is highly doubtful whether this state could have existed as long as it has. This is why the Arabs continually maintain that their opposition is not so much to Israel's existence as a Middle Eastern state per se, but to Israel, the product of Western Zionism.

Evangelical Christian Thought and the Restoration of Israel

It is interesting to examine the attitudes of European and American Christians regarding the establishment and the future of Israel. Although Zionism was essentially Jewish in its origins, there were also non-Jewish movements which assisted in furthering the concept of a Jewish national home. These groups have often been labeled with the general classification of Christian Zionism. Alfred M. Lilienthal, one of the better known anti-Zionist American Jews, points out the strange admixture of elements comprising this:

> For just as all Jews are not Zionists, so all Zionists are not Jews. Christian Zionists have been an essential part of this closely knit, well-financed, and efficiently run movement which, in its control of American media of information, has won for Israel the unique position that country occupies today. . . .
>
> Basic psychology has been applied to achieve an admixture of support: the conscience of the disturbed Christian world, desirous of making amends for its role in perennial Jewish persecution; the liberal's sympathy for the underdog; the philanthropy of the rich; and the religious sentimentalism of Biblical literalists who viewed the establishment of Israel as a necessary precursor to the second coming of Jesus. These elements blended together molded inexorable support for Israel.[17]

A recent study published in Israel by Claude Duvernoy dealing with Christian and Jewish Zionism shows that there was an intimate relationship between the Rev. William Hechler, an Anglican clergyman, and Theodor Herzl, the founder of political Zionism. After the two met in 1896, Hechler was instrumental in setting up meetings with government officials for Herzl and extended to him counsel and advice. Duvernoy pictures Herzl as the prince and Hechler as his prophet. Hechler's interest in the Jewish restoration grew out of a millenarian interpretation of the Scriptures which closely connected the second advent of Jesus Christ with the return of the Jews to Palestine. A good example of his approach to the Scriptures was his explanation of numbers mentioned in chapters 11 and 13 of Revelation. Here it states that the holy city would be under the control of Gentile nations for forty-two months or 1260 days while the "beast" is depicted as ruling also for forty-two months or 1260 days. Hechler interpreted these days as prophetic years and believed that the Muslims were the Gentile nation which would control Jerusalem for 1260 years. Since Jerusalem was conquered by the Muslims in 637, the beginning of the Messianic age would have to fall in 1897, 1260 years later, and that was the year in which the World Zionist Organization was created. He thus saw this as a direct indication from God that he should support Theodor Herzl.[18]

To classify Christian support in its various forms under the general heading of Christian Zionism is not very useful. In comparing it to Jewish Zionism, one can immediately see that the two differ in many ways. Jewish Zionism involves a world-wide organization with many affiliated groups and substantial financial resources. Christian Zionism, on the other hand, is not sponsored by an international organization specifically created for this purpose. The belief in the restoration of Israel is a part of the doctrinal position of a number of Christian denominations, organizations, and even individuals which are connected only by the common practice of basing their convictions on prophetic passages in the Bible. These groups did not contribute financially to the establishment of the state of Israel but they did lend moral support because of their belief in the second coming of Jesus Christ. It should, of course, be mentioned that many Christian groups and individuals do not assume this position in regard to the return of Israel. They believe that the prophetic portions of the Bible dealing with this topic refer to a world-wide spiritual Israel which will include Jews and Gentile alike and that this spiritual kingdom will result from the preaching of the Gospel through the Church.

Two nineteenth century English publications particularly exemplify the conflicting Christian opinions about the restoration of Israel. In 1849 William Ewbank delivered a talk at a meeting of the London Society for the Promotion of Christianity Amongst the Jews. Ewbank was an anti-restorationist who felt that any attention given to the subject of the Jewish national home was a "serious impediment to their conversion to the pure faith of Christ."[19] He frankly admitted that the question of the national restoration was a recurring theme in Jewish conversations in the 1840's, but he was convinced that Christians who are genuinely interested in evangelistic efforts among the Jews should discourage all talk of a Jewish political state. In his address Ewbank freely used Scripture to reinforce his position as, for example, James' quotation from the prophet Amos: "After this I will return, and I will rebuild the dwelling of David which has fallen; I will rebuild its ruins, and I will set it up, that the rest of men may seek the Lord, and all the Gentiles who are called by my name, says the Lord, who has made these things known from of old." (Acts 15:16, 17; Amos 9:11, 12).[20] Ewbank argued that this referred to the church and could not be interpreted as meaning the possibility of a restored Jewish state in Palestine. Isaiah 60:7 was another stumbling block for a Jewish restoration.

The context of the passage emphasized the future glory of Zion and it read as follows: "All the flocks of Kedar shall be gathered to you, the rams of Nebaioth shall minister to you; they shall come up with acceptance on my altar, and I will glorify my glorious house." It is perfectly logical, contended Ewbank, that since Christ was God's eternal lamb, there would be no need for sacrificing animals in Israel's future golden age. Israel, as a Jewish state, would neither accept Jesus as Messiah nor temple sacrificing. Therefore, the Gospel could not be fulfilled by a further institutionalization of Jewish practices such as would take place in a political state.

The opposite view of the restoration can be seen in a published lecture which David Baron, a European Jew converted to Christianity, delivered in 1890 during a visit to the United States. He discussed chronological events predicted by the Old Testament which would involve the Jewish people just before the messianic age and said: "The first item in that programme is restoration."[21] This statement set the theme of his work and he endeavored to prove it from the Biblical sources. Baron dissented strongly from those who spiritualized the prophetic portions concerning Israel by asserting that the future Israel does not refer to the church; the Jews will not be nationally gathered into the church, and the Old Testament prophecies do not refer to the restoration of Israel under Nehemiah after the Babylonian captivity. On the positive side Baron made the following claims: (1) The restoration would be so complete that even the promised land would not have room enough for the Jews; (2) Israel would enjoy national independence and maybe even supremacy over other nations; (3) the universal restoration of the Jew would be the second restoration mentioned by Isaiah (Isa. 11:11, 12); and (4) Israel had never yet possessed in all its fulness the Palestinian land which God promised to it. From the various boundaries mentioned in the Old Testament, Baron calculated that Israel would occupy an area of 300,000 square miles.[22]

Christian backing for a restoration of Israel was evident even prior to the nineteenth century. At least twelve works appeared before 1700 which on religious grounds supported the return of the Jews to Palestine. John Milton, the English poet, endorsed the idea of a Jewish restoration to Palestine. Oliver Cromwell, the Puritan leader of England, did likewise. Roger Williams, the founder of Rhode Island, was a firm believer in the restoration of Israel. Even the second president of the United States, John Adams, expressed a desire to see the return of the Jews to Palestine.[23] An American Christian spokesman, William E. Blackstone, presented a petition to President Benjamin Harrison signed by hundreds of clergymen, national and local government officials, and businessmen which asked him to call a conference of the Western powers to consider the claims of the Jews

concerning Palestine. Blackstone personally felt that the Eastern Mediterranean area possessed a great potential for agricultural and commercial
development.[24]

The twentieth century saw increasing enthusiasm among various Christian groups on both sides of the Atlantic for a Jewish national state. Zionism played a part in this, but so did a number of evangelical and fundamentalist groups in Protestant circles, especially those spawned during
conservative theological struggles in the earlier part of the century. Splinter
groups broke off from every major Protestant denomination and formed
their own denomination or fellowship because they felt that the establishment within each denomination was coercing them to accept liberal theological tenets. Because most of these groups were firmly committed to a
literal interpretation of the Bible they believed fervently that the prophetic
portions of the scriptures provided for the definite political restoration of
Israel, and for this reason they lent strong moral support to the Zionist
movement. Even the more liberal National Council of Churches has
backed Israel in a number of ways. Some of these are: resolutions calling
for the safeguarding of the security of the state of Israel, the hindering of
certain studies on the Arab refugee problem, and the dissemination of
educational materials to help the average layman understand the Jewish
community in the United States and its relationship to Israel.[25]

Evangelical feeling in the United States and Europe has been an important factor in the Zionist quest to establish and strengthen the state of
Israel. The strongest Zionist movements have taken place in those nations
identified as Christian. Without this Christian support it is doubtful that
the Jewish goal of a national restoration could have been realized.

The Christian's Dilemma

Before one can discuss the problems which an evangelical Christian
faces as he attempts to interpret international affairs in general and the
Israeli-Arab question in particular, it is necessary to mention briefly what
constitutes his basis of belief. The foundation of an evangelical's faith is
the authority of the Scriptures and the necessity for personal regeneration
through faith in Jesus Christ. Beyond these basics one finds innumerable
variations on secondary issues. The editors of *Christianity Today* expressed these differences in the following way:

> This common ground is crisscrossed by many fences. Evangelicals
> differ not only on secondary doctrines but also on ecclesiology, the
> role of the Church in society, politics, and cultural mores. No honest
> observer would minimize the extent to which they are divided.[26]

From this it is apparent that the evangelical does not have a set of cut-

and-dried answers at his disposal for the problems of international politics. Rather, he must extrapolate ethical principles from the Bible and his own personal Christian faith. Thus, he views contemporary problems from an ethical or "Christian" frame of reference and seeks for solutions which will harmonize with his value system. Statesmen and experts in international affairs do not have all the answers either, hence they gather at conferences and international bodies such as the United Nations in order to search for satisfactory ways to resolve their differences. Unfortunately, international politics do not function on a moral basis. Statesmen may give lip service to rational judgment and moral principle but the concessions they seek will always be those which they believe will benefit their national interest.

The recent conflict (June 1967) between the Jews and Arabs is an excellent example of this. The Arab leaders were more interested in upholding Arab pride, regardless of the price, than they were in dealing with the plight of their people. This position cannot be defended either on rational or moral grounds despite Arab attempts to do so in the United Nations. The Israelis, on the other hand, had been planning for this war since the last conflict in 1956. The war was well-planned and executed, and it resulted in the loss of many lives and the confiscation of large amounts of Arab territory. The Israeli response to the Arabs' request for the return of their land was that part of it would be retained and the fate of the remainder determined by negotiations which naturally could be expected to benefit Israel. To defend this action on a moral basis is extremely difficult but to advocate it on nationalistic grounds is quite easy.

Because of his belief in divine providence, the committed Christian cannot look upon world affairs as being totally divorced from divine direction. He must take into account God's existence in every aspect of life, and must reject the idea that man's only responsibility is to mind his own business. The Christian is truly his "brother's keeper." This motivating force causes him to realize that he must project these attitudes from the personal level to the national and international level. It is unacceptable for him to be a complete isolationist in any realm of life.

In a book which attempts to explain the various interpretations which Christians adopt in politics, Denis Baly states that many Christians use the New Testament as their basis of thinking while excluding the Old Testament. Although these people believe they should study the Old Testament through the eyes of the New Testament, nevertheless they ought to accord equal authority to both sections of the Bible. Baly asserts that the Christian stands on weak ground if he uses only the New Testament as his basis of authority in political affairs because it is primarily concerned with *persons*, while the Old Testament is oriented toward *nations*. A philosophy based purely on the latter could result in concepts of strict segregation or isolation. A philosophy based purely on the former could lead to a strict moralism. Whereas the two can and do overlap, a balanced Christian position has to regard nations and individuals on a somewhat different basis. A person can die a martyr's death for what he believes, but it would be difficult to comprehend a nation experiencing martyrdom.[27] Moral standards must be used in the understanding of international affairs, but the Christian must be realistic enough to see that many nations and individuals will feel no obligation to abide by such standards.

The more deeply one probes into international problems, the more likely it is that he will discover evidences of immoral behavior. Whether in Biblical times or in the twentieth century one still finds men's attitudes to be consistently selfish. Yet, the Christian has the responsibility to uphold that which he considers to be right.

As one directs attention to the Israeli position in the Middle East, it is difficult to justify by moral standards certain national decisions and actions. During the events leading up to independence in 1948 the Zionist Jews mercilessly evicted the Arab residents of Palestine. The crimes which the so-called Christian nations of Europe committed against the European Jews were duplicated to some degree by the Zionists as they pursued their conquest of Palestine. The Arab here became the persecuted and the threatening voice which had to be silenced.[28] The refugee problem following the 1948 war produced a festering sore which remains yet unhealed. The Israelis did not consider it their responsibility to help solve the question since the refugees were residing in the surrounding Arab states. There they have lived for twenty years in appalling poverty and filth.

To justify Israel's role in the 1956 conflict is also difficult, particularly since it was linked with a Western imperialistic venture, the recapture of the Suez Canal. It is true that her ships were excluded from the use of the canal, but perhaps the taking of the Sinai Peninsula could have been justified better on the nationalistic premise that it demonstrated Israeli armed might. Her expression of strength did gain the southern port of Eilat, thus giving Israel the much-needed southern access to the Indian Ocean and East Asia. Perhaps the justification can be found, relatively speaking, in the greater good which was provided for the citizens of Israel by the opening of this Negev port.

In the most recent crisis the Israeli actions have again demonstrated an aggressive stance toward the Arabs. This does not mean that the Arabs were not also at fault since the Egyptians just prior to the outbreak of hostilities had blockaded the Gulf of Aqaba. Foreign correspondents were denied access to Sharm el Sheik at the southern end of the gulf by the Egyptian government. This left all news coverage to *Al Ahram*, the semi-official newspaper in Cairo. *Al Ahram* announced the mining of the entrance to the Gulf to deter Eilat-bound vessels. This mining, however, never took place and this was known by Israeli intelligence. Similarily, *Al Ahram* proclaimed that Egyptian patrols halted two German ships because they were supposedly bound for Eilat. This report was also known to be false by the Israelis for one ship never entered the Straits of Tiran and the other ship telegraphed its owners that it had had a normal voyage and had not been boarded. Not one ship was stopped and goods continued to flow under non-Israeli flags as they had in normal times.[29] It was a blockade that essentially blockaded nothing but did afford a provocation which could lead to war. One should not condemn the Israelis for their over reaction to this because any highly nationalistic people could have responded in the same way.

The Arab position in Palestine is not without fault and in many ways is a most tragic one. In the twentieth century the Arab awakened suddenly to the technological advances and the military potentialities offered by modern science. In his rush to bridge the gap between his world and that of the technologically advanced nations, he failed to master the ideas on which this modern world was based. The Arab peasant was bewildered by the economic support and the international contacts which were at the disposal of the Palestinian Jews. Unable to compete on this level, the Arabs resorted to terrorist activities. During the two decades after the establishment of Israel the Arabs were not able to face reality. The Arab states could only agree on one solution, namely, pushing Israel into the Mediterranean Sea. Of all these states, only Jordan made any attempt to integrate the Palestinian refugees into its society. The Arab countries continued to fan the fires of nationalistic pride which looked toward the reconquest of Palestine, but they manifested little concern about the welfare of the average Arab peasant.

The Arab world has now lost its third conflict with the Palestinian Jews. Economically, it is in the worst possible position, especially in those states surrounding Israel. Outside assistance is absolutely necessary if these governments are to meet even the minimal needs of their citizens. Perhaps this situation would not have come about if the Arab states had faced the reality of the existence of Israel, established diplomatic relations with the Jewish state, and attempted to share the technological knowledge that could increase agricultural production. Unfortunately, this did not happen and probably will not in the immediate future.

How does the evangelical relate his understanding of the Scriptures with current events in the Middle East? One must admit that there are many passages in the prophetic writings of the Old Testament which have not been fulfilled. For example, if one considers Israel and Jerusalem as described in the Book of Zechariah, he might wonder about the future of Israel. "And the Lord will become king over all the earth; on that day the Lord will be one and his name one," (Zech. 14:9) describes a situation which has never taken place. The destinies of Egypt and Israel are discussed in a number of other passages such as Deuteronomy 28:63–67, Jeremiah 43:8–13, and Isaiah 9. Isaiah struck an encouraging note when he wrote about the future millennium when there will be no conflict between the Jew and the Arab:

> In that day there will be a highway from Egypt to Assyria, and the Assyrian will come into Egypt, and the Egyptian into Assyria, and the Egyptians will worship with the Assyrians. In that day Israel will be the third with Egypt and Assyria, a blessing in the midst of the earth, whom the Lord of hosts has blessed, saying, "Blessed be Egypt my people, and Assyria the work of my hands, and Israel my heritage." (Isa. 19:24–5).

The Christian should not push aside these predictions as idealistic dreaming because they do provide a basis of hope for the future of the Middle East.

When Jesus was discussing future times in the Olivet discourse, he made some definite statements about Jerusalem. The holy city was to face desolation and suffering which he described in these words: "For great distress shall be upon the earth and wrath upon this people; they will fall by the edge of the sword, and be led captive among all nations; and Jerusalem will be trodden down by the Gentiles, until the times of the Gentiles are fulfilled." (Luke 21:23–4) In June 1967 control of the old city of Jerusalem passed from Gentile to Jewish hands for the first time since these words had been uttered. There is no guarantee that the Israelis will continue to control the old city, but it is interesting to note the possible fulfillment of this statement by Jesus.

The Apostle Paul dealt with the relationship between the future of Israel and the Gospel in Romans 9–11. He strongly emphasized the point that God deals with all individuals equally as far as the message of reconciliation is concerned. Yet at the same time, Paul mentioned that God has not forgotten his own people, the nation of Israel: "Lest you be wise in your own conceits, I want you to understand this mystery, brethren: a hardening has come upon part of Israel, until the full number of the Gentiles come in, and so all Israel will be saved." (Rom. 11:25–6) The Scriptures seem to support the prophetic idea of a national restoration for Israel.

Even if one does accept this as a valid possibility, is he automatically entitled to assume a pro-Israel stance in the present Middle Eastern situation? A recent article in *Christianity Today* forcefully demonstrated that the American support of Israel has dealt a virtual death blow to Christian missionary endeavor in Arab lands. The bitterness which Muslim Arabs have toward America has been directed at the Christian church because they feel the United States government and the church are inseparable.[30] The fact of the matter is that the Christian cannot simply categorize himself as pro-Israeli or pro-Arab because he is obliged to stand for that which is right and just in this as well as every international question. He should condemn unrighteous deeds whether they be committed by his own or any other nation. Just because a Christian feels that Israel has a future does not mean that he cannot be critical of the many unethical and criminal acts committed by the Israelis. The same holds true for the person who feels that Israel has no future in God's plan for mankind. He cannot lightly dismiss or overlook actions on the part of the Arabs which violate the principles of God's moral law. He must condemn the stubborn determination of the Arab leaders to obtain revenge at any cost and their failure to meet the pressing physical needs of their own population, and he can in no way excuse the violence directed against pro-Israeli public figures, so tragically exemplified in the assassination of Robert Kennedy.

For the Christian the Israeli-Arab problem is a definite dilemma. Although his sympathies may lie with one side or the other and his position may be influenced by his interpretation of the prophetic Scriptures, he must nevertheless look at the question in light of the moral issues involved. The result is that he cannot give wholehearted allegiance to either side because both parties have transgressed God's moral law. If the Christian can somehow lead them to recognize this, perhaps a way of reconciliation for these two peoples can be opened.

NOTES

1. For a concise but adequate history of Zionism, see Israel Cohen, *The Zionist Movement* (London: Frederick Muller, 1945).

2. The English translation of this work is Theodor Herzl, *The Jewish State: An Attempt at a Modern Solution of the Jewish Question* (3rd ed., London: Central Office of the Zionist Organization, 1936).

3. Oscar I. Janowsky, *Foundations of Israel* (Princeton: D. Van Nostrand, 1959), p. 134.

4. Janowsky, *Foundations of Israel*, pp. 136–37.

5. Philip K. Hitti, *The Near East in History* (Princeton: D. Van Nostrand, 1961), p. 509.

6. Great Britain, *Parliamentary Papers*, 1939, Cmd. 6019, pp. 1–12.

7. Peretz, *Middle East Today*, p. 275.

8. Two rather complete histories of the Arab peoples are Carl Brockelmann, *History of the Islamic Peoples* (New York: Capricorn Books, 1960), and Philip K. Hitti, *History of the Arabs* (New York: St. Martin's Press, 1963).

9. William A. Williams, *America and the Middle East* (New York: Rinehart, 1958), p. 1.

10. *Ibid.*, p. 40.

11. Nadav Safran, *The United States and Israel* (Cambridge: Harvard University Press, 1963), pp. 38–39.

12. Harry S. Truman, *Memoirs by Harry S. Truman* (Garden City: Doubleday, 1956), II, p. 133.

13. Williams, *America and the Middle East*, p. 41.

14. Safran, *United States and Israel*, p. 42.

15. Truman, *Memoirs*, II, pp. 158, 160.

16. This was stated in an address by President Johnson to the National Foreign Policy Conference for Educators as reported by Associated Press. *Christian Science Monitor*, June 21, 1967, p. 9.

17. Alfred M. Lilienthal, *The Other Side of the Coin: An American Perspective of the Arab-Israel Conflict* (New York: Devin-Adair, 1965), p. 4.

18. Claude Duvernoy, *Le Prince et le Prophete* (Jerusalem: The Jewish Agency, 1966).

19. William W. Ewbank, *The National Restoration of the Jews to Palestine Repugnant to the Word of God* (Liverpool: Dreighton and Laughton, 1849), p. 4.

20. The Revised Standard Version of the Bible is used throughout this essay even though Ewbank quoted from the King James Version.

21. David Baron, *The Jewish Problem: Its Solution or Israel's Present and Future* (Revised ed., London: Morgan and Scott, c. 1896), p. 20.

22. *Ibid.*, pp. 19–22.

23. Arthur W. Kac, *The Rebirth of the State of Israel* (Chicago: Moody Press, 1958), pp. 48–51. The author's strong dispensationalist approach often shades his interpretation, but the book does contain a rather detailed discussion of the restoration question.

24. *Ibid.*, pp. 51–52.

25. Lilienthal, *The Other Side of the Coin*, pp. 7–10.

26. "Somehow, Let's Get Together," *Christianity Today*, XI (June 9, 1967), p. 24. Another interesting editorial on this subject is "Who Are the Evangelicals?" *Ibid.*, XI (June 23, 1967), pp. 22–23.

27. Denis Baly, *Multitudes in the Valley* (Greenwich, Conn.: The Seabury Press, 1957), pp. 247–49.

28. The British historian, Arnold J. Toynbee, has strongly accused the Zionist Jews of a "more tragic fall" than the Nazi Gentiles because of their persecution of the Arabs. See *A Study of History* (New York: Oxford University Press, 1954), VIII, pp. 288–92; and *Ibid.*, (1964), XII, pp. 627–28.

29. "Why the Worst Happened" from *The Sunday Times* [London], reprinted in *Atlas Magazine*, VII (July 1967), pp. 14–17.

30. James L. Kelso, "Perspective on Arab-Israeli Tensions," *Christianity Today*, XII (June 7, 1968), p. 9.

Robert G. Clouse is Associate Professor of History at Indiana State University, Terre Haute, Indiana. Born in Mansfield, Ohio on August 26, 1931, he attended the public schools of that city. Mr. Clouse was a student at Ashland College and received the B.A. degree with honors from Bryan College in 1954. He obtained the B.D. degree magna cum laude from Grace Theological Seminary in 1957 and the M.A. and Ph.D. in history from the University of Iowa in 1960 and 1963. In the summer of 1964 he was a postdoctoral fellow at the Folger Shakespeare Library in Washington, D. C., and he pursued research in England and Germany in 1968.

As an ordained Brethren minister, Mr. Clouse has served churches in Iowa and Indiana. He was a teaching assistant in the Department of History at the University of Iowa for three years and a visiting professor at Indiana University, Bloomington during the fall semester of 1965–66 and 1968–69. He joined the history faculty of Indiana State University, Terre Haute as an assistant professor in 1963 and was promoted to associate professor in 1967.

Mr. Clouse is interested in the history of the Christian Church, particularly in the Reformation period. As a student of the history of doctrine, he has paid close attention to millennialism and has written on the seventeenth century appearance of this phenomenon. His articles have appeared in the *Teachers College Journal*, the *Grace Journal*, and the *Westminister Dictionary of Church History*. Professor Clouse belongs to numerous professional organizations, including the American Historical Association, American Society of Church History, Indiana Academy of Religion, Society for Reformation Research, Central Renaissance Conference, Renaissance Society of America, and American Association of University Professors. He served as the 1967–68 president of the Central Renaissance Conference. Mr. Clouse also was chosen as an Outstanding Young Man of America in 1967 and is an active member of the Republican Party.

ROBERT G. CLOUSE

The Vietnam War
in Christian Perspective

One of the more pressing problems of the present time is that of armed conflict. Never have the issues of war been brought so sharply into focus as by the current struggle in Vietnam. If evangelical Christians wish to communicate the Gospel to men today, they must apply their faith to this problem. Certainly the threat of nuclear destruction has made any resort to the use of force to settle international problems a very delicate business. The Christian ought to model his attitude toward war on the teachings of the New Testament, but it has so little to say about this vital topic that one can only formulate general principles from its pages rather than find specific directions for action. Historically, Christians have drawn three different approaches to the problems of war and peace from the teaching of Jesus and the Apostles.

The early church assumed a pacifist stance down to the time of the Emperor Constantine (c. 300 A.D.). This view of society traditionally emphasizes withdrawal from the world and a hopelessness or pessimism toward human government. Although this attitude was not prevalent during the Middle Ages, it reappeared at the time of the Reformation among the Anabaptists and Quakers and is seen today in some of the "peace churches" such as the Quakers, the Church of the Brethren, and the Mennonites.

A second approach, that of the "just war," developed after the time of Constantine. This idea, borrowed heavily from classical teaching, was encouraged by the identification of church and state in the late Roman Empire and the threat of the barbarian invasions. St. Augustine taught that the "just war" should be fought according to a code of good faith and humanity but monks and priests were nevertheless to be exempted from participation in the conflict. The view of many Christian groups with respect to World War II is a contemporary illustration of this approach.

During the high middle ages, the period when the church occupied the foremost position in western society, the idea of the crusade prevailed. The crusades were religious wars fought at the command of the church or in response to the wishes of certain religious leaders in an effort to facilitate the spread of Christian ideology. In more recent times the crusading approach has been exemplified by the attitude which a great many American churches took toward World War I.

The "Crusade" in Vietnam

While most of the major Protestant denominations do not view the current struggle in Southeast Asia in crusading terms, it appears that this spirit is rather prevalent in evangelical circles. Far too many Gospel ministers are being led astray by a facile equation of any enemy of the United States of America with an anti-Christian, materialistic, godless communism. They find it easy to see the war in Vietnam as a gigantic, apocalyptic struggle between the forces of Christ (America and South Vietnam) and the forces of antichrist (the Viet Cong and their allies). The Christian crusaders against communism who wish to defend American "liberties" readily brand anyone who opposes this war as a "pink" or "red" or a foolish dupe of communist propaganda. All who listen to very conservative preaching have been exposed to this kind of reasoning. Moreover, the argument continues that since many liberal theologians object to the war in Vietnam, those who have questions about it had best be cautious or they too will fall into the trap that has been set and be enticed away from the true faith. As one noted fundamentalist puts it: "Then theologically the Bible is no longer the guide and standard by which people generally settle matters. There is little hatred for sin. There is no recognition of the high duty and responsibility of putting down sin. Our consciences have been blurred. We do not believe in a hell for sinners."[1]

It would be well to examine with some care one argument which has been widely circulated among Christian people for the unqualified support of the present policy in Vietnam. This tract, written by John R. Rice, makes the initial assertion that "no one, acting for himself, has a right to kill."[2] The Biblical condemnation of killing cited to support this includes the Sixth Commandment and such New Testament statements as Revelation 21:8: "But as for the cowardly, the faithless, the polluted, as for murderers, fornicators, sorcerers, idolaters, and all liars, their lot shall be in the lake that burns with fire and brimstone, which is the second death." However, it is also pointed out that God himself kills at certain times. He slew the firstborn of Egypt (Ex. 12:29), Nadab and Abihu

(Lev. 10:1, 2), Korah, Dathan, Abiram, and their families when they rebelled against him (Num. 16:31, 32), and Ananias and Sapphira (Acts 5:1–10). God has delegated this power to kill to organized society in order to deal with murderers and those guilty of other crimes. (Gen. 9: 6; Ex. 21:15–17; Rom. 13:1–6) Rice continues:

> To deny the right, yea, the duty of the government, to assess and inflict the death penalty is to deny the authority and right of God, and that course leads to anarchy. The governments of the world have the right and duty to put to death criminals and rebels against the government and against society. Kings and governors carry the sword of God and they are the ministers of God to execute His wrath and vengeance upon sinners. That is the united teaching of both the Old and New Testaments, and all citizens should pay tribute, that is taxes, for this very cause, that the government may have strength to protect us from criminals and to enforce the laws. Those who resist the powers that be, resist the ordinance of God and the ministers of God.[3]

Just as God justifies the killing of criminals, he sometimes wishes nations to go to war; for, so the argument goes, there is no distinction between a police force and an army. War, though a horrible business, is to be preferred to compromise with evil. "In God's sight, sin is always worse than bloodshed."[4] The armies of Moses, Joshua, and David show how God can use war to carry out his policy. "The Modernist and unbeliever says that that teaching is in the Old Testament, and that therefore it will not do for us today. But the Old Testament is the Word of God just the same as the New Testament."[5] Therefore, Christians should not hesitate to fight in the army and engage in conflicts such as the current one in Vietnam. Romans 13:1 teaches that the powers that be are ordained of God and that one should obey them. Furthermore, some of the most godly men of the Bible have been soldiers including Abraham, Moses, Joshua, Gideon, David, and Asa. And if one still should doubt that good company can be found in the army, Rice mentions some more recent soldiers who would be well-liked by most American Christians. These famous American military men include Abraham Lincoln, who served in the Black Hawk War, Stonewall Jackson, Robert E. Lee, and George Washington.

Tucked in among all these references to godliness on the part of soldiers is a statement which reveals the theoretical basis for most of these remarks. Dr. Rice informs his readers:

> I believe that the enslavement of millions of people by communism is indescribably wicked. Any good Christian ought to have a

holy indignation over it. I think that America sinned through our government in holding back General MacArthur and preventing outright victory in the Korean War. I believe our government sinned against God in holding back and letting Russian troops occupy Berlin and divide Germany. I believe that before that, the American government greatly sinned in being soft on communism, and turning the mainland of China principally over to the Communists and thus betraying our friend, Chiang Kai-shek. I have no doubt that if there is ever holy and righteous cause for war, it is to prevent godless communism with its murder and torture and persecution from taking over other lands which ask our help.[6]

The only way the Christian can work for peace, according to this line of thinking, is to pray (cf. I Tim. 2:1, 2) and to look for the second coming of Jesus Christ when peace on earth will be restored.

This view concerning the present conflict in Vietnam is not shared, however, by all Christians. For some believers it seems to be heartless and impersonal, and it is matched in the secular sphere by those who preach power politics and discuss nations and peoples as though they were chessmen to be manipulated rather than cared for as human beings. Anyone who wants to form a balanced opinion of the war should begin, of course, by inquiring into the details of the nation of Vietnam. It is interesting to observe that in the above-mentioned pamphlet the name Vietnam does not appear except in the title. This utter lack of understanding of the situation in Southeast Asia makes it virtually impossible for such an individual to apply Christian morality to the struggle there.

A Brief History of Vietnam

Vietnam has known much conflict and many conquerors.[7] From 208 B.C. to 939 A.D. the northern part of the country was ruled by the Chinese. By 40 A.D. they had introduced the bureaucratic system of government which had evolved in China. Despite some abortive revolutions they ruled much of the land until the fall of the T'ang dynasty when Vietnam gained its independence. This long period of domination gave a distinct Chinese cast to Vietnamese civilization. The Vietnamese used Chinese written characters, studied the Confucian classics in order to pass through an examination system into high public office, and believed in the government of enlightened men who would rule by persuasion rather than force. Besides the Confucian tradition the Vietnamese were also affected by Buddhism, and the early civil service included many Buddhist monks. The increasingly Confucian emphasis in the royal court, however, led to the isolation of the Buddhists from the government. Still, the mass of the people accepted a religious synthesis among several faiths which continues to the present day. "Buddhism then becomes the common denominator in the beliefs of the Vietnamese people. A Vietnamese who professes to be a Confucian does not deny his belief in Buddhism, nor must a convinced Budhist declare that he disbelieves Confucianism. That is why we cannot say with accuracy how many Vietnamese are Buddhist. When we examine the beliefs of a typical peasant we find elements of Buddhism, Taoism, and Confucianism intimately mixed together, along with still other elements belonging to native beliefs that existed even before the three great religions were introduced into Vietnam."[8]

With the exception of a twenty year interlude of Chinese rule in the fifteenth century, Vietnam existed as an independent country from 940 until 1883. In that year the French completed their conquest of the land. Prior to 1400 the state centered in the north around the Red River Valley, but beginning in the fifteenth century the power of Vietnam extended into the south as well. Later there were periods of strife and division in the country but the essential cultural unity of Vietnam remained. The most serious division came about 1620 when a powerful noble family, the Nguyen, was established in the south while the Trinh clan ruled from Hanoi. It took the northern dynasty fifty years of military efforts to realize that force could not unify the land. This led to a century long truce which ended in 1774. About that time, however, a nationalist movement overthrew both ruling houses. During these years the rulers of both the north and the south never ceased to proclaim their belief in the unity of Vietnam. This was evidenced by the fact that both sides claimed to recognize the Le dynasty as the legitimate rulers of the land although neither side paid much attention to the monarchs.

The Vietnamese who pushed to the south during the seventeenth and eighteenth centuries found a very rich area in which to settle, namely, the Mekong Delta. This gave them an opportunity to enlarge their lands and challenged them in much the same way that the western frontier vitalized American life. However, this spread of the people away from the Red River Valley and the centralizing influence of Hanoi led to an increase in power by local landowners. They found it to their interest to keep the village economy as it had been for centuries, though the forces rooted in the Vietnamese villages made for a certain unity in the country's life. Since the geographical and climatic conditions in the south were similar to those in the north, agriculture could be practiced in much the same way in both areas. Also, when the immigrants moved south, they usually came in relatively large, well-organized groups so that they could successfully engage in the work of clearing the fields, draining swamps, and building irrigation systems for crops. These peasants created the Vietnamese national spirit for they not only helped the country grow by their pioneering push to the south but they also kept alive a sense of national unity. Unfortunately, they were cruelly oppressed by the elite mandarin class. An old Vietnamese peasant song sums up his treatment: "I am always bathed in sweat, and of my torn garments only the collar survives."[9] They often revolted against the landlords but always ineffectively.

A new factor was introduced into Vietnamese life when the Portuguese arrived in 1535. They traded with the country, which they called Cochinchina, during the sixteenth century. The commercial position which the Portuguese held in the east was lost to the Dutch who became the leading European exploiters of the Orient during the seventeenth century. The Dutch established trading posts in Vietnam and later in the century both the English and the French joined them. During the eighteenth century all the westerners except the Portuguese withdrew from Vietnam and even their trade was carried on in a very weak way. Not only did the rivalry between the powers make conquest by any one of them difficult, but also it did not appear that the area was worth the expense of conquest.

Western influence might have died out entirely had it not been for the work of Christian missionaries. Although much of the Roman Catholic evangelism in Asia was not successful, it met with more success in Vietnam than in any other Asiatic area except the Philippines. An outstanding Catholic leader, Monsignor Alexander of Rhodes, came to Vietnam in the early seventeenth century, learned the language, and wrote a catechism and a Vietnamese-Latin-Portuguese dictionary. The path of missions was a rough one for Rhodes because the mandarins realized that he would undermine the foundation of their society with his new doctrines. Expelled from the country, he continued to direct the work from the Jesuit headquarters in Macao.

Before he died, Rhodes devised a plan to train indigenous priests who would not be required to learn Latin and would be subject to the authority of the Roman Catholic Church but not that of the Vietnamese state. This plan was adopted in 1658 and the work of evangelization was eventually placed under the control of the Society of Foreign Missions founded at Paris in 1664. The Society was to give spiritual strength to the French East India Company founded in the same year. François Pallu, one of the early directors of the evangelization of Vietnam, illustrates the close cooperation between the religious and economic interests of the French in the east. He served as the East India Company's principal adviser on how to meet competition in the Orient, and even directed Colbert's military campaign against the Dutch in the Far East. The French effort to take over Southeast Asia received a setback in 1658 when their attempt to conquer Siam failed. The Christian communities which were established in

Vietnam did not receive the formal backing of a western government until the nineteenth century.

The official French lack of concern about Cochinchina did not mean that individuals were not interested in seeing western influences spread in that area. In the latter half of the eighteenth century Pigneau de Béhaine, French bishop of South Vietnam, aided the Nguyen ruler of Vietnam who was driven from his throne by rebels. The bishop organized a few hundred western volunteers who fought for the reunification of Vietnam in 1801–1802. Pigneau had hoped to educate the king's son in the Christian religion and to see a church-oriented ruler on the throne of the country, but the young prince died before his father and Minh Mang, who came to the throne in 1820, proved to be anti-Christian. In many ways a capable ruler, Mang reorganized the social basis of the land and deprived the landlords of their power. His new allies were an even more backward-looking class of mandarins.[10] These government functionaries were selected from the ranks of the educated on the basis of a knowledge of classics modelled after the Chinese system. This isolationist mentality led to the persecution of Christians who were associated with western ideas. In 1836, after a French priest was caught with a group of rebels, the government threatened to execute all priests, and Vietnam, with the exception of Da Nang, was closed to Europeans.

The Vietnamese were able to pursue this independent policy because the Europeans were preoccupied with the problems caused by the Napoleonic Wars. After the Vienna settlement and the restoration of the Bourbons in France, it was possible for the Westerners once again to consider enlarging their influence in the Far East. French national concern for the Roman Catholic missions in East Asia grew, and this enthusiasm had an impact on the government during the regime of Napoleon III. This interest was shown by the occupation of Tourane (Da Nang) and Saigon in 1858. The Vietnamese emperor in 1862 signed a treaty with France ceding the three provinces adjacent to Saigon, allowing passage on the Mekong River, giving missionaries freedom of action throughout Vietnam, opening three ports for trade with the west, and agreeing to pay the French a large indemnity. The ruler assented to this humiliating treaty because of a rebellion which threatened his control over the Red River Valley. By 1867 the French had conquered all of Cochinchina and had extended their "protection" to the Kingdom of Cambodia to the west.

The Europeans had hoped that the Mekong River might prove to be a highway into China, but when they discovered that it was not navigable beyond southern Vietnam, they redirected their imperialist efforts to the north. By 1883 French officials had gained control of the Red River Valley and Annam, and in 1887 the administrative unit of Indochina was organized. This consisted of Cochinchina (the Mekong Delta). Cambodia, Annam, and Tongking (the Red River Valley). Laos was added to this union in 1893. The Vietnamese people hated the new French colonial masters, but gradually their will to resist was broken and a new regime molded their future.

The colonial outlook of the western people in the later nineteenth century was an extension of nationalism. The European nation-states had so glorified their own past that they had come to believe they were destined to bring "civilization" to all the world. The new rulers of Vietnam felt that they should help the brown-skinned people of the world to become more like Europeans. After conquering the country, the French introduced an educational system, staffed by French-trained teachers, which was designed to instill western culture into Vietnamese life. Besides education, the Europeans also fostered economic development and soon Indochina became the richest colonial possession of France. They built railways and roads, started coal mines and cotton mills, and established coffee, tea, rubber, and rice plantations. Most of this commercial enterprise was in the hands of French and Chinese merchants and entrepreneurs because the Paris government felt that Vietnamese nationals might hinder French exploitation of the country.

The Vietnamese deeply resented the foreign domination and not only because of economic exploitation. Although enlightened as far as racial attitudes were concerned, the French created dissatisfaction by their practice of granting citizenship to a very small number of colonial subjects. Hostility against foreign rule was often expressed through the old religious systems of Buddhism and Confucianism, and thus the colonial masters tended to favor the Roman Catholics. Meanwhile, an early leader of the resistance movement to French rule, Phan Boi Chau, directed his propaganda and revolutionary work from China. The Japanese victory over the Russians in 1905 encouraged Chau and other Vietnamese to rebel, hence giving this period of history the title "the era of plots." The new revolutionary groups adopted the ideology of such western writers as Rousseau and Montesquieu against the French rulers. French policy seemed utterly unable to cope with the real problems of Vietnam.

World War I added its unsettling effects to Southeast Asia. Over one hundred thousand Vietnamese soldiers and laborers were sent to Europe during the war, and on their return they brought a knowledge of the West and a desire to improve conditions in their homeland. The French tried to satisfy some of their demands by authorizing elected assemblies but these were chosen by such a small electorate that they did little to quiet the unrest. In 1925 a young revolutionary named Nguyen Ai Quoc (Ho Chi Minh) founded the Revolutionary Youth League which became the nucleus for the future Indochinese Communist Party. Quoc was educated in France where he became a Marxist, only later travelling to Moscow. For the next forty years he was to show a single-minded dedication to the cause of revolution in Vietnam. In 1927 Ho joined with a number of other Vietnamese revolutionary parties to form the Vietnam Quoc Dan Dang or VNQDD with the advice and assistance of the Kuomintang Party of China. The VNQDD fomented a series of uprisings in 1930 which the French ruthlessly suppressed. Villages were strafed and bombed, prisoners tortured, hostages executed, and finally almost the entire leadership of the VNQDD was caught and liquidated.

In 1933 a new emperor, Bao Dai, returned from his schooling in France. (The French continued to keep a puppet emperor on the throne during the years they occupied the land.) The imperial court was for a short time a center of attempts to loosen French control. Ngo Dinh Diem, a reform-minded nationalist, was appointed Minister of the Interior and made secretary of a commission reform. When he realized the insincerity of the French he resigned in disgust and went into exile. World War II brought Japanese control to Vietnam, but they ruled through the French and little change occurred. In fact, it should be noted that the French were the only Western power to retain control in Asia during World War II. When defeat in the conflict appeared imminent, the Japanese promoted the establishment of an independent Vietnamese government at Hué in the south in 1945.

Two Vietnams

This independent Vietnamese state which the Japanese encouraged Bao Dai to form had a serious rival in the north. In late 1944 Ho Chi Minh, who had been directing guerrilla activity in North Vietnam during the war, formed a provisional government and was chosen president of the Vietnamese Republic. The Chinese refused to let French troops go north of the sixteenth parallel after the fall of Japan and this helped Ho consolidate his regime. In March 1946 the French recognized the northern Republic and promised to hold a referendum in the south to see if the country could be unified. They hoped to make the Indochinese Federation part of a world-wide French Union on the order of the British Commonwealth of Nations. This did not gain much support in Vietnam so France organized a separate state in Cochinchina and declined to hold the election. The Vietnamese reply to this was to attack the French garrisons in 1946. The leadership in the fight for independence was taken by the Vietminh organization of Ho Chi Minh which aligned itself with more moderate resistance groups.[11]

The French persuaded Bao Dai to head an opposition government. However, Dai's dependence upon the French and the fact that he continued to live the life of a playboy in France cost him a great deal of support. Still, there was considerable anti-communist sentiment behind his government, especially among the Catholics of Tongking and the different religious sects in the area of Saigon. The Tongking Roman Catholics numbered two and one half million out of a population of nine million. The bishops held political as well as religious power in the rural villages and they organized militia units to fight the communists. Bao Dai and his representatives distrusted these forces and refused to cooperate with them. The religious sects in the south also seemed to offer a vital power group which Bao Dai and his troops did not care to encourage. An example of these exotic sects was the Caodaists who had their own hierarchy including a pope and cardinals and a theology which contained Buddhist and Christian elements and featured such patron saints as Victor Hugo. Only one sect found favor with Bao Dai, namely, the Xuan which operated a mafia-type organization in the Saigon area that controlled such activities as prostitution and gambling. Another obstacle to an effective government was the French demand that the Vietnamese army should not be allowed to organize into large forces but rather serve in small companies with the Europeans.

Thus the Bao Dai government was handicapped by internal dissension and French caution, while Ho Chi Minh received considerable help from his communist allies. By 1949 Mao Tse-Tung had seized control of China and in 1950 he recognized the government of Ho. This communist aid went beyond politics and before long there were training centers in South China where Vietminh forces were taught to use modern weapons. These newly trained troops enabled Ho to change his tactics from guerrilla warfare to open battles with large concentrations of manpower. To prevent the movement of Ho's forces out of Hanoi to the west and south, the French had placed a garrison at Dien Bien Phu. In the spring of 1954 this fortress was besieged and captured. Not only did the Vietminh win a decisive military victory when this center was overrun but they also scored a decisive psychological success against the French. This enabled the Vietnamese to obtain a settlement at a conference in Geneva (May to July 1954) that ended the sixty year domination of France over the area. The nations represented at this meeting included Britain, the Soviet Union, France, the United States, China, Cambodia, Laos, and Vietnam. (There were representatives of both the French-backed South Vietnamese government and the North Vietnamese Democratic Republic.)

The decisions at this conference included the following: (1) Vietnam was to be divided temporarily along the seventeenth parallel until general elections could be held in July 1956 to reunify the country; (2) French troops were to be withdrawn from the north; (3) the Vietnamese people were to have three hundred days to move to either the North or South zone as they chose; (4) military personnel and supplies were not to be increased in either zone; (5) an International Control Commission consisting of India, Canada, and Poland was to see that these agreements were followed; and (6) Laos and Cambodia were to be established as independent nations. Although the United States did not sign these agreements, it did agree verbally to refrain from the use of force to disturb the Geneva settlement.[12]

As a result of these decisions, there was a dramatic move of approximately one million Catholic refugees from North Vietnam to the south. These people had enjoyed a privileged status under the French, and since they had fought against the Vietminh, they feared reprisals. The United States sent a team to aid the refugees, and one of the young naval officers assigned to this duty was Thomas A. Dooley. He came not only as a naval officer but also as a Roman Catholic who sympathized with his co-religionists.[13] Tom Dooley's experiences led him to write about them, and he exerted considerable influence on American public opinion.[14] According to the Gallup Poll of 1960, he was one of the ten most admired Americans. Tragically mistaken about the realities of Southeast Asia, this young man believed that America had not really been involved in Vietnam. Actually, during the years 1950–54 the United States had given the French 2.6 billion dollars to restore western influence in that area. Perhaps depending too much on ill-informed advice like Dooley's, America increased her commitment and gave large amounts of aid directly to the government of South Vietnam. Many believed that out of this an Asian counterpart to West Germany would develop.

However, South Vietnam continued to be racked with problems. Besides the difficulties of the refugees from the north there were still communists in the south and sects such as the Caodaists who considered themselves autonomous. A strong leader was needed and in 1954 Bao Dai asked Ngo Dinh Diem to become prime minister. Diem acted vigorously to secure the withdrawal of French troops, put down the rebellious sects, and delay the election for reunification of the country. By 1955 he had become head of state in place of Bao Dai and had replaced the empire with a republic. From this date the United States assumed the role of the French in supporting the government of South Vietnam. With the establishment of the Republic the people of the south had expected economic development and social reform. This was slow to come, and aside from an improvement in the legal status of women, which was achieved at the insistence of his sister-in-law, Madame Nhu, Diem made few improvements. To an ever-increasing degree the goal of Diem became simply the abolition of opposition so that orderly reform could be carried out in his own way. Diem also halted exports to the north, and since the rice production of South Vietnam was necessary to feed the industrial population of the North this was a serious blow. Finally, the refusal to allow elections in 1956 sparked the resumption of intensive guerrilla warfare in the country. It should be remembered that the Geneva agreements did not provide for two Vietnams but rather for a truce in order that something other than a military solution could be found for the nation. Now it looked as though the only hope for those non-communist opponents of the southern region lay in the use of violence. The insurgents were not primarily communists but rather members of religious sects, Buddhists, and former Vietminh fighters who would have been annihilated by Diem's policy of crushing opposition. Thus, the North Vietnamese entered the conflict in the south only after local peoples had started fighting. (As recently as 1966 the Northerners constituted only about ten percent of the guerrilla forces operating in the south.) By 1963 the situation under the Diem regime had become so serious that a Buddhist-supported military coup overthrew his government. Despite all the attempts to legalize this new regime, it has remained essentially an authoritarian military rule.

While the southern part of the country continued to suffer the agonies of civil war, North Vietnam rebuilt her economy with Soviet and Chinese aid. Land was consolidated into collective farms, and while the industrial output increased, food production did not. The Lao Dang or Workers Party tightened its hold on North Vietnamese life, especially with the establishment of a new school system. Morale has been high enough and prosperity sufficiently adequate that Ho has been able to aid the guerrillas in the south despite the intensive United States air raids on his country since 1965.

The United States and Vietnam

As has already been indicated, the United States became concerned about Vietnam after the fall of China to the Communists. This nation had been supplying weapons to her NATO ally, France, and after the French debacle gave support to the Diem regime. This commitment started with the sending of advisors and financial aid to the Saigon government. One side in the civil war was chosen and backed. At first, the American support was cautious. President Dwight Eisenhower indicated as early as 1954 that the United States would aid South Vietnam in an economic way so that it could become a strong and viable state. John F. Kennedy reiterated this promise of aid, but in a CBS interview shortly before his tragic death he said: "I don't think that unless a greater effort is made by the government to win popular support that the war can be won out there. In the final analysis, it is their war. They are the ones who have to win it or lose it. We can help them, we can give them equipment, we can send our men out there as advisors, but they have to win it—the people of Viet-Nam—against the Communists."[16] These statements have been construed by President Lyndon B. Johnson as a moral commitment to send soldiers to fight in Vietnam. In 1966 he declared: "We are there because we have a promise to keep. Since 1954 every American President has offered support to the people of South Vietnam. . . . To dishonor that pledge, to abandon this small and brave nation to its enemies and to the terror that must follow, would be an unforgivable wrong."[17]

Many feel that this aid is necessary to stop the spread of world communism. They reason that nations fall to communist domination like dominoes and that once the monolithic structure of world Marxism has triumphed, there will be no place for Christianity or the American way of life. Actually, this reflects a serious misunderstanding of the events of recent history because the domino theory simply has no basis in fact. No country became communist when the Russian Revolution succeeded in 1917 or when communism won out in China in 1949 or in Vietnam in 1954 or Cuba in 1960. In reality, the domino theory is a replica of a crude Marxism which teaches the inevitable victory of communism. One has every reason to believe that a victory by Ho in Vietnam, rather than helping the spread of communism from China, would probably block it. The Vietnamese have for generations wished to be free not only of Western but also of Chinese domination. Ho would in all likelihood become an Asian Tito.

The American position in Vietnam has turned into an enigmatic one. Motivated by a pathological fear of communism, all of this nation's good intentions are being blighted. Although the United States fervently wants peace, she is bogged down in a bitter civil war. This country professes that she desires economic betterment of the Vietnamese yet has become identified with a hated, graft-ridden, parasitic landlord class. The United States, a land that loves liberty, has become entangled with a regime characterized by nepotism and tyranny.

The Christian and Vietnam

How will those who profess to follow Jesus Christ react to Vietnam? Certainly, as a citizen one should be interested in his nation's war policies, and a Christian will recognize that there are times when a nation needs to fight.[18] However, it seems that such occasions are sharply limited if one is to understand life through the teachings of Jesus Christ. There is a consistent emphasis in the New Testament on peace. The Lord Jesus Christ was styled "the Prince of Peace" and he counselled his followers to live as peacemakers. A person must start by being at peace with God by the removal of sin's enmity through faith in the sacrifice of Jesus Christ. (Rom. 5:1; Col. 1:20) Inward peace will follow (Phil. 4:7) and will extend in an outward fashion between man and man. (Eph. 2) Peace is thus viewed as one of the initial products of the work of God's Holy Spirit. (Gal. 5:22, 23) Christ and the Apostles never limited this fruit of the spirit and a Christian should not try to confine it merely to an inward state. An outworking of this peace should help to counteract the war attitude which has swept over the United States in recent years.

This war mentality has a vicious and brutalizing effect on American society both in internal and external affairs.[19] Much of the traditional Christian basis of national life seems to be eroding in Vietnam. The United States has blasted that little land with a severity seldom equalled in modern warfare. Napalm, white phosphorous bombs, rockets, gases, anti-personnel bombs, B-52 raids, chemical warfare—a whole science fiction arsenal has been unleashed on that unfortunate Southeast Asian nation. Not only are American troops concerned with fighting an armed enemy but they are also working at "pacification" attempts. Correspondents have noted the revulsion of American fighting men when ordered to burn villages and shoot chickens, ducks, water buffalo, and family pets. These same writers report that the United States is losing the battle in Vietnam against prostitution and bar girls and that Southeast Asian cities are being made into gigantic brothels to satisfy the desires of American troops. How, a Christian should ask, will all this affect American character? Can minds twisted by brutality and accustomed to violence ever be normal again? As one observer stated: "I simply cannot help worrying that, in the process of waging this war, we are corrupting ourselves. I wonder, when I look at the bombed-out peasant hamlets, the orphans begging and stealing on the streets of Saigon, and the women and children with napalm burns lying on the hospital cots, whether the United States or any nation has the right to inflict this suffering and degradation on other people for its own ends."[20] A Christian is forced to agree with Morley Safer when he called the war in Vietnam "a brutal absurdity . . . a black comedy."[21] The war encourages the growth of the Military Establishment and a type of right wing fascist mentality. "We support our boys in Vietnam" read the bumper stickers. "All right," the Christian replies, "then let us help them return home. Let the Vietnamese civil war take its course without us."

An evangelical must view with concern some further implications of the American war in Vietnam. Does this mean the beginning of a world police force, a "pax Americana"? If this is the case, then where did the United States obtain the mandate for such action? The possibility of revolt and unrest exists in several lands today. Many of these revolutions will be financed and led by communists. Does this mean that American soldiers will be deployed every time an uprising occurs against a "friendly" government. (We have some strange friends such as Franco of Spain, the Greek military dictators, and the Shah of Iran.) Shall the United States send men to new Vietnams in Spain, Greece, Iran, Peru, Bolivia, or Colombia? This will certainly detract us from pressing needs at home and give a violent and imperialist emphasis to our foreign policy.

Besides the danger of the brutalizing influence and the temptation to become involved in policing the world, a Christian must also wonder what this nation can hope to gain by a possible victory in Vietnam. If America wishes to stop communism, this is hardly the way to do it. As a matter of fact, all of the "hard line" arguments taken by some Americans have their counterpart among fanatics on the communist side. The idea of a compromise peace is called by Peking a "Munich" solution and communists say that a "capitalist" Vietnam would be the beginning of the fall of the communist world. The Chinese could well believe that we are trying to surround them with bases. David Schoenbrun has made this point quite clearly:

> We charge China with being aggressive and expansionist, but most of the world believes that *we* are the expansionist power. American soldiers, businessmen, and technicians are seen almost everywhere in the world. Hardly a single Chinese soldier is seen outside China, and few Chinese diplomats or technicians are seen anywhere. We believe we are not expansionist because we clearly do not covet territory, but we fail to see that others regard the extension of influence on a global scale as a new form of expansionism. They do not believe that we are in Vietnam only to prevent a South Vietnamese Communist victory over a South Vietnamese military clique. They have long believed—and feel their suspicions confirmed by President Johnson's Asian tour—that the United States, a Pacific power, now has a new objective: to extend its power from the Pacific to the continent of Asia.[22]

Actually, the nearer the United States comes to victory in the war the closer she draws to an ultimate confrontation with China or Russia

and World War III. The American war in Vietnam has given credence
to the Chinese idea that peaceful coexistence can not work and that good
Marxists should fight to the death against capitalists. It is also extremely
significant that very few friends and allies of the United States have
moved to give assistance to the Vietnam venture. A victory in the war
would be a hollow one indeed if this country came to be regarded as a
brutal aggressor by the other democratic nations of the world.[23]

Good people certainly may disagree but it seems that a thinking
American Christian should encourage deescalation of the war. Bombing
of the north ought to stop and our troops should be pulled back to
coastal enclaves. An all-Asian Conference could be called to bring the
combatants together in an atmosphere of neutrality so that a political
settlement might come about. Also, the United States should begin now
to prepare Vietnam for the transition from a war to a peacetime economy.
It could be made clear that it would be economically profitable for the
country to have peace.

An eloquent statement by an outstanding American leader, Senator
Mark Hatfield of Oregon, sums up the Christian perspective toward the
war in Vietnam:

> My views are naturally influenced by my beliefs, by my faith,
> because no man can isolate or divide himself into tight little com-
> partments that do not relate to one another. We're an organism in
> which there are interdependencies, interrelationships. We are also
> related to our environment, and our environment tends to in-
> fluence us.
>
> My concern about Vietnam is primarily a political concern be-
> cause I feel that we are involved there in a situation which has
> been going on for twenty years. During the period the French were
> there they lost 96,000 dear soldiers. The United States gave millions
> of dollars to support the French. Now we are doing the battle of
> the civil war; and in twenty years a policy that has brought neither
> victory or solution, I think, needs careful review.
>
> And then I also am deeply concerned because I have been in
> Hanoi and have fought in the area during the time I was involved
> in the Chinese Civil War back in 1945. And I have a feeling clearly
> that God created every human being on this earth in his own image
> and I hate to see the cheapness of life, the awesome loss of life
> through starvation or through war. I just cannot accept the idea
> that ultimate victory will be achieved by killing more people, killing
> more people, and killing more people.
>
> I think we should take peace, prosperity, and food and love to
> these people. Paul teaches us that love is the most powerful instru-

ment in the world. I think it is far more powerful than the atomic bomb, and we ought to use our genius and our ingenuity to find a honorable way to solve this problem. If we have the genius to put a man on the moon by 1970, surely we have the genius to find the solution to this horrible war. . . .

I believe that the Christian answer to any problem is to recognize first that God is sovereign and that all things happen either with His direction or with His permission. But I also believe just as deeply, in fact, that God has created all these men and women on this earth and that we have a responsibility to share the blessings that God has given us. Our material possessions, our wisdom, our education, are all things that we must share with other people because we are all our brother's keeper. I would much rather be a keeper than a destroyer, and that to me is what America is doing today, destroying people.[24]

NOTES

1. John R. Rice, *War in Vietnam: Should Christians Fight?* (Murfreesboro, Tenn.: Sword of the Lord Publishers, 1966), p. 3.

2. *Ibid.*, p. 5.

3. *Ibid.*, p. 11.

4. *Ibid.*, p. 13.

5. *Ibid.*, p. 16.

6. *Ibid.*, p. 18.

7. For those desiring to learn more about Vietnamese history see Joseph Buttinger, *The Smaller Dragon: A Political History of Vietnam* (New York: Praeger, 1958); Bernard B. Fall, *The Two Viet-nams* (New York: Praeger, 1963); Van Chi Hoang, *From Colonialism to Communism: A Case History of North Vietnam* (New York: Praeger, 1964); and Robert Scigliano, *South Vietnam: Nation under Stress* (Boston: Houghton Mifflin, 1964).

8. Thich Nhat Hanh, *Vietnam: Lotus in a Sea of Fire* (New York: Hill & Wang, 1967), p. 12.

9. Buttinger, *The Smaller Dragon*, p. 173.

10. "The mandarins' character as a governing elite was emphasized both by the nature of the training they received and by the tests they had to undergo. These tests, which were competitive and strictly impartial, made sure that only the fittest among all students received their diplomas as 'men of letters,' and that the best of these men, in terms of the established criteria, could obtain the highest official degrees. But before a Vietnamese youth could compete for the highest honors, the years of study and the passing of preliminary examinations might well have made him a middle-aged or elderly man. Only the very brilliant were able to get to the summit as young men, after absorbing no less than all the knowledge that existed, or was recognized as existing under the prevailing Confucianist views.

Thus it came about that the country's ruling class, after the seedbeds of feudal power were destroyed, became identical with the country's educated minority. Vietnam was administered and ruled by its intellectuals, and no Vietnamese intellectuals existed who were not either members or associates of the country's ruling elite.

Indeed, a closer examination of Vietnamese society during the first half of the nineteenth century reveals a surprising historical phenomenon: a state had come into being in which the ancient dream of a government by philosophers was literally fulfilled; the training of the mandarins was philosophical in the fullest sense of the word. There were no special courses in administration. No instruction in any kind of technical skill was required for the official tests. The subjects to be mastered were exclusively literary, and the skills to be acquired purely rhetorical and scholastic. The bulk of the curriculum consisted of ancient Chinese philosophy, with history and poetry as mere handmaidens of Confucianism. The aim of all studies was to absorb the accumulated wisdom of the past, in order to achieve the moral perfection that qualified a man to rule. Minh Mang himself, the most scholarly of the Nguyen emperors, expounded these views in his remarkable political and poetic writings. He was the truest mandarin-emperor Vietnam has known, a king who based his own qualifications for government and his right to exercise absolute power not on royal blood but on his role as moral philosopher and head of the nation's intellectual elite." Buttinger, *The Smaller Dragon*, pp. 290–91.

11. Viet Minh is a shortened form of the party's name Vietnam Doc Lap Dong Minh Hoi. This was formed in China in 1941 by a group of émigré political organizations to fight French-Japanese fascism. Ho was the general secretary and under his leadership the party built cells in Japanese-occupied Vietnam.

12. "Final Declaration of Geneva Conference, July 21, 1954" in *The Viet-Nam Reader*, edited by M. G. Raskin and B. B. Fall (New York: Vintage Books, 1965), pp. 96 ff. Other books which provide useful information on the period 1946–65 include Bernard B. Fall, *The Two Viet-Nams: A Political and Military History* (5th ed., New York: Praeger, 1965); Ellen G. Hammer, *The Struggle for Indochina* (Stanford: Stanford University Press, 1955); and Jean Lacouture, *Vietnam: Between Two Truces* (New York: Vintage Books, 1966).

13. For the Catholic hierarchy's effect on American intervention in Vietnam, notice Robert Scheer and Warren Hinckle, "The Viet-Nam Lobby" in *The Viet-Nam Reader*, pp. 66 ff.

14. Thomas A. Dooley, *Deliver Us From Evil* (New York: Farrar Strauss, 1956); *Edge of Tomorrow* (New York: Farrar Strauss, 1958); and *The Night They Burned the Mountain* (New York: Farrar Strauss, 1960). These books are still widely read in the United States.

15. The learned Buddhist monk, Thich Nhat Hanh comments: "Many of the Diem projects were well-conceived in themselves and could have been valuable, but the government became increasingly corrupt and inefficient through Diem's desire to control everything himself, and through his failure to enlist the help of talented non-Communist nationalists in his government. From the moment of his assumption of power, Diem spared no effort to eliminate every form of opposition to his regime, and had no faith in anyone except members of his own family and of his own church. With a few talented exceptions, the coterie who surrounded him were incompetent sycophants, seeking to reenforce their own positions by leaning on the government and the Church.

Various groups in South Vietnam at this time sought to participate in the government in the hope of making it a genuinely representative one. Such groups as the Cao Dai and the Hoa Hao, who had their own armies and controlled certain areas of Vietnam, used these as a base from which to seek participation in government. However Diem and his American advisers chose instead to suppress all of these groups forcibly, maintaining that a state could not exist within a state. The Diem government became obsessed with the problem of eliminating all opposition, but gave no thought to the consolidation of the various non-Communist forces in South Vietnam. Diem put his entire reliance on violent suppression instead of resorting to more humanistic political means of consolidating the state's existence." *Vietnam*, p. 57.

16. John F. Kennedy, CBS interview with Walter Cronkite, September 2, 1963.